# TEACHER'S MANUAL

## to

# CALIFORNIA LEGAL ETHICS

## Seventh Edition

▪ ▪ ▪

By

## Richard C. Wydick

*Professor of Law, Emeritus*
*University of California, Davis*

## Rex R. Perschbacher

*Daniel J. Dykstra Chair in Law*
*University of California, Davis*

## Debra Lyn Bassett

*Justice Marshall F. McComb Professor of Law*
*Southwestern Law School*

*This book is a California edition of*
*Schwartz, Wydick, Perschbacher & Bassett,*
*Problems in Legal Ethics, Ninth Edition*

### AMERICAN CASEBOOK SERIES®

### WEST®

A Thomson Reuters business

Mat #40877236

*American Casebook Series* is a trademark registered in the U.S. Patent and Trademark Office.

COPYRIGHT © 1992 WEST PUBLISHING CO.
© West, a Thomson business, 1997, 2001, 2003, 2005, 2008
© 2010 Thomson Reuters

    610 Opperman Drive
    St. Paul, MN 55123
    1–800–313–9378

Printed in the United States of America

**ISBN:** 978–0–314–20740–1

# TO THE TEACHER

*How to Fit the Book To Your Course*

This casebook is intended for use in California law schools with two-unit or three-unit legal ethics courses that provide from 30 to 45 hours of classroom instruction.

The book contains 14 chapters, and each chapter covers one or two discrete topics. We cover one chapter per week. Reviewing the cases and other excerpts typically requires one class hour; the Discussion Problems generally require another class hour.

If you have the luxury of a three-unit course, you can devote more time to the policy issues behind the rules, you can show video clips raising ethical issues, and you can weave in outside materials if you wish.

*Reading Assignments*

At the beginning of each chapter, we have suggested a reading assignment for the students. The chapters and reading assignments vary in page length, but they are intended to be roughly equal in difficulty and to consume roughly equal amounts of class time. Thus, we suggest that you ask the students to prepare a chapter at a time, rather than ask them to read a set number of pages at a time.

*Supplemental Readings*

Each chapter suggests supplemental readings in books that should be available in your law school library:

- G. HAZARD & W. HODES, THE LAW OF LAWYERING (3d ed. 2001 with yearly supplement); and

- The RESTATEMENT (THIRD) OF THE LAW GOVERNING LAWYERS (2000), prepared by the American Law Institute.

The supplemental readings will enlighten those students who care to dip into them, and they will help you as teacher when you prepare for class. For valuable guidance on the law and ethics rules that are unique to California lawyers, you will also wish to consult P. VAPNEK, M. TUFT, E. PECK & H. WIENER, CALIFORNIA PRACTICE GUIDE: PROFESSIONAL RESPONSIBILITY (The Rutter Group 1999) (looseleaf with yearly updates).

*What this Teacher's Manual Contains*

The chapters of this Teacher's Manual correspond to the chapters of the book. Each Teacher's Manual chapter includes briefs of the principal cases, plus dialogues for each of the discussion problems. The dialogues do not reflect what goes on in our (or anybody's) classroom. We chose the dialogue format, not for realism, but because it offers a convenient, colloquial way to say what we wanted to say.

California instructors will want to be aware that numerous proposals to amend the California Rules of Professional Conduct are in the process of being reviewed. The progress of those proposals can be monitored at http://calbar.ca.gov/state/calbar/calbar_generic.jsp?cid=10145&n=96433.

Richard C. Wydick
Rex R. Perschbacher
Debra Lyn Bassett

Los Angeles, California
January 2010

# TABLE OF CONTENTS

# CHAPTER ONE
# INTRODUCTION TO LEGAL ETHICS

## ADVANCE ASSIGNMENT

To prepare for the first class hour, the students should read Chapter One of CALIFORNIA LEGAL ETHICS.

## HOUSEKEEPING DETAILS

- *Required Materials.* Each student should have a copy of CALIFORNIA LEGAL ETHICS. In addition, each student should have a current copy of either the Abridged Edition or the Complete Edition of SELECTED STATUTES, RULES, AND STANDARDS ON THE LEGAL PROFESSION (Thomson West). The Abridged Edition is somewhat less expensive and contains all the source materials the students are likely to need when using PROBLEMS IN LEGAL ETHICS.

- *Class Preparation.* At the beginning of each class, we note on the blackboard what chapter the students are to prepare for the following class. Each chapter begins with a reading assignment; we ask our students to read that assignment and to come to class ready to talk about the discussion problems.

- *Supplemental Reading.* On the first day of class, we show our students samples of the supplemental reading materials and explain that the supplemental reading is not mandatory but is helpful. We tell the students where the supplemental reading materials can be found in the law school library.

- *Final Examination.* We have found it useful to tell the students on the first day of class what kind of final examination to expect. That helps them decide how to prepare for class, how to take class notes, and how to study the material.

## CLASS DISCUSSION

After covering the housekeeping details, we turn to the primary object of the first class—sparking the students' interest in legal ethics. There are several ways to do that with the readings in Chapter One of CALIFORNIA LEGAL

ETHICS. One approach would be a general class discussion progressing through each of the readings from Chapter One. We favor a different approach, diving straight into the discussion problems in Chapter One, like this:

## Discussion Problem 1

[This problem is based on ABA Model Rule 4.4(b) and Comments 2 and 3 thereto, as amended in 2002, and on ABA Formal Ethics Opinions 92–368 (1992) (now withdrawn), 94–382 (1994), and 06–440 (2006). As the teacher you should read those materials when preparing for class, even though your students will not be aware of them. If you have time, you will find the following additional material helpful: Anno., *Waiver of Evidentiary Privilege by Inadvertent Disclosure—Federal Law,* 159 A.L.R.Fed 153 (2000); RESTATEMENT (THIRD) OF THE LAW GOVERNING LAWYERS § 79, comment h (2000); RONALD ROTUNDA, PROFESSIONAL RESPONSIBILITY: A STUDENT'S GUIDE 162–164 (2002); Maryland State Bar Ass'n Comm. on Ethics Op. 2000–04, 16 ABA/BNA LAWYERS' MANUAL ON PROF. CONDUCT 179 (2000); SEC v. Cassano, 189 F.R.D. 83 (S.D.N.Y. 1999) (attorney–client privilege *lost* because of in-house attorney's inadvertent disclosure); State Compensation Ins. Fund v. WPS, Inc., 70 Cal.App.4th 644, 82 Cal.Rptr.2d 799 (1999) (attorney–client privilege *not lost* despite in-house attorney's inadvertent disclosure). *See also* Fed. R. Civ. P. 26(b)(5)(B) ("If information is produced in discovery that is subject to a claim of privilege or of protection as trial–preparation material, the party making the claim may notify any party that received the information of the claim and the basis for it. After being notified, a party must promptly return, sequester, or destroy the specified information and any copies it has and may not use or disclose the information until the claim is resolved. ...").]

A] In Discussion Problem 1, you are the plaintiff's lawyer in a suit against five corporate defendants, each with its own lawyer. One of the defense lawyers has mistakenly faxed you a memo about settlement. You have read the fax cover sheet and the opening paragraph of the memo, and they make it obvious that the memo was not supposed to go to you: it is a very sensitive document that reveals the settlement posture and proposed tactics of one of the defendants. After reading that opening paragraph of the memo, what should you do?

B] I guess the ethics issue is what should I do with a piece of my adversary's privileged material that has fallen into my hands without any wrongdoing on my part? To resolve it, I'd first need to figure out what my choices are. I see three choices here:

- I could continue reading the memorandum and use it for whatever advantage it may bring to my client; or

- I could stop reading, put the memo in a safe place, and say nothing about it to anybody; or

- I could stop reading, call the defense lawyer who sent it, tell that lawyer what happened, and ask what that lawyer wants me to do with it.

A] That's a good start. What next?

C] Can't we eliminate the second choice immediately? If I am not going to read the memorandum and use it for my client's benefit, then I don't see any purpose in keeping it. Keeping it looks suspicious—somebody may find it later and think that I read it, even though I didn't.

B] I agree, the second choice is no good; I was just trying to be complete. We can eliminate the second choice and focus on the other two: (a) reading the memo and using it, or (b) calling the defense lawyer and asking for instructions about what to do with it.

C] I think it would be dishonest for me to read it and use it. I realize that I got the fax transmission by mistake. We have assumed that the memo is privileged and remains privileged despite the defense lawyer's mistake in faxing it to me. I realize that the defense lawyer sent it to the other defense lawyers for a limited, legitimate purpose—devising a settlement strategy. It would be dishonest for me to take advantage of the defense lawyer's mistake.

A] Wait a minute. Don't you have an obligation to do whatever you can to help your client win?

B] *Whatever* I can? No! Do I have an obligation to tap the defense lawyer's phone, so I can listen in on privileged conversations? Do I have an obligation to sneak a look into the defense lawyer's briefcase while she is in the restroom? Do I have an obligation to bribe a key witness? Perhaps I have an obligation to do everything that's *lawful and ethical* to help my client win, but that's the extent of it.

A] Based on the case you read in Chapter One [*Rico v. Mitsubishi Motors Corp.*], which option would appear to be the lawful and ethical choice?

B] I think it would be to advise the plaintiff's lawyer to stop reading, to notify the sender, and to follow the sender's instructions about the fax.

A] You might be interested to learn that in 2002, the American Bar Association came to the same conclusion. ABA Model Rule of Professional Conduct 4.4(b), added in 2002, says this:

> A lawyer who receives a document relating to the representation of the lawyer's client and knows or reasonably should know that the document was inadvertently sent shall promptly notify the sender.

[*See also* ABA Model Rule 4.4, comments [2] and [3].]

A] What practical steps can a lawyer take to avoid the kind of mistake the defense lawyer made here?

C] Learn how to operate the fax machine correctly, and make sure your assistants know how to use it correctly.

B] Get organized and work carefully. Fax machines, e-mail, and high speed copying machines can save work for lawyers, but they also create many possibilities for serious error.

D] The law firm I clerked for last summer used a fax cover sheet that would have been helpful here. The cover sheet said something like this:

> This transmission is confidential between the sender and the intended receiver. If you are <u>not</u> the intended receiver, please do not copy this transmission, and do not read past this cover sheet. Rather, do one of the following:
>
> 1) Destroy this transmission; or

2) Forward this transmission to the intended receiver; or

3) Return this transmission by mail to the sender.

A] Did the firm have any policy about when to use that cover sheet?

D] Yes. We were told to use that cover sheet only for confidential communications. For ordinary communications, we used a different cover sheet that did not have that language on it.

A] Good idea. If the boilerplate is used on every fax, it may not work when you really need it.

## Discussion Problem 2

[To prepare for the discussion of Problem 2, you as teacher should read ABA Model Rule 1.14; ABA Formal Op. 96–404; Cal. Bar Op. 1989–112 and RESTATEMENT (THIRD) OF THE LAW GOVERNING LAWYERS § 24 (2000).]

A] In Problem 2, you are the lawyer for Samuel, who has inherited a large sum of money from his family. In years past, you have represented other members of the family in a variety of matters. You now represent Samuel in business, investment, and estate planning matters. He is a single parent who has an eleven-year-old daughter, Clara, under his care. From things Samuel has told you in confidence, and from things you have observed about him, you have concluded that he is addicted to drugs and is unfit to take care of himself, his estate, and his daughter. Samuel's sister Dena has asked you to petition the court to appoint a conservator for Samuel. You know from your past dealings that Samuel will adamantly oppose a conservatorship. The problem asks you what you will do in response to Dena's request. Before we tackle that ethics issue, let's make sure everybody knows about this conservatorship business. What is a conservatorship?

B] Under the law of most states, a relative such as Dena is allowed to petition the court for appointment of a conservator for a person in Samuel's condition. [See, e.g., CAL. PROBATE CODE § 1801.] If the court appoints a conservator, then the conservator would take charge of Samuel's affairs—run them as a fiduciary—until Samuel is able to take over for himself. If Samuel does not want a conservator, he can oppose the petition. That turns it into an adversary proceeding. Samuel would have a lawyer, and he would be allowed to show why a conservator should not be appointed.

A] Moving to the ethics issue, assume that you wholeheartedly agree with Dena that Samuel needs a conservator. May you petition the court for the appointment of a conservator, as Dena has asked you to do?

C] I'd tell Dena to look for a different lawyer. I have been representing Samuel in business, investment, and estate planning matters, and that puts me in a conflict of interest.

B] There's no conflict of interest here. Applying the utilitarian analysis, the greatest happiness will be produced if Samuel has a conservator. Consider the interests of all those who will be affected:

> ● Samuel: He's an addict and cannot look after himself, or his money or his daughter. His interest is best served if he has a conservator.

> ● Dena: She's the concerned sister who doesn't want to see Samuel harm himself and others. Her interest is best served if he has a conservator.

> ● Clara: She's the eleven-year-old daughter. Samuel is not fit to look after her anymore. Her interest is best served if he has a conservator.

> ● Me: I'm the lawyer who has served members of this family for years. I have a personal interest in the well-being of these people, and that interest is best served if Samuel has a conservator.

C] You have built a trick into your response. You say that Samuel's best interest is served if he has a conservator. Doubtless we would all agree with that. But apparently Samuel does not agree! Until the court decides otherwise, Samuel must be treated as an autonomous human being who has the right to decide for himself what his interests are. You, his lawyer, should not assume that power for yourself.

B] Your approach turns the lawyer into a moral blob. If the lawyer is convinced that the client is under a disability and cannot act in his own best interest, then the lawyer should follow his own judgment instead of his client's judgment on this limited issue. Here that means bringing the matter before the court and letting the court decide whether Samuel should have a conservator.

C] I can't agree. Samuel is your present client, and you can't allow the interests of yourself or others (like Dena or Clara) to undercut your loyalty to him. Further, in the course of representing Samuel, you have observed things about him, and you have learned things in confidence from him; based partly on that material, you have now concluded that he needs a conservator. You cannot use the information you learned in confidence to harm him. The most you can do here is advise Dena to seek another lawyer.

A] You two have uncovered a disagreement that will come up several times in this course. One view is that the lawyer is the faithful agent of the client and must not go against the client's wishes. The other view is that the lawyer is an independent moral actor and must sometimes substitute her own judgment for that of the client. These opposing views are reflected in a split of authority on the very ethics issue presented in Problem 2:

The Activist View: ABA Model Rule 1.14(b) (which has been adopted in most of the states) permits a lawyer to seek the appointment of a guardian (custodian) for a client when the lawyer "reasonably believes that the client cannot adequately act in the client's own interest." [The rule is discussed in Hazard & Hodes §1.14:301-303.] The RESTATEMENT (THIRD) OF THE LAW GOVERNING LAWYERS § 24 (2000) is in accord. ABA Formal Op. 96–404 provides a small refinement—you yourself could properly petition for appointment of a guardian, but you should not represent a third party petitioner, such as Dena. According to the ethics committee, representing Dena would be "more adverse" to Samuel's interest than petitioning on your own behalf.

The Conservative View: The conservative view is reflected in the opinions of three California ethics committees that have considered the problem presented in Problem 2; each of them has concluded that the lawyer must not petition the court to have a guardian appointed for her client. The reasons given are those that C expressed. First, to petition for the guardianship might involve misuse of information the lawyer received in confidence. [See Cal. Bar Op. 1989–112; Los Angeles Bar Op. 450 (1988); San Diego Bar Op. 1978–1.] Second, the petition would put the lawyer into a conflict of interest. A lawyer must not bring a legal action against a present client. Further, a lawyer must not allow the interests of himself or others (such as Dena and Clara) to undercut his loyalty to his client. [Id.]

B] So what is the <u>right</u> answer?

A] The introductory material in Chapter One suggests that the rules of legal ethics do not always provide a clear "right" answer. In hard cases, you may get some guidance from the three general moral theories you read about in Chapter One. In a situation such as Problem 2, where reasonable lawyers have studied the issue and reached opposite conclusions, you will follow any guidance provided by the jurisdiction in which you are practicing. This means that for those of you planning to practice law in California, you will need to follow the California Bar Opinions just discussed. For those of you who do not plan to practice in California, but instead plan to practice in a jurisdiction that has adopted the ABA Model Rules, you must make your own moral judgment about what is right (note that ABA Model Rule 1.14 says that the lawyer "may" take protective action—not that she "must" do so). One object of this course is to help you recognize those situations and make those judgments.

## **Discussion Problem 3**

A] This problem is a modified version of the set of facts discussed in Arizona State Bar Comm. Op. 91–2 (1991). Here we have a lawyer named Leon, who arranged a settlement for his client Curtis a few years ago. Under this settlement, the insurance company sends lawyer Leon a monthly check. Leon deducts 10% as his legal fee and sends the rest on to client Curtis. Now Leon has discovered a mistake: each month the insurance company has been sending almost twice the amount that it owes. Leon tells Curtis about the mistake, and Curtis responds that he knew something must be wrong, but he really needs the extra money. Client Curtis tells Leon: "Don't rock the boat." Suppose you were Leon. What should you do here?

B] The first thing I'd do is some good hard lawyering. I would check my computations. Maybe I am the one who made the error, and the insurance company figure is the correct one. Then I would re-check the settlement agreement. Perhaps I misinterpreted it; maybe my client is really entitled to the higher amount. If neither of those steps solves the problem, then I'd do some legal research, to find out the legal consequences if Curtis keeps money that he knows has been paid to him by mistake.

A] Once again, "good hard lawyering" is an excellent way to approach any ethics problem. Often you will discover that what seems at first to be an ethics problem is not an ethics problem at all. It may be a fact problem that you can resolve by finding out what really happened. Or, it may be a law problem that resolves itself when you do some legal research. So "good hard lawyering" is always the place to begin solving an ethics problem. For the sake of argument, let's assume that your calculations are correct and that you have correctly interpreted the settlement agreement. Thus, your client is clearly not entitled to the higher payment.

What would your legal research produce—what are the consequences if your client keeps money that he knows has been paid to him by mistake?

B] A person commits larceny by accepting money that has been delivered to him by mistake, if: (a) he realizes the mistake at the time of delivery; and (b) he simultaneously intends to keep the money, thus permanently depriving the owner of it. [*See* WAYNE R. LAFAVE, CRIMINAL LAW § 8.2(g) at 801–02 (3d ed. 2000).] Curtis said that he "knew something must be wrong" but that he needs the money and doesn't want Leon to rock the boat. That strikes me as strong evidence of the two mental elements of larceny.

A] Because this is your first class and you have not yet studied the rules of legal ethics, let me give you a quick statement of three principles that would be on my mind if I were the lawyer in this situation:

● Honesty. As a lawyer, I must act honestly and lawfully, and I should encourage my client to do likewise. If it is larceny for Curtis to accept these overpayments, I should encourage him to set the matter straight. If he won't do so, then at a minimum I do not want to be a part of his unlawful conduct.

● Loyalty. As a lawyer I am an agent for my client, and that gives me a duty of loyalty to the client. First, I should not act in a way that harms the client (unless the law requires me to). Second, I should pursue my client's interests, to the extent that I can do so within the bounds of the law.

● Confidentiality. As lawyer, I have an ethical duty not to disclose and not to misuse confidential information that I learn about my client's affairs. Here my knowledge about the mistaken payments and my communication with Curtis about those payments are both confidential.

B] Aren't those three principles in conflict in this problem? How can you act honestly in this situation and still maintain the confidentiality and act loyally to your client if your client wants to keep on milking the insurance company?

A] Can anybody see how to harmonize those three principles in this situation?

C] I think so. If I were Leon, I'd give Curtis three pieces of advice.

First, I'd advise Curtis about the payments he has accepted in the past. I'd tell him that he has a moral obligation to return the overpaid amount. If their roles were reversed, Curtis would want the insurance company to pay him back, so he should pay them back. I would advise Curtis that besides the moral obligation, he probably has a legal obligation as well. I would advise him that if he in fact realized that he was not entitled to the money at the time he received it, and if he then intended to keep it, then he could be found guilty of larceny. Further, I would advise him that if the insurance company brought a civil suit against him, he would probably have to pay back the money. [*See* RESTATEMENT OF RESTITUTION § 20 (1936) (overpayment of money through mistake of fact entitles payor to restitution); *Messsersmith v. G.T. Murray & Co.*, 667 P.2d 655 (Wyo. 1983).]

Second, I'd advise him about collecting overpayments in the future. I'd tell him that he now clearly knows that he is not entitled to the overpayments and that to continue accepting them would be larceny.

Third, I'd advise him that I cannot continue being his lawyer if he wants to go on taking overpayments from the insurance company. I would hope that after getting these three pieces of advice, Curtis will decide to tell the insurance company about the mistake and offer to pay back the past overpayments.

A] Suppose Curtis listens to your advice and responds this way: "Leon, I don't care whether you continue as my lawyer. I certainly will not pay back the past overpayments, and I will take my chances on the insurance company continuing the overpayments in the future. I know that as a lawyer you are not allowed to reveal my confidential information, so you can't blow the whistle on me. So quit if you wish." What would you do then?

C] For starters, I would quit as his lawyer, for two reasons. First, to continue as his lawyer and to continue processing the monthly checks from the insurance company would involve me personally in his larceny. Second, I don't want to be the lawyer for a person who is bent on dishonest conduct.

A] Your decision would comport with the legal ethics rules that we will study later in this course. [*See* ABA Model Rule 1.16(a)(1) (mandatory withdrawal where to continue would involve lawyer in a crime); ABA Model Rule 1.16(b)(1) (permissive withdrawal where client persists in criminal or fraudulent conduct).] If you withdraw as the lawyer for Curtis, could you also "blow the whistle" on him by telling the insurance company about the mistake?

C] I don't know—I assume we will be studying the confidentiality rules in this course. From what we learned in the evidence course about the attorney–client privilege, I suspect there is a distinction between revealing future crimes and revealing past crimes.

A] Yes, the rules of legal ethics also distinguish between future crimes and past crimes. Generally, a lawyer must not reveal confidential information concerning the client's past crimes. The rule on future crimes varies from state to state. The 2003 version of ABA Model Rule 1.6(b) allows a lawyer to reveal a client's confidence in order to prevent death or substantial bodily harm, and also allows a lawyer to reveal a client's confidential information to prevent the commission of a crime or fraud reasonably certain to cause substantial financial injury in furtherance of which the client has used (or is using) the lawyer's services. [*Accord* RESTATEMENT [THIRD] OF THE LAW GOVERNING LAWYERS §§ 66–67 (2000).]

C] I don't understand how the distinction between past and future crimes works. If Leon reveals Curtis's intent to continue taking overpayments in the future, he will necessarily also have revealed that Curtis has taken overpayments in the past. What should a lawyer do in that situation?

A] The authorities are divided on that issue. In the case on which Problem 3 is patterned, the Arizona Ethics Committee said that the lawyer should <u>not</u> reveal a future crime if doing so necessarily reveals a past crime. [Arizona State Bar Comm. Op. 91–2 (1991).] The California State Bar Ethics Committee reached the same conclusion on analogous facts. [Cal. Bar Op. 1988–96 (1988); *see also* CHARLES WOLFRAM, MODERN LEGAL ETHICS 674–75 (1986).] In contrast, the Restatement gives the lawyer discretion to reveal the confidential information where necessary to prevent impending harm from acts that have already taken place. [RESTATEMENT, *supra,* §§ 66 and 67.]

There is one more point here under the 2003 amendments to ABA Model Rule 1.6. The 2003 amendments permit a lawyer to reveal a client's confidential information to mitigate or rectify substantial financial injury caused by the client's crime or fraud when the client used the lawyer's services. This would appear to fit the circumstances here. Note, however, that again the rule is permissive rather than mandatory—creating an option, not an obligation. But this is available only in jurisdictions that have adopted the ABA Model Rules. The exception to the duty of confidentiality in situations involving the client's fraud that is set forth in ABA Model Rule 1.6 does not currently exist in California! [*See* CRPC 3–100 (creating an exception to the duty of confidentiality only "to prevent a criminal act that the [lawyer] reasonably believes is likely to result in death of, or substantial bodily harm to, an individual"); CAL. BUS. & PROF. CODE § 6068(e)(2) (providing an exception to the duty of confidentiality where "the attorney reasonably believes the disclosure is necessary to prevent a criminal act that the attorney reasonably believes is likely to result in death of, or substantial bodily harm to, an individual").]

B] You folks have been ignoring an issue that bothers me. The problem says that every month lawyer Leon has received a check from the insurance company and has deducted 10% of it as his legal fee pursuant to the settlement agreement. If the insurance company has been paying too much, then Leon has been getting a larger legal fee than he's entitled to. What should he do about that?

A] Remember the three ethics principles I outlined at the beginning—honesty, loyalty, and confidentiality. With those three principles in mind, what do you think the lawyer ought to do?

B] He could not continue representing Curtis and continue collecting a larger fee than he's entitled to. To do so would be larceny, just as it would for Curtis. So if Curtis won't agree to tell the insurance company about the mistake, then Leon must withdraw as the lawyer for Curtis. That leaves him with the problem of what to do about the overpayment he has received in the past— 10% of the total overpayments made by the insurance company. I don't know what a good utilitarian would say about that, but I think that the Golden Rule approach and Kant's approach would require Leon to pay back the insurance company.

A] Suppose the problem arises in a jurisdiction where the duty of confidentiality does not permit Leon to inform the insurance company about the overpayment. How can Leon refund his 10% of the overpayment without tipping off the insurance company?

B] Well, I guess he could send them cash in a plain brown envelope, but that has the smell of underworld tactics. Another way to do it would be for Leon to hire another lawyer, and to have her make the refund to the insurance company without disclosing the identity of either Leon or Curtis. [*Cf. Baird v. Koerner*, 279 F.2d 623 (9th Cir. 1960); *see also* GEOFFREY C. HAZARD, JR., SUSAN P. KONIAK & ROGER C. CRAMTON, THE LAW AND ETHICS OF LAWYERING 254-55 63 (3d ed. 1999) (discussing *Baird*).]

A] Like the cash in the brown envelope, it seems devious to use another lawyer as "bagman" for an anonymous return of the money to the insurance company. But perhaps it is the only practical way to reconcile Leon's duty of honesty with his duty of loyalty and confidentiality. The Arizona Ethics Committee couldn't come up with anything better—they said the lawyer should send the money back to the insurance company through an intermediary so that the client's confidential information would be preserved. [Arizona State Bar Comm. Op. 91–2 (1991).]

## RICO v. MITSUBISHI MOTORS CORP.
### California Supreme Court, 2007

Facts: Plaintiffs' counsel obtained a defense counsel document containing notes from a strategy session with defense experts. The court ultimately concluded that plaintiffs' counsel acquired the document through inadvertence. Plaintiffs' counsel scrutinized the document and distributed copies to co-counsel and plaintiffs' experts. Defense counsel moved to disqualify plaintiffs' counsel and experts.

Issue: When counsel receives a document subject to attorney-client privilege through the inadvertence of opposing counsel, may counsel use the contents to his client's advantage?

Holding: No.

Discussion: A lawyer receiving such a document should refrain from examining the materials any more than is essential to ascertain if the materials are privileged, and immediately notify the sender that he or she possesses material that appears to be privileged. Here, plaintiffs' counsel realized the significance of the document and that it had been produced inadvertently, but used the document to full advantage nevertheless. The appropriate sanction in this circumstance is disqualification of both plaintiffs' counsel and plaintiffs' experts.

# CHAPTER TWO
## SOURCES AND APPLICATION OF
## LEGAL ETHICS RULES

### Discussion Problem 1

A]  Problem 1 asks what legal requirements you will have to meet to practice law in California.  What did you discover?

B]  I found that for a law student like me there are four main requirements:

> 1)  I must be at least 18 years old;
> 2) I must have completed some education requirements, and graduation from this school meets those requirements.
> 3) I must pass the bar examination; and
> 4) I must be a person of "good moral character." [*See* CAL. BUS. & PROF. CODE § 6060.]

A]  Why do you limit your answer to "a law student like me"?

B]  Because if I were an out-of-state attorney already practicing elsewhere and had been for four of the past six years, I could be admitted to practice in California if I am at least 18, have "good moral character," and take a bar examination that is shorter than the exam given to fresh law school graduates.

A]  In both cases you mentioned you must have "good moral character."  What does that mean?

B]   Professor Wolfram says it's a slippery term that has many different meanings.  [CHARLES WOLFRAM, MODERN LEGAL ETHICS § 15.3.2, (cited hereafter as "Wolfram").]  One definition I saw says that it means honesty, fairness, candor, trustworthiness and a respect for the law, the judicial process, and the rights or others.  [*See* Anno. 64 A.L.R.2d 301 (1959).]  One Supreme Court opinion says it all boils down to "lack of manifest dishonesty." [*Konigsberg v. State Bar*, 353 U.S. 252, 262-64 (1957); for a critical view of the good moral character standard, *see* Deborah Rhode, *Moral Character as a Professional Credential*, 94 YALE L.J. 491 (1984).]  *Kwasnik v. State Bar of California*, in the casebook, defines it similarly as "the absence of proven conduct or acts which have been historically considered as manifestations of 'moral turpitude.'" Professors Hazard and Hodes go behind the terminology and list matters the disclosure of which by a bar applicant, "will trigger further investigation, and might lead to delayed or denied admission: serious or repeat violations of the criminal law, dishonesty in college or law school academic work, tax fraud or tax evasion, substance abuse, serious mental disorders, unpaid financial obligations, bounced checks or bankruptcies, and dishonesty on the admission questionnaire itself." [GEOFFREY C. HAZARD, JR. & W. WILLIAM HODES, THE LAW OF LAWYERING § 62.7, at 62-14 (3d ed. 2001) (cited hereafter as Hazard & Hodes).] (see below)

A] Suppose that a long time ago, before you ever thought of becoming a lawyer, you were convicted of a crime—say, grand larceny. Does that mean that you cannot become a lawyer?

B] I don't know. I guess it would create a problem. Kwasnik got into trouble because he declared bankruptcy and avoided paying a judgment for $232,000 as a result of a serious traffic accident in which someone was killed.

A] Yes. The Committee of Bar Examiners will certainly want to know the background. But rehabilitation is the key. The important question is: What is your character at the time you seek admission? If you can demonstrate that you have a good moral character now, that will overcome past misconduct. [*See* Anno., 88 A.L.R.3d 192 (1978).] The Bar Examiners will look at the nature of the conduct, the number of times the conduct occurred, the passage of time since the conduct occurred, and your showing of rehabilitation. This is how Kwasnik overcame his past.

B] I have to demonstrate it? You mean I carry the burden of proof if my character is questioned?

A] Yes. [*See Kwasnik.*] Which brings up another point. How does the bar find out about your moral character?

B] Those of us who applied for the California bar had to fill out a long, complicated questionnaire. It asked about trouble with the law, trouble with schools, trouble in the military service, trouble with employers, all manner of things. And it asked for references. I suppose they use all that to check up on you.

A] Yes, they do. What happens if the character investigation turns up something that looks questionable?

B] That happened to one of my former roommates. He had to go down to the state bar office to explain his side of the story. I guess that did not satisfy them, because later they held a hearing before a panel of lawyers. He said it was just like a court hearing. [*See* Rules Regulating Admission to Practice Law in California, Rule X; *Kwasnik*, in the casebook.] Ultimately they found there was no problem with my roommate, but it held him up for several months before he could be admitted to practice.

## Discussion Problem 2

A] Discussion Problem 2 asks about the *Kwasnik* case which deals directly with the question of "good moral character." Character issues come up in both bar admission and discipline.

## Part (a)

A] Part (a) asks you to look at the character investigation procedure. How did the bar learn about Kwasnik's past?

B] It looks like the bar got its start with information Kwasnik himself listed on his California Bar application—that long questionnaire you mentioned in Problem 1. Kwasnik would have had to list any court proceedings to which he was a party and probably the bankruptcy and his previous admissions in New York and Florida. When the bar examiners looked into his past, they would have discovered the unpaid judgment and Kwasnik's mixed success in getting admitted in Florida. Eventually, the bar examiners had lots of information about Kwasnik, including details about the Smilanich litigation, the wage garnishment that resulted, the bankruptcy, and the Florida bar proceedings. These facts were apparently a part of the "stipulation of facts" used before the hearing panel of the State Bar Court.

A] Just what procedure did the California bar follow?

B] Apparently sometime before Kwasnik took the California Attorney's Examination in July 1987, he completed the character application. Then the bar examiners delayed certifying him for practice, even though he passed the examination, until they could complete the investigation. Almost a year later, in June 1988, Kwasnik had a hearing before the State Bar Court in which he had the burden to show he had "good moral character." At this hearing, using the stipulation of facts, the panel found he had proved he had good moral character and recommended he be admitted to the bar. The Committee of Bar Examiners, or someone dissatisfied with the outcome, must have sought a rehearing, but the hearing panel issued findings of fact again recommending he be admitted to the bar. There followed still another level of review. The Review Department of the State Bar Court later made its own findings, among them that Kwasnik lacked good moral character by failing to accept any responsibility for the Smilanich family "victimized by his drunken driving." By an 11-4 vote the review department recommended Kwasnik not be admitted to the bar. Apparently, this finding was accepted by the Committee of Bar Examiners, and Kwasnik then appealed to the California Supreme Court.

A] In all this convoluted procedure, who had the burden of proof, and who should have that burden?

B] According to the California procedure, Kwasnik had the burden to show his good moral character. At first, that didn't seem right. Why should I have to prove I have good enough character to be admitted to the bar? Shouldn't there be a presumption of good character until it's proven otherwise? At the same time, it is important to me and everybody practicing law that we do not admit unfit persons—lawyers have a bad enough image already. Reading a bit between the lines of *Kwasnik* I think that in effect there is a presumption of good character. The bar examiners don't require all applicants to prove they have good character; all they require is a candid application that may disclose areas for further investigation. Although they do try to contact references and run our fingerprints through some checks, unless something special comes to their attention, you will be admitted if you pass the bar exam. Only when something *does* come to their attention (as it did in Kwasnik's case) is the bar likely to ask the applicant to show that the problem doesn't exist, or isn't as serious as it looks, or has been overcome with time and rehabilitation. It is at this stage of the investigation that the burden is on the applicant to demonstrate his or her good character. That seems a reasonably fair system: only when the issue is raised and a cloud exists should an applicant have to dispel the cloud. [According to Wolfram, § 15.3.2, at 858 (citing Rhode, *supra*) in the entire country, only about 50 persons a year are denied admission to the bar on character grounds.]

## **Part (b)**

A] What about specifics? Was the court right or wrong to admit Kwasnik?

B] I think the court was wrong. Kwasnik may have only made one mistake, but so do plenty of murderers. He got into a serious automobile accident that killed the father of a family, and rather than doing all he could to pay the court judgment that resulted, he declared bankruptcy and seemingly washed his hands of the matter. I don't want to have to explain to my family, friends, and the public that we should overlook this one mistake and recognize what a good lawyer he has been most of the time. The profession is in enough trouble without having to explain away members like Kwasnik.

C] I disagree. The purpose of the good character requirement isn't to make our lives more comfortable by imposing exceptional character requirements. It is to ensure that persons admitted to the bar are likely to act as responsible members of the profession *now*. Plenty of good lawyering can be done by people who may have committed careless acts—youthful or later—but who are now prepared to act responsibly. The former District Attorney of San Francisco was nearly prevented from being admitted to practice because of a series of fistfights (9 from 1953-1964 including one as a Hastings student) and numerous arrests (including 6 in one 7-month period) during pro-civil rights public demonstrations. Despite the bar's finding that he lacked good moral character due to a "fixed and dominant propensity for lawlessness whenever violation of the law suits his purposes of the particular moment," the California Supreme Court held these acts did not demonstrate moral turpitude and that he possessed good moral character. [*Hallinan v. Committee of Bar Examiners,* 65 Cal.2d 447, 55 Cal. Rptr. 228, 421 P.2d 76 (1966).] He has gone on to a distinguished career at the bar and in politics. This entire character question makes me uncomfortable. Surely there are many lawyers in the bar skating by on the edges of ethical practice whose misdeed just don't come to the attention of the bar examiners or disciplinary authorities. And in bar admissions, we make a decision often based on only a few years of adulthood, that someone will be presumed to be of good character to practice law for 40 or more years. How can anyone make that kind of determination with any certainty?

A] Certainly a good question. Professor Rhode reaches much the same conclusion and highlights the danger that invidious criteria are often applied as well. [Rhode, *supra.*]

## Part (c)

A] Am I correct in assuming that you are equally suspicious of "bright-line" rules that make certain offenders ineligible for the bar as well as rigid rehabilitation (or no rehabilitation) standards?

C] Yes. As great a burden as it is on the bar, I believe each case rests on its own peculiar facts, and we should avoid any hard and fast rules.

B] That's a cop out. We need clear rules. I would deny admission to anyone who has been convicted of fraud or other serious financial misdeeds, and to those convicted of violent crimes, and any kind of drug dealing.

## Part (d)

A] No matter when the conduct occurred—how long ago or what the age of the applicant at the time? What about the 15 or 16-year-old from the urban ghetto who throws a rock at a firefighter during a riot and is convicted or the youngster who gets picked up with enough drugs in her possession to convict her on weight alone of possession with intent to sell? Ten years later, they've straightened up their lives and want to go to law school. Are they out of luck in your system?

B] I'll have to think about it. [Wolfram states that "very few, if any, offenses are so disabling that a person will be excluded from the bar in every state because of the offense." Wolfram, § 15.3.2, at 862.]

### Discussion Problem 3

A] We'll return to the character question again in Problem 5. For now, let's look at another of the requirements for the practice of law in California.

## Part (a)

A] Will you have to become a member of the State Bar of California?

B] Yes, because California has a "mandatory" or "compulsory" bar (sometimes also called a "unified bar" or "integrated bar"), meaning that to practice in this state you must be a member of the State Bar of California.

A] That's right. After you learn that you have passed the bar examination, you will be sworn into practice before the Supreme Court of California. That gives you the right to practice before any state tribunal in California. (For example, you don't have to be admitted separately to practice in the Superior Court in Fresno.) At the same time, you will become a member of the State Bar of California, and to be a member you will have to pay annual dues. What is the dues money used for?

B] Running the discipline system, communicating with bar members and educating the public about the bar, monitoring the Minimum Continuing Legal Education (MCLE) program, running the Ethics Hotline, and overseeing pro bono and IOLTA programs that provide legal services to low-income Californians. Before 2002, a small portion of the annual dues was used for lobbying, mostly on issues relating to the legal profession or the quality of legal services. The amount that was used for lobbying on other issues was almost negligible, and after the decision in the *Keller* case, a lawyer who didn't want to pay for that activity could deduct a ratable amount from his or her dues bill.

But when, following *Keller*, litigation and disputes over lobbying activities between the Bar and dissenting members continued, the California legislature and the California State Bar finally agreed to create a separate Conference of Delegates of California Bar Associations. The Conference, incorporated in June 2002, will hold annual meetings jointly with the Bar through 2007, sharing expenses and meeting revenues. The Bar will collect donations to the Conference as part of its dues bills. The Conference will be free to debate and approve proposals to change California law, limited only by its own bylaws and agreements. [*See The Daily Recorder*, September 24, 2002, at 1, 10.]

A] Did the decision in *Keller* have any impact on lawyers' attitudes about having a mandatory state bar?

B] After the *Keller* decision, California lawyers had a plebiscite about whether to continue having mandatory bar membership. The plebiscite resulted in an almost 2-1 vote to retain the mandatory bar.

A] Where does the *Keller* decision leave mandatory bar membership?

B] Just about where it was. Mandatory bar membership is constitutional, but the members cannot be required to pay dues to support political or ideological activities that have little or nothing to do with regulating the legal profession or improving the quality of legal services. [*Morrow v. State Bar of California*, 118 F.3d 1174 (9th Cir. 1999).]

## Part (b)

A] Part (b) of Problem 3 asks if you will have to join the city or county bar association in the area where you open your office. Will you?

B] No, those are voluntary organizations. But in the firm where I clerked last summer, most of the lawyers did belong. They said it was a good way to meet other members of the local bar, keep up on current legal developments, and even earn MCLE credit. A partner took me to a county bar association lunch; I met some lawyers from other firms, and we heard an interesting program on civil discovery proceedings.

## Part (c)

A] Part (c) of Problem 3 asks whether you will have to join the American Bar Association. Will you?

B] No. Only about one-third of the lawyers in the country belong to it. I heard someone say that California has both more ABA members and more nonmembers than any other state. I think I will join it because I understand the ABA does a lot with continuing legal education and has been a strong voice for promoting both federally-supported legal services and pro bono programs. I hope to become a litigator, so I will probably join the Litigation Section of the ABA. That section puts out a valuable periodical and offers useful continuing education programs.

## Discussion Problem 4

A] In Problem 4, you've already been admitted to practice before all the California state courts.

## Part (a)

A] What would you have to do if you wished to represent client Arnold in the United States District Court for the Northern District of California (San Francisco/San Jose)?

B] That depends on the local rules of the federal district court; the local rules vary considerably from court to court. In the Northern District of California (San Francisco/San Jose) you must have good moral character and must be an active member in good standing of the Bar of the State of California. [Local Rule 11-1.] In the Eastern District of California (Sacramento/Fresno), the local rules also say you must be an active member in good standing of the State Bar of California. [Local Rule 83-180.] In each case, you must file a petition to be admitted. In the Northern District the petition must be accompanied by a certified copy of certificate of membership in the Bar of the State of California and you must certify your knowledge of the Federal Rules of Civil and Criminal Procedure and Evidence and the local and Ninth Circuit Court of Appeals' rules of court; your familiarity with the Alternative Dispute Resolution Programs of the court; and your understanding of and commitment to abide by the court's Standards of Professional Conduct. In the Eastern District the petition must state your residence and office addresses; the courts in which you have been admitted to practice and the dates of admission, whether you are active and in good standing in each of the courts, and whether you have been or are being disciplined; and the petition must be accompanied by satisfactory proof that you are an active member of the State Bar and give your State Bar number. Then you can be admitted, either on oral motion or without even appearing, but you must sign up with the clerk, take an oath, and pay the prescribed fee.

## Part (b)

A] Part (b) of Problem 4 asks about being admitted to practice before the United States Court of Appeals for the Ninth Circuit (that includes California). What does that require?

B] That's covered by a uniform rule for all of the federal circuits—Federal Rule of Appellate Procedure 46(a). It says that you can be admitted if you have good moral character and are a member of the bar of any other federal court or the highest court of a state. Again, you have to file an application, take an oath, pay a fee, and get a present member of that court's bar to move your admission, either orally or in writing.

## Part (c)

A] Part (c) of Problem 4 asks what it takes to be entitled to practice before the United States Supreme Court. What did you discover?

B] That's governed by Rule 5 of the Revised Rules of the United States Supreme Court. It says you must be of good moral and professional character, you must have been admitted to practice before the highest court of any state, commonwealth, territory, or possession of the United States or of the District of Columbia for at least three years immediately before applying, and you must have been free of any disciplinary action whatsoever during that 3-year period. You need proof of your previous admission and good standing. Two present members of the Supreme Court Bar must sponsor you and swear to your good moral character, and again you must take an oath and pay a fee. All of that can be accomplished by mail, unless you happen to be in Washington, D.C., and want to be admitted on oral motion in open court.

*[Teachers may wish to take up subparts (d) and (e) together. Part (d) deals with representing a client in a dispute that appears destined for non-judicial resolution; while (e) specifically refers to representation in a judicial dispute. In both cases the dispute involves a state in which the lawyer has not been admitted to practice.]*

## Part (d)

A] In part (d) of Problem 4, we are asked about representing a California client of yours whose business activities in Colorado have resulted in a dispute there. She would like you to represent her in connection with that dispute in Colorado. It also looks like the Colorado dispute may end up in arbitration or other alternative dispute resolution proceedings in Colorado. Currently, you are not admitted to practice in Colorado. Can you represent her?

B] I don't think so. I know that practicing law in a jurisdiction without being admitted to practice there is grounds for discipline [ABA Model Rule 5.5(a); and it may also be a violation of Colorado law. *See, e.g.,* CAL. BUS & PROF. CODE §§ 6125-6126 (misdemeanor).] Unless you can make some sort of argument that what you will do in Colorado isn't the practice of law—and that seems a stretch—I think you're going to have to say sorry, but you'll need to find a lawyer admitted in Colorado to help you out.

A] You're certainly right about the basic rules, but that doesn't really answer the question. Before you tell your client you can't help her, and possibly lose not just this representation, but maybe the client as well, since you didn't help her out in her time of need, let's look at what you can do if you do want to undertake the representation and stay within the rules.

B] OK. Well, if I am interested in regularly representing clients in Colorado, I might want to become regularly admitted to the Colorado bar. If California and Colorado had a reciprocity agreement, then it would be simple, provided I could meet some basic requirements, such as a minimum period of law practice in California. Unfortunately, California does not recognize reciprocity agreements at all, so I will have to do it the hard way, by taking the Colorado bar examination. Until recently, this might have presented another problem. Many states had residency requirements of one kind or another. For example, New Hampshire wouldn't admit a Vermont resident to the New Hampshire bar unless she took up residence in New Hampshire. [*Supreme Court of New Hampshire v. Piper*, 470 U.S. 274 (1985).] But beginning with the *Piper* case, the United States Supreme Court has found residency requirements violate the Constitution's privileges and immunities clause by depriving lawyers of their right to practice their profession. The Court has rejected all the reasons offered by the states as not substantial enough to bar nonresidents from taking the bar examination and practicing law. If the special circumstances present in *Barnard v. Thorstenn*, 489 U.S. 546 (1989), cited in the casebook, weren't enough to justify the Virgin Islands' residency requirement, it's hard to see what would. Neither the Islands' geographic isolation, nor their caseload pressures, nor difficulties in access to their sources of law, nor administrative burdens, nor the need for all bar members to accept court appointments to represent indigent criminal defendants justified a blanket exclusion of nonresident lawyers.

A] So neither the Virgin Islands nor Colorado can keep you out of their state bars just because you live in California. Is there any downside to this new world of nationwide practice?

B] As I understand it, I can take as many bar exams as I want and join as many state bar associations as I want, but I'm going to have to pay my dues in each of those states—both the money dues and the figurative dues (MCLE, court-appointments, *pro bono* obligations and the like) the states impose. And, the more out-of-state lawyers that must be monitored and regulated, the higher the fees are likely to be for everyone.

A] There may be more costs here than the Court recognized, but it's hard to see what the alternative would be. If strictly interpreted, the unauthorized practice rules would put the modern nationwide practice of law at risk and leave lawyers tied to localities when their business clients are not. The business of law practice has simply outgrown its state-based regulation, but there is no general federal regulation either. But relief may be at hand. In connection with its Ethics 2000 Commission, in 2000, the ABA appointed a Commission on Multijurisdictional Practice. The Commission proposed a major revision to ABA Model Rule 5.5 to create a set of "safe harbors" that allow lawyers admitted elsewhere and not under any disciplinary injunction in their state(s) of admission to engage in limited or temporary activities in another state in which they are not admitted. Under amended Model Rule 5.5, "(c) A lawyer admitted in another United States jurisdiction, and not disbarred or suspended from practice in any jurisdiction, may provide legal services on a temporary basis in this jurisdiction that: . . . (3) are in or reasonably related to a pending or potential arbitration, mediation, or other alternative dispute resolution proceeding in this or another jurisdiction, if the services arise out of or are reasonably related to the lawyer's practice in a jurisdiction in which the lawyer is admitted to practice and are not services for which the forum requires pro hac vice admission . . .." This seems to fit perfectly. So, if I want to avoid becoming a regular member of the Colorado bar, but still represent Deborah in her consulting fees dispute, I may be able to take advantage of the provisions of Rule 5.5(c)(3), *if Colorado adopts the amended Rule.* Even without the Rule's safe harbor provisions, most states have some limited exemptions established by rule, statute, or case law. However, it is critical that you check on the law of the particular state in which you seek to provide limited services but not seek full bar admission. Just a few years back, the California Supreme Court, in *Birbrower, Montalbano, Condon & Frank, P.C. v. Superior Court*, 17 Cal.4th 643a (1998), found lawyers doing what your client wants here were engaged in the unlawful practice of law in California and denied them the right to collect unpaid fees from their client. In response, the legislature enacted Cal. Civ. Proc. Code § 1282.4 specifically allowing lawyers not licensed in California to represent clients at arbitration proceedings if they file a timely certificate.

The California Supreme Court recently adopted the recommendations of the "Advisory Task Force on Multijurisdictional Practice" to allow in-house counsel and public interest lawyers not yet admitted to practice in California to practice on a limited basis without obtaining full admission to the bar. In addition, although the task force recommended against a system of full reciprocity, the new rules allow out-of-state lawyers to practice in California under limited circumstances. [*See* Cal. S.Ct. Rules on Multijurisdictional Practice, Rules 9.45-9.48.]

By the way, this is not a problem limited to the United States. The European Union is faced with a similar problem in an international context. The treaties and rules that tie the EU nations together mandate freedom to do business, including professional business, but the EU is having difficulty accommodating the radically different forms of law practice among its member states.

### Part (e)

A] Part (e) of Problem 4 asks about representing a client in a negligence action against him pending in the Arizona courts, just across the river from where you have your law office in California. Under what circumstances may you do that?

B] Just like in Part (d), I might want to take the Arizona bar examination and become regularly admitted to the Arizona. If California and Arizona had a reciprocity agreement, then I may be able to take advantage of that—but they don't.

A] If you want to find some way of avoiding becoming a regular member of the Arizona bar, but still represent Edgar in his automobile negligence case, do you have an alternative?

B] There is always the possibility of getting the Arizona court to admit me specially—*pro hac vice*—for the purpose of litigating Edgar's case only. [*See* Wolfram § 15.4.3.] In California, admissions *pro hac vice* are governed by a rule of court that requires a written application, payment of a fee, and requires that I associate an active member of the California State Bar as counsel of record. [*See* Cal. Rules of Court 983.] Since Arizona's rule may differ, I will check closely and follow its particular requirements.

A] Suppose that while representing Edgar in that case in Arizona, after being admitted *pro hac vice*, you do something unethical—perhaps you destroy some documents that the court has ordered your client to produce. Which state could discipline you?

B] Both California and Arizona could. Arizona could discipline me because I've interfered with the process of justice in the Arizona court, and because I'm admitted there *pro hac vice*. And, of course, California could discipline me as well, because I'm a member of the California bar and have my office in California. [*See* CRPC 1-100(D); ABA Model Rule 8.5.]

## Part (e)

A] Part (e) of Problem 4 asks about joining with your California law partner, Thomas, to open a branch office in Nevada. Thomas is admitted in Nevada, but you are not. Could you open that branch office with Thomas?

B] Yes, but there would be limitations on how we could hold ourselves out to the public. According to ABA Model Rule 7.5(b), Thomas and I could open the branch office in Nevada under the same name that we use in California. But on the letterhead for the branch office, and in advertisements and other firm listings in Nevada, we'd have to indicate that Thomas is the only one licensed to practice in Nevada. For instance, the letterhead might have a note after my name saying "Admitted in California only" or something to that effect. The CRPC have no exact counterpart, but California's advertising rule prohibits the use of untrue statements and false, deceptive, or misleading matter in any "communication," including a firm name. [CRPC 1-400(A) and (D).]

## Discussion Problem 5

A] In Problem 5, you are asked to serve as a lawyer's lawyer. Lawyer Lawrence has embezzled money from a real estate investment venture in which he and his friends were involved. You are asked to assume that Lawrence was not acting as a lawyer but rather as a purely private citizen, a business person, in connection with that real estate investment venture.

## Part (a)

A] Is he subject to discipline by the bar for what he did? Even though he wasn't acting in his lawyer capacity?

B] Yes. The capacity makes no difference—if Lawrence is a crook in his personal capacity, he is likely to be a crook in his lawyer capacity as well. ABA Model Rule 8.4(b) lists as "professional misconduct" the commission of "a criminal act that reflects adversely on the lawyer's honesty, trustworthiness or fitness as a lawyer in other respects." Stealing money from friends surely ought to qualify. Second, he would be disciplined for conduct involving "dishonesty, fraud, deceit, or misrepresentation." Embezzlement involves dishonesty and fraud. [ABA Model Rule 8.4(c).] I've seen the term "moral turpitude" mentioned in cases and older authorities, but I haven't seen that term used in the ABA Model Rules—was it abandoned at some point?

A] "Moral turpitude" is still used in California and some other jurisdictions, but it's a fuzzy term without well-agreed boundaries. [*See, e.g.,* CAL. BUS. & PROF. CODE § 6106 (commission of an act of moral turpitude is grounds for suspension or disbarment).] The Comment to ABA Model Rule 8.4 explains that the drafters believed lawyers should be professionally disciplined only for "offenses that indicate lack of those characteristics relevant to law practice"— for example, dishonesty, breach of trust, and acts of violence. But notice that the drafters also say that a "pattern of repeated offenses," even minor ones, can indicate "indifference to legal obligation." [*See generally* Hazard & Hodes, § 65.4.]

## **Part (b)**

A] Now consider part (b) of Problem 5. Do you have an ethical duty to turn in Lawrence?

B] Under the ABA Model Rules, a lawyer generally does have a duty to turn in another lawyer who has committed a disciplinary violation implicating the lawyer's "honesty, trustworthiness or fitness as a lawyer." [*See* ABA Model Rule 8.3(a).] But that duty does not apply if the information is privileged. And in this case the information would be protected by the attorney-client privilege. The question states that Lawrence consulted me in my capacity as a lawyer, and that he consulted me in confidence. Therefore I have no duty to turn him in— in fact, I could be disciplined myself if I revealed his confidential information. [ABA Model Rule 1.6(a).] In California, there is no disciplinary rule that requires one lawyer to turn in another lawyer for a disciplinary violation. Instead, California has an extensive self-reporting requirement. [*See* CAL. BUS. & PROF. CODE § 6068(o).]

C] Didn't we previously discuss an exception to the duty of confidentiality under the ABA Model Rules when the client has committed a fraud?

A] There are exceptions to prevent a fraud, and to mitigate or rectify the client's fraud, "in furtherance of which the client has used the lawyer's services." [*See* ABA Model Rule 1.6(b)(2), (3).] Here, Lawrence's fraud was a done deal before he came to you for legal advice, so these exceptions are inapplicable. And, remember, there are no such exceptions for fraud under the

California Rules of Professional Conduct.

## Discussion Problem 6

A] Discussion Problem 6 asks about two lawyer discipline cases you read—*In re Mountain* and *Drociak v. State Bar of California.* Before we look at the cases, you might want to consider whether certain *types* of lawyers are more likely to get into disciplinary difficulty than other types. A recent study by the *California Lawyer* magazine of all 285 discipline cases in the California Supreme Court from June 1988 to June 1989 described the typical attorney punished by the bar as "middle-aged, male and inclined to take on more work than he can handle effectively or competently." Fully half were sole practitioners. Ninety-two percent were male (versus 76 percent of the bar); 82 percent had been in practice for at least 11 years; 57 percent for 11-20 years (versus 46 and 30 percent, respectively); 75 percent were between the ages of 36 and 55; and 27 percent between 41 and 45. [James Evans, *Lawyers at Risk,* California Lawyer 45-48 (October 1989).]

### Part (a)

A] Returning to *Mountain* and *Drociak*, Part (a) asks in each case how the state bar probably became aware of the lawyer's misconduct.

B] In *Mountain*, the adoption case, I'd guess that the first couple (Mr. and Mrs. M) complained to the state bar. Or else lawyer G, who had been hired by the M's to investigate the matter, reported Mountain to the state bar. In the blank verification forms case, *Drociak,* the opinion does not tell us what the source of the bar's information was. It might have come from the adversary lawyer or from the judge who dismissed the case when the client failed to appear, or it could even have come from Drociak himself or someone in his office— Drociak admitted that he used presigned forms in other cases as well before the disciplinary panel.

### Part (b)

A] Part (b) asks what procedure was followed in each case.

B] The procedures in these two cases seemed quite similar but not identical. We assume that in each case, somebody informed the state bar of the questionable conduct. Then, presumably after some investigation, the state bar commenced a proceeding. In *Mountain* the proceeding started with a complaint filed by the Kansas "disciplinary administrator." We are not told precisely how the *Drociak* proceedings began. The California State Bar may begin an investigation either with or without a complaint to the State Bar. The State Bar then investigates, and if The Office of Investigation or Trial Counsel believes there is reasonable cause, the office issues an order to show cause directed to the bar member. [*See* Rules of Procedure of the State Bar of California; Title III, General Provisions; Division II; Chapter 4, Investigations; Chapter 6, Disposition of Inquiries, Complaints and Investigations (1996). An earlier set of rules was in effect in *Drociak*.]

A] What was the next step in each case?

B] In both *Mountain* and *Drociak* there were hearings before a disciplinary panel (in *Drociak*, part of the State Bar Court); Mountain and Drociak apparently attended in person; Mountain had a lawyer representing him. The hearing panels listened to evidence from the lawyers and made findings of fact and conclusions of law—much as a judge would do after a court trial in an ordinary civil case. The panels also made recommendations about the appropriate discipline—that Mountain should be disbarred and that Drociak should be suspended from practice one year, stayed, and placed on probation for two years under certain conditions, including 30 days' actual suspension.

A] Each case eventually ended up in a court; how did that happen?

B] In *Mountain*, the hearing panel wrote its final report with the findings of fact, conclusions of law and recommendation for disbarment. Then Mountain took exceptions to the panel's report and appealed to the Supreme Court of Kansas. In *Drociak*, the procedure was only slightly different, with one more step. The panel's findings were reviewed by the Review Department of the State Bar Court. The review department adopted the panel's findings and recommendation on a nine-to-four vote (three of the dissenters found the discipline excessive; one believed it was too lenient). Drociak then challenged the findings and recommendation in the Supreme Court of California. In each case, the state supreme court apparently looked carefully at the particular facts and exercised its own judgment about the kind of discipline to impose. In Drociak's case, the California Supreme Court agreed that the findings had cast him in a "false light," but it upheld the disciplinary recommendation nevertheless.

## Part (c)

A] Part (c) asks what you think of the discipline imposed on Mountain. Was it too lenient, or too harsh, or just about right?

B] Mountain was disbarred, and that's the most that could have been done to him—the maximum disciplinary sanction. He started out representing the M's, but then he convinced the natural mother that he was representing her, and in the end he represented the other couple who finally adopted the baby. He had a three-way conflict of interest going there! [*See* ABA Informal Op. 87-1523 (1987).] Further, he lied to the M's about the baby and about what he'd done, and later he lied to attorney G. Finally, he was apparently doing it all out of personal greed. I'd say disbarment was just right.

[Note: For a closer look at adoption lawyers in California, see Stephen Pressman, *The Baby Brokers*, California Lawyer 30-34, 105 (July 1991). California law prohibits lawyers from representing both the adopting parents and the birth parents without detailed written consent from both parties. CAL. FAMILY CODE § 8800.]

## Part (d)

A] Part (d) asks about Drociak. Was the discipline imposed on Drociak too lenient, too harsh, or just about right?

B] Again, I think it was just right. Drociak apparently was not acting out of greed or personal interest, but believed he was actually helping his clients by using presigned verifications. Given his clean 25-year record, harsh punishment would have been inappropriate. On the other hand, mere reproval would have been too lenient. I think the California Supreme Court wanted to send a strong message to all California lawyers that this kind of deception of the court and other counsel is a serious matter and will not be tolerated, and that it's no excuse to say you were doing it for the client's sake.

## KWASNIK v. STATE BAR OF CALIFORNIA
### Supreme Court of California, 1990

Facts: Petitioner Kwasnik, a member of the New York Bar, was involved in an automobile accident in 1970 that resulted in the death of Steven Smilanich.

Petitioner pleaded guilty to a traffic infraction ("driving while impaired") and received a $50 fine, but no criminal charges were filed against him. Smilanich's widow and children filed a wrongful death action against him in 1974. The court found for Smilanich in the amount of $232,234.16. Petitioner's insurance carrier paid the $10,000 policy limit. The court enforced the judgment by garnishing petitioner's wages when he refused to pay. Petitioner attempted to make a settlement offer with Smilanich in November 1980 for a fraction of the remaining judgment. Smilanich refused and petitioner filed for bankruptcy in Florida asking only for discharge of the Smilanich judgment. The judgment was discharged in March 1981.

The Florida Bar denied petitioner admission when he applied in 1979, finding he had engaged in three instances of wrongful conduct. The Florida Supreme Court denied review. When the Florida State Bar once again refused to admit petitioner in 1986, the Florida Supreme Court reviewed the recommendation and held that the petitioner met the moral character requirements due to his "sufficient rehabilitation" and ordered the Florida Bar to admit petitioner if he passed the bar exam. Kwasnik was admitted to practice in Florida in 1988.

In 1987, Kwasnik applied to the California State Bar and passed the Attorney's Examination of the California Bar Examination. The State Bar Court held a formal hearing to investigate petitioner's moral character. The three judge panel found that he had sustained his burden of proof and recommended his admission to the California Bar. The Review Department of the State Bar made its own findings and determined that petitioner did not possess good moral character based on his conduct in Florida regarding the Smilanich matter. The review department recommended that the California Bar refuse Kwasnik admission. Petitioner sought review by the California Supreme Court.

Issue: Did petitioner sufficiently establish good moral character despite a prior wrongful death judgment against him that he discharged in bankruptcy?

Holding: Yes. The State Bar requires a showing of good moral character in order to protect the public, not to impose punishment. The petitioner has the burden of proving that he conducted himself in a manner consistent with good moral character. If he can do so, the State Bar must rebut the petitioner's showing of rehabilitation from previous misconduct or his prima facie case. In Kwasnik's case, the State Bar has presented no evidence that petitioner's previous conduct would affect his ability to practice law in any way.

Discussion: The court has defined "good moral character" as "the absence of proven conduct or acts which have been historically considered as manifestations of moral turpitude." In order to determine if an attorney possesses good moral character, the court looks to previous acts of the attorney and to the propensity of the attorney to commit wrongdoing. The applicant has the burden of proving good moral character.

In a situation when an applicant has committed an act labeled as contrary to good moral character, the applicant can prove rehabilitation has occurred. The court accords significant weight to testimonials by attorneys and judges because they have a stake in the integrity of their profession. Petitioner had eight such letters written on his behalf on the occasion of his second application to the Florida State Bar. An applicant can also prove rehabilitation by showing an unblemished record other than the act in question. In addition, since the petitioner's misconduct did not in any way relate to the practice of law, it should receive less weight in evaluating petitioner's moral character.

Finally, the purpose of the moral character requirement is to protect the public and the public's confidence in the legal punishment rather than to impose punishment. Preventing the petitioner from admission to the bar would not protect the public, it would only serve to punish the petitioner.

## DROCIAK v. STATE BAR OF CALIFORNIA
### Supreme Court of California, 1991

Facts: Petitioner Drociak represented a party in a personal injury action against Greyhound Bus Lines, Inc. Petitioner had his client sign undated blank verification forms. Petitioner filed a complaint on behalf of his client. When Greyhound made a discovery request, petitioner wrote to his client four times between May and August 1986 requesting that she visit his office to prepare answers to the questions. He received no reply. Petitioner told counsel for Greyhound that he had "temporarily lost contact" with his client. Petitioner received numerous extensions for discovery but finally used the undated presigned verifications and answered the interrogatories himself. He also served responses to a request for documents with one of the presigned verifications. The court dismissed the trial when the petitioner's client failed to appear. Petitioner found out shortly after that his client had died in October 1985. The Review Committee of the State Bar recommended discipline for violation of California Business and Professional Code section 6106 (commission of an act involving moral turpitude), section 6068(d) (failing to

34

employ "such means only as are consistent with the truth"), and Rules of Professional Conduct 5-200 (same as 6068(d)). Drociak sought review by the California Supreme Court.

Issue: What is the appropriate discipline for an attorney who uses presigned verification forms to respond to discovery without the client's participation?

Holding: The Review Department's finding of unprofessional conduct was supported by the evidence. The decision to suspend Drociak for 30 days with two years probation is appropriate punishment.

Discussion: Drociak violated sections 6106 and 6068(d) of the California Business and Professional Code by attaching the presigned verification to the response to the discovery request and to the answers to the interrogatories. The state bar can punish violations of sections 6106 and 6068(d) with disbarment or suspension. Petitioner did not provide any reason for the court to make an exception to sections 6106 and 6068(d). Hardship on the attorney's office staff due to the attorney's suspension and absence of any harm to the client do not suffice to mitigate the importance of protecting the public by deterring future misconduct. The court found the recommended discipline necessary and appropriate to protect the public and deter future misconduct.

## SHELLER v. SUPERIOR COURT
### California Court of Appeal, 2008

Facts: A Texas attorney, appearing *pro hac vice* in a California class action, sent a communication to class members containing a misrepresentation. The trial court formally reprimanded the attorney and imposed attorney fees as a condition of permitting the attorney to retain his *pro hac vice* status.

Issue: Do the California state trial courts have the authority to revoke an attorney's *pro hac vice* status?

Holding: Yes. However, the trial court did not have the authority to reprimand the attorney or impose attorney fees.

Discussion: The California state trial courts have the inherent power to revoke a lawyer's *pro hac vice* status when the lawyer has engaged in conduct that would be sufficient to disqualify a California attorney.

## IN RE MOUNTAIN
### Supreme Court of Kansas, 1986

Facts: This is a state bar discipline proceeding against attorney Mountain, arising from his handling of an adoption. Mr. and Mrs. M wanted to adopt a baby from expectant mother, A.S. The M's contacted attorney Mountain who agreed to represent them for $500 ($250 in advance). Mountain then contacted A.S. and her grandmother. He convinced them that he represented them. The grandmother decided that the M's were not wealthy enough to adopt the baby. Mountain suggested other couples and told the grandmother she would receive $5,000 under a new arrangement with a different couple. Mountain then lied to the M's, telling them that A.S.'s baby showed fetal abnormalities. Mountain had never talked to A.S.'s physician, and the physician had never said the fetus was abnormal. Mountain also told the M's that there was family resistance to the adoption. Mountain advised the M's not to go through with the adoption, and they reluctantly agreed not to. Meanwhile, Mountain had already made arrangements for a different couple to adopt the baby. This second couple paid Mountain $17,000.

The M's then hired another attorney, G, to investigate the matter. Mountain lied to G about several aspects of his role in the adoption. After G started investigating, Mountain refunded the $250 fee advance to the M's, but he did not refund other money the M's had advanced for the expectant mother's financial support.

Issues: Has Mountain violated the ethics of the profession? If so, what is the appropriate discipline?

Holding: Mountain violated the conflict of interest rules by representing the M's and the second couple at the same time in the same matter. He lied to the M's about the health of the fetus, and he failed to carry out his agreement to represent the M's in the matter. Further, Mountain lied to attorney G about the matter, and he collected a clearly excessive fee from the second couple. The appropriate discipline is disbarment.

Discussion: Note the procedure followed in this discipline case. Somebody, probably the M's or attorney G, informed the state bar about Mountain's conduct. After investigation, a state bar official filed a formal complaint. In due course, a hearing panel heard evidence, entered findings of fact and conclusions of law, and recommended that Mountain be disbarred. Mountain then appealed. The Supreme Court of Kansas decided that the evidence supported the findings of fact, that the findings of fact supported the conclusions of law, and that disbarment was the appropriate sanction. The order of disbarment was entered directly by the Supreme Court, and the clerk was instructed to strike Mountain's name from the rolls.

# CHAPTER THREE
# BEGINNING AND ENDING THE
# LAWYER-CLIENT RELATIONSHIP

## Discussion Problem 1

A]  Problem 1 asks about lawyer Sheila who has been asked to defend a member of the American Nazi Party in a criminal case involving an allegedly illegal street rally.  Let us begin with a much simpler case.  Suppose you have decided to devote your professional life to representing plaintiffs who get injured by dangerous products.  A wealthy chainsaw manufacturer swaggers into your office and demands that you defend him in a pending products liability case.  Must you do so?

B]  I'm not sure.  The closest authority I could find is Comment 1 to ABA Model Rule 6.2, which says that ordinarily a lawyer is not obliged to accept a client whose character or cause is repugnant to the lawyer.  I'm not sure whether the chainsaw guy qualifies as "repugnant."

A]  Based on your own experience, does a lawyer have a duty to serve anybody who walks in the door with the fee in hand?

B]  I'm still not sure.

A]  The ABA Model Rules and the CRPC aren't much help here, but the general rule in the United States is this:  A lawyer is not a public utility.  That is, a lawyer has no duty to serve just anybody who wants service and can pay for it.  [*See* Wolfram § 10.2.2.]  Thus, you could decline to represent the chainsaw manufacturer for whatever reasons might suit you.  That's the general rule.  But you read about some exceptions to the general rule; what's one of them?

B]  If you are in a state like California that uses the Attorney's Oath [quoted in the casebook], one of the things you swear is that you will not reject, for personal reasons, "the cause of the defenseless or the oppressed."

A]  Do you find anything similar in the ABA Model Rules?

B]  Yes,  a similar approach is found in the Comments to ABA Model Rule 6.2.

A] In Discussion Problem 1, do you think that the Nazi Party falls in the category of "defenseless or oppressed"?

B] That's debatable. The problem says that the American Nazi Party has ample funds to pay for his defense. On the other hand, it also says that the other skilled trial lawyers in the city have refused to serve as counsel. I think this differs from the wealthy chainsaw manufacturer; he should be able to pay the fee, and many good firms of tort defense lawyers would probably be willing and anxious to serve him. I think the Nazi Party in Problem 1 is an example of the "unpopular client" mentioned in Comment 1 to ABA Model Rule 6.2. If so, then I should not turn him down simply because I find him and his beliefs odious.

A] Can anybody think of a second exception to the general rule that a "lawyer is not a public utility"?

C] Yes. A lawyer is obliged to accept a fair share of work *pro bono publico.*

A] Let's postpone that important one until we get to Discussion Problem 2. Any other exceptions?

C] Yes, there's one suggested by part (b) of Problem 1; if the court *appoints* Sheila to serve as defense counsel, then there are limits on her ability to turn down the appointment.

A] Can you give us an example of those limits?

C] If taking the case would require the lawyer to violate a disciplinary rule, then the lawyer must decline the case. For example, suppose the court appoints Sheila as defense counsel without realizing that she was the only eyewitness to a key contested fact in the case. Generally, a lawyer cannot serve as trial counsel in a case in which she must also testify as a witness. [*See* ABA Model Rule 3.7; CRPC 5-210.] Therefore, Sheila should respectfully decline the court appointment. [*See* ABA Model Rule 6.2(a).]

A] Is there anything else that would excuse Sheila from accepting a court appointment as defense counsel?

B] The problem states that some of Sheila's business clients are prominent citizens who opposed the rally. What if they decide that they don't want to do business with a lawyer who represents Nazis? ABA Model Rule 6.2(b) says Sheila could be excused if taking the case would "result in an unreasonable financial burden" on her. Perhaps Sheila could argue that she should be excused because some of her regular clients will take their business elsewhere, and that will impose an unreasonable financial burden on her.

A] Do you find that argument persuasive?

B] No. It's contrary to the admonition in Comment 1 to ABA Model Rule 6.2 that a lawyer should accept a "fair share of unpopular matters or indigent or unpopular clients." I think Rule 6.2(b) was intended to apply when the appointed case would consume so much time and energy that it would create a precarious financial situation for the lawyer.

A] Does anybody see any other ground on which Sheila could be excused from accepting a court appointment as defense counsel in this case?

C] Yes. ABA Model Rule 6.2(c) states that if your personal feelings about a case are so strong that you could not give the client proper legal service, then you should decline the appointment. The problem states that Sheila is Jewish and that her grandparents narrowly escaped from Austria in 1939. I think we'd need to know more about Sheila's personal feelings about Nazism to decide whether that provision would apply. If her feelings were strong enough, they might even create a conflict of interest. [*See* ABA Model Rule 1.7(a)(2); CRPC 3-310.]

## Discussion Problem 2

A] In Discussion Problem 2, the newly-hired associates in your law firm have asked the firm to adopt a policy that every lawyer should devote the equivalent of 100 hours a year to representing poor people. As a young partner in the firm, how are you going to vote on that proposal?

B] I'm going to vote in favor of it. ABA Model Rule 6.1 says that lawyers ought to do *pro bono* work. ABA Model Rule 6.1 provides in its first sentence: "Every lawyer has a professional responsibility to provide legal services to those unable to pay." Since 1993, ABA Model Rule 6.1 has incorporated as an aspiration the House of Delegates' sense that each lawyer should render 50 hours of *pro bono* work a year, with a substantial majority of that work directed to the economically disadvantaged. The State Bar of California also urges all lawyers to give at least 50 hours of *pro bono* services annually to the indigent. There's no disciplinary rule that requires it, but it's strongly encouraged. We can do better and give 100 hours.

A] Sure, but why focus our efforts solely on representing poor people in civil and criminal cases? The earlier version of ABA Model Rule 6.1 (pre-1993) gave a broad definition to *pro bono*; it included not only representing poor people, but also covered just about anything a lawyer could regard as a "worthy cause." That would include having the lawyers in the firm help organize a charity ball to support the civic light opera. Will you vote for this proposal if it requires every lawyer in the firm to spend 100 hours a year representing indigents in civil and criminal cases?

B] My answer is still yes. Indigent people need representation, and the government programs are drastically underfunded. Since lawyers enjoy a monopoly of the right to practice law, I think each lawyer has a corresponding obligation to do a fair share of the free legal work that needs doing.

C] I disagree. Why should we be bound by what the ABA, a highly political organization, decides is the "right" kind of *pro bono* work? I'm not sure we have any obligation to work for free at all, much less an obligation to work for free only for the indigent. My expertise might be in corporate advising and mergers; why should I have to do work for indigent clients; I may not even be competent to do that kind of work. And isn't offering incompetent legal service just as much a failure of professional ethics as not living up to what the ABA wants to promote as a P.R. project? [*See* ABA Model Rule 1.1 (incompetence as a disciplinary violation.] If this really turns out to be a matter of conscience and not professional regulation—the rule says I "should aspire" to render *pro bono* services, not that I "shall" do so—then I am entitled to be guided by my own conscience.

A] What did you think of the *Bothwell* case, which holds that a federal district court can appoint unwilling counsel to serve without a fee in a civil matter, but, at the same time, declines to make the appointment under its facts?

B] I agreed with the court's conclusion. As important as volunteer efforts are, courts can and should require lawyers to share in the necessary provision of legal services to those who cannot afford them. Many lawyers are required to pay dues to bar associations as a condition of practice. [*See Keller v. State Bar of California*, cited in Chapter 2 of the casebook]. Why can't they also be required to make a small portion of their time available to those who cannot otherwise afford legal services? The *Bothwell* court drew upon the need to ensure a "fair and just" adjudicative process, the need to maintain the integrity of the judiciary and civil justice system, the lawyers' role as "officers of the court," the lawyers' effective monopoly on judicial access, and the ethical obligations we noted earlier to conclude it possessed inherent power to compel appointments to represent indigent civil litigants.

C] I think the *Bothwell* case supports my argument. None of the arguments it presented were compelling in themselves, yet the court concluded somehow that, put together, they supported its power. Then, after I don't know how may pages, the court ended up concluding its authority had to be exercised with "restraint and discretion" and denied compelled representation to Bothwell after a lengthy "marketability" (economic) analysis. This doesn't help a bit. It means that some lawyers will be compelled to provide free services and others won't depending on what is really the whim of the court and judge involved. At least one California case, *Cunningham v. Superior Court*, 177 Cal.App.3d 336, 222 Cal. Rptr. 854 (1986), is contrary to the result reached in *Bothwell*. Further, the case law precedents deal only with representation of indigents *in court*; they don't address the problem of the legal service needs of indigent persons in their day-to-day lives outside of court. If we Americans believe that everyone needs a lawyer regardless of income, then it is up to the legislature to provide funding for such a system, and I see no such prospect on the horizon. Moreover, if courts cannot *force* lawyers to work without a fee, then it gives added dignity to those lawyers who do the work voluntarily. [For a thorough discussion of these issues, *see generally Symposium on Mandatory Pro Bono*, 19 HOFSTRA L. REV. 739-1270 (1991).]

A] How do you think the law firm in Problem 2 ought to fund this 100 hour per year program?

B] Fund it? What's to fund? Each lawyer in the firm will simply do the 100 hours work.

A] It's harder than that. Notice that the problem says that the lawyers in the firm average 1,800 billable hours a year. That's a fairly common, civilized pace, although some workaholics rack up nearly double that number of hours. If you assume that each lawyer in the firm takes a two-week vacation each year, then 1,800 hours means roughly 35 billable hours per week. Most lawyers need perhaps 50 or 55 hours in the office to end up with 35 hours that can in good conscience be billed to a client. 100 hours a year on *pro bono* work is about 5.5% of each lawyer's billable time. Now let me suggest to you some of the possible ways to compensate for that loss of billable hours. The firm could eliminate the two-week vacations.

B] Terrible idea. We need vacations.

A] The firm could lay off some secretaries, or cut their salaries.

B] No—that would wreck the place quicker than anything.

A] The firm could stop buying so many materials for the library.

B] No—you can't do legal work if you don't have the tools.

A] The firm could cut the lawyers' salaries.

B] That's the worst idea you've mentioned so far.

A] The firm could raise its fees to paying clients enough to offset the 5.5% loss in billable hours.

B] That has a nice ring to it. We learned about the benefits of loss-spreading in torts class. If the nation's taxpayers are unwilling to pay for legal services for the poor, perhaps we can at least spread the cost among those who are wealthy enough to use and pay for legal services.

C] I think there's a hitch in that idea. Perhaps other firms in town are not as high-minded as our firm. They will not provide the *pro bono* services we provide; they will be able to charge lower fees, and they will steal all our paying clients.

A] Anybody else got an idea?

B] It's simple. We will all put in two more billable hours per week. According to the figures you gave us earlier, that will mean 58 or 60 hours per week in the office rather than 55.

A] Do the rest of you like that solution?

C] I don't. It means I'm robbing my family of time I would otherwise spend with them. For me, law practice is a way to support my family—it's not a substitute for my family.

A] What's the moral to be extracted from Problem 2?

C] There's no free lunch. The *pro bono* program has to be supported somehow, whether by lower salaries, or lower overhead costs, or longer work hours, or higher fees.

A] Are there any other approaches to fulfilling a sense of obligation and commitment to *pro bono* work?

B] ABA Model Rule 6.1 mentions providing legal services "at a substantially reduced fee," as well as making financial contributions to legal aid organizations, so there are alternatives to providing legal services for free. I like the idea of being able to make a financial contribution. That removes potential competence issues and does not require additional time away from my family. I like the idea of giving something back to the profession, and most lawyers can afford to make a charitable contribution—especially since it's tax-deductible.

C] Personally, I plan to do my fair share of *pro bono* work when I get into law practice. But I think that ought to be left to each lawyer's own conscience, and that's precisely where the ABA Model Rules and the CRPC leave it.

## Discussion Problem 3

A] Before we start on Problem 3, let me summarize what we have concluded about a lawyer's duty to accept cases. We began with a general rule that a lawyer is not a public utility—a lawyer has no duty to serve every client who walks in the door with the fee in hand. Then we saw some exceptions to that general rule. First, a lawyer cannot, for selfish reasons, refuse to represent somebody who is "defenseless or oppressed." Second, a lawyer cannot turn down a court-appointed case, except for a compelling reason. Those reasons would include: a) violation of a disciplinary provision; b) imposition of an unreasonable financial burden on the lawyer; and c) inadequate representation because of the lawyer's personal feelings about the case. Third, we saw that the ABA Model Rules urge every lawyer to carry a fair share of *pro bono* work.

Under the California Rules, an additional limitation is mentioned in the casebook—under CRPC 2-400, in the management or operation of a law practice, a lawyer must not unlawfully discriminate in "accepting or terminating representation of any client." [*See* CRPC 2-400(B)(2).]

Problem 3 asks us to look at the opposite side of the coin. Are there some situations in which a lawyer has an ethical duty to <u>reject</u> an offer of employment?

B] Suppose that taking a case will put me in a conflict of interest; I can't take a case if it would cause me to violate a disciplinary rule. [*See* ABA Model Rule 1.16(a)(1); CRPC 3-700(B)(2).]

A] Another example?

B] Suppose a person is in such poor physical health that she couldn't do a proper job in the case. In that situation she'd have a duty to reject the case. [*See* ABA Model Rule 1.16(a)(2); CRPC 3-700(B)(3).]

A] Another example?

C] If the lawyer had a substance abuse problem that interfered with his work, he would have to decline. [*See* ABA Model Rule 1.16(a)(2); CRPC 3-700(B)(3).]

A] Another example?

B] If the lawyer was suffering from depression, that could constitute a "mental condition materially impair[ing] the lawyer's ability to represent the client." [*See* ABA Model Rule 1.16(a)(2); CRPC 3-700(B)(3).]

A] Another example?

C] According to ABA Model Rule 3.1 and CRPC 3-200(A), you can't take a legal position that is frivolous. In this context, "frivolous" means that you cannot support the position under present law and that you cannot even make a good faith argument for changing the present law.

## Discussion Problem 4

A] In Problems 1, 2, and 3, we talked about the *beginning* of the attorney-client relationship—when you have a duty to take a case, and when you have a duty to reject a case. Problem 4 concerns the *ending* of the attorney-client relationship. Ordinarily when you take on a legal matter, you have to stick with it until it is over. But there are three situations in which the attorney-client relationship can prematurely end. First, sometimes you *must* withdraw. Those situations are covered by ABA Model Rule 1.16(a) and CRPC 3-700(B). Second, sometimes you *may* withdraw. Those situations are covered by ABA Model Rule 1.16(b) and CRPC 3-700(C). Does anybody have any questions about what those provisions mean?

A] Hearing no questions, we will consider a third situation. Judicial opinions sometimes assert that the client always has the right to *fire* the lawyer, with cause or without cause. [*See, e.g., Fracasse v. Brent*, 6 Cal.3d 784, 494 P.2d 9, 100 Cal. Rptr. 385 (1972) and the *Rosenberg* case in the casebook.] Does that make any sense to you?

B] Yes. If the client loses faith in the lawyer, then the relationship isn't going to work. Even if the client doesn't have a good reason for the loss of faith, it seems wise to let the client call off the relationship and get a new lawyer, or have no lawyer at all.

A] Problem 4 asks if there is any situation in which the client cannot freely fire the lawyer. Did you find one?

B] Yes, *Ruskin v. Rodgers*, in the casebook, illustrates that situation. In that case, for no apparent reason, the defendant tried to fire his lawyer two days before trial was set to start, and again as the attorney was just starting to cross-examine the first trial witness. The trial judge would not allow a continuance or substitution of attorneys, and the appellate court sustained that exercise of discretion. I think the reason behind it was to avoid prejudice to the other side. Apparently the other side was all ready to proceed with trial, and the defendant was just trying to delay justice.

## Discussion Problem 5

A] Discussion Problem 5 concerns the client's liability to the lawyer for the work the lawyer has done up to the time the lawyer is fired. How much did you conclude lawyer Simon is entitled to recover from client Noreen?

B]  Under Florida law, as expressed in the *Rosenberg* case, I think the most Simon can get is $5,000.  *Rosenberg* relied on a leading California case, *Fracasse v. Brent*, so the result should be the same in California.

A]  How did you come to $5,000 from what you learned in *Rosenberg*?

B]  *Rosenberg* says that a fired attorney is entitled to the reasonable value of the services rendered, but subject to a top limit—the amount the attorney would have received under the fee contract had the client not fired him.  In Simon's case, the reasonable value of his services is stated to be $6,000.  But if Noreen had not fired him, then he'd be entitled to the larger of $5,000 (the minimum fee stated in the contract) or 20% of the amount covered by settlement.

A]  In this case, what is 20% of the amount recovered by settlement?

B]  The problem says that the "percentages were to be computed after deducting litigation expenses."  I suppose that means that the $1,000 worth of litigation expenses will be subtracted from the $13,000 settlement before multiplying by 20% to compute Simon's fee.  If that's true, then Simon's share would be 20% of $12,000, or $2,400.  Since $5,000 is larger than $2,400, Simon would have gotten $5,000 if he hadn't been fired.  *Rosenberg* says that the lawyer should not come out better by getting fired than if he'd stayed with the case.  Thus, I conclude that Simon gets only $5,000, not the full $6,000 value of his services.

## Discussion Problem 6

A]  Discussion Problem 6 asks you to compare two cases you read, *Holmes* and *Kriegsman*.  Did you disagree with the result in either case, and why was the attorney allowed to withdraw in *Holmes* but not in *Kriegsman*?

C]  I agreed with the result in both cases. The Comment to ABA Model Rule 1.16(b)(5) and (6) mentions withdrawal because of the client's refusal to abide by a fee agreement with the lawyer.  That's exactly the situation in *Holmes*. Abrahams and his corporation could apparently afford to pay Goldman's fee— but they refused to do so.

A]  And in *Kriegsman*?

C] There the client had to go on welfare because her divorce case was taking so long. She didn't "deliberately disregard" her promise to pay the fees—she simply could not afford to pay them at that time.

A] Were there any other factors that might distinguish the two cases?

C] In *Holmes*, the case was not ready for trial, and apparently neither side would be prejudiced by a delay to allow defendants to get other counsel. In *Kriegsman*, the wife's lawyers had already poured a lot of time into the case. Much of that time would have to be duplicated if she had to get a new lawyer. I think the judge in *Kriegsman* did exactly the right thing by setting the case for early trial. That will end the husband's delaying tactics, and the matter will get resolved as economically as possible.

## BOTHWELL v. REPUBLIC TOBACCO CO.
### United States District Court,
### District of Nebraska, 1995

Facts: In March 1994, plaintiff Earl Bothwell, then an inmate at a correctional facility, submitted a request to proceed in forma pauperis, a civil complaint, along with a motion for appointment of counsel. The magistrate judge granted the motion and ordered the complaint to be filed.

Bothwell sued the tobacco company on ground of strict liability and breach of implied warranty of fitness claims. Bothwell claimed that when warning labels appeared on cigarette packages in 1969, he switched from factory-manufactured cigarettes to his own rolled cigarettes, mistakenly believing that loose tobacco was safer because it had no warning label. In 1986, Bothwell was diagnosed with emphysema, asthma, heart disease, and "bronchial and other respiratory diseases." Afterwards, he learned that the loose tobacco he smoked was actually stronger and more harmful than factory-manufactured cigarettes.

The magistrate judge required the defendants to respond to the complaint and granted the motion for appointment of counsel. The judge appointed Paula Metcalf, who then moved for reconsideration and vacation of his order appointing her. Metcalf argued that the court did not possess any statutory or inherent authority to force an attorney to represent an indigent client in a civil case. For other reasons, the judge granted the motion and vacated the order of appointment.

Issue: Does a federal court possess the inherent power to compel an unwilling attorney to accept a civil appointment?

Holding: Yes. Although the judge found it unnecessary to exercise its inherent authority in this case, enough policy reasons and theories existed to establish that federal courts had the power to compel an unwilling attorney to represent an indigent client in a civil matter.

Discussion: In *Mallard v. United States*, 490 U.S. 296, 109 S.Ct. 1814, 104 L.Ed.2d 318 (1989), the United States Supreme Court held that section 1915(d) did not authorize a federal court to require an unwilling attorney to represent an indigent client in a civil case. However, the *Mallard* decision focused on the statutory language of section 1915(d), leaving open the question of whether courts had the inherent power to compel an attorney to accept an appointment.

The magistrate judge held that federal courts did possess that inherent authority. The inherent power to compel representation of indigent clients served two primary purposes: "(1) to ensure a 'fair and just' adjudicative process in individual cases; and (2) to maintain the integrity and viability of the judiciary and of the entire civil justice system."

Although no constitutional right to counsel in civil cases exists, attorneys are necessary to ensure fairness and justice. The adversarial system provides an effective method for "ferreting out the truth." However, the system only works if both sides have adequate legal representation. If a client has not waived their right to representation by choice or by other factors other than indigency but cannot obtain representation due to indigency, the principles of equality are offended. Although the indigent can sometimes obtain legal assistance in the private market, legal aid organizations are oftentimes not able to meet the legal needs of the indigent due to budget cuts. Such failure to obtain representation threatens the viability of the results of the adversarial system.

In addition to policy arguments for the inherent power of courts to compel representation, other theories exist which support such a finding: the lawyer as an officer of a court, the monopoly of lawyers, and finally, the ethical obligations of lawyers.

The notion of the lawyer as an officer of the court is based in English common law. Historically, the English court system provided for such a need, having "serjeants-at-law," officers of the court, who were required to represent the poor. *United States v. Dillon*, 346 F.2d 633, 636-37 (9th Cir. 1965). Critics of this view contest that American lawyers are more like barristers than "serjeants-at-law" and thus are not officers of the court. However, the claim that no direct counterpart to the "serjeant-at-law" exists in America serves to underscore the need for such a lawyer. Also, courts have compelled representation for the indigent for centuries. Today, the officer-of-the-court doctrine has become part of the American judicial system. Consequently, the magistrate judge refused to discard it.

The monopoly theory also supports mandatory compliance with appointment orders. Since attorneys have been granted the exclusive privilege of practicing law, they must provide representation to indigents. Although individuals are free to represent themselves, "meaningful access to the courts" often requires representation by someone trained in the law. Additionally, the prohibitive costs and "rigid training program" compromise an individual's ability to pursue a legal education in order to represent themselves. Critics point out that other licensed groups such as doctors, teachers, brokers, and pharmacists are not required to provide their services to the poor. "While that is true, it misses the point." Lawyers have a unique symbiotic relationship with the government and provide the necessary link between the courts and the public. "Lawyers are essential in maintaining the system because the only realistic way the populace at large can obtain 'equal justice' is through the advocacy of those trained in the law." Lawyers instill a measure of tranquillity by allowing individuals the opportunity to resolve conflicts in a more civil manner.

Finally, lawyers have an ethical obligation to represent indigent clients. Canon 2 of the Code of Professional Responsibility states that lawyers should not seek to be excused from an appointment to represent an indigent client "except for compelling reasons." Code of Professional Responsibility, EC 2-29. Although not expressed in mandatory language, the canon indicates that service to the indigent is a necessary part of an ethical attorney. These obligations are a recognition of the essential nature of a lawyer's services in the judicial system. Attorneys' ethical obligations to provide services to the indigent is the "'flip side' of the court's inherent authority to provide 'instruments' to ensure fairness and justice."

Although the court possesses the power to compel representation, "appointment of counsel must be necessary to bring about a fair and just adjudicative process." In determining whether to appoint counsel, the court should consider factors such as the factual and legal complexity of the case, the plaintiff's ability to investigate the facts, the existence of conflicting testimony, the plaintiff's ability to present his claims, and the plaintiff's ability to obtain counsel on her own.

Examining the case before him, the judge found it unnecessary to exercise the court's inherent authority to compel Metcalf to represent Bothwell. The judge found the plaintiff's claims lacked "marketability." The "marketability" analysis consisted of several steps: (1) was there a market of lawyers who practice in the legal area of the plaintiff's claims, (2) did the plaintiff have ready access to that market, (3) what are the possible fee arrangements in such a case, and (4) was the market's rejection of the plaintiff's claims due to indigency, which triggers the court's ability to compel representation. In this case, a number of lawyers practiced in the products liability area. The plaintiff had ready access to them, since he was not incarcerated when this opinion was given and did not allege any other barriers. Additionally, contingent fee arrangements could have been made. Plaintiff tried unsuccessfully to retain an attorney in the area. The judge ruled that such rejection was more likely due to the enormous cost of pursuing litigation against the tobacco companies rather than Bothwell's financial status. Since the rejection was due more to the prohibitive cost of such a suit, the judge elected not to exercise the court's power to compel Metcalf to represent Bothwell.

## RUSKIN v. RODGERS
### Appellate Court of Illinois, 1979

Facts: Plaintiff sued defendant for specific performance of a written contract for purchase of an apartment building and its conversion into condominiums. Plaintiff prevailed at trial. On appeal, defendant charged numerous errors because the trial court denied motions for continuance and substitution of attorneys.

Issue: Does a client have an absolute right to dismiss his lawyer at any time, with cause or without cause?

Holding: No. The trial judge was correct in ordering the trial to proceed on schedule.

Discussion: The defendant had attempted to discharge his lawyer before trial and again during the lawyer's cross-examination of the first witness. To allow a substitution of attorneys would have been extremely disruptive and would have resulted in significant and prejudicial delay. Here the effort to discharge the attorney appeared to be predicated on emotional whim rather than sound reason. The trial judge handled the matter correctly.

## ROSENBERG v. LEVIN
### Supreme Court of Florida, 1982

Facts: Defendant Levin hired plaintiffs Rosenberg and Pomerantz to perform legal services under a contract that provided for a $10,000 fixed fee, plus a contingent fee equal to 50% of all amounts recovered in excess of $600,000. Defendant later fired plaintiffs without cause and then settled the case for $500,000. Plaintiffs sued in quantum meruit, seeking to recover the reasonable value of the legal services they rendered up to the time they were fired.

The trial court awarded the plaintiffs $55,000, based on the quantum meruit theory. The district court agreed that quantum meruit was the correct theory, but it lowered the recovery to $10,000, the maximum the plaintiffs would have recovered under their fee contract.

Issue: Where there is a fee contract between a client and a discharged lawyer, is quantum meruit the appropriate basis upon which to calculate what fee is due to the lawyer?

Holding: Yes, but the lawyer's recovery in quantum meruit cannot exceed the amount that the lawyer would have recovered under the fee contract had he not been discharged.

Discussion: Quantum meruit is the appropriate basis for recovery when a lawyer on contingent fee is discharged before the end of the case. Following the California rule, the Florida court holds that the lawyer's claim does not arise until the contingency has come to pass—the client recovers something in the case by settlement or judgment.

In calculating the reasonable value of the lawyer's services, the court can consider the totality of the circumstances, including the amount of time spent, the recovery sought, the skill demanded, and the results ultimately obtained.

But the quantum meruit recovery must be limited by whatever maximum figure the lawyer and client have set in their fee contract. Otherwise, the client would be penalized, and the lawyer might recover more by getting fired than by carrying out the contract!

## HOLMES v. Y.J.A. REALTY CORP.
### Supreme Court of New York, Appellate Division, 1987

Facts: Plaintiff slipped and fell in an apartment house maintained by defendant Y.J.A. Realty Corp. Plaintiff sued the corporation and its sole shareholder, Yori Abrahams. The defendants hired attorney Goldman to represent them, and they promised to pay him $125 per hour for office work and $400 per day for court appearances.

Goldman billed the defendants periodically for work done. At one point, defendants paid $3,500 that was then due, but later an additional sum of $2,275.30 remained due and unpaid for over five months. Though able to pay, defendants simply did not do so. At that point, Goldman asked the court's permission to be relieved as counsel for defendants, both because of the unpaid bill and because defendant Abrahams had berated him and accused him of disloyalty and conflict of interest. The trial judge denied Goldman's motion.

Issue: Was the trial judge correct in refusing to allow Goldman to withdraw as defense counsel?

Holding: No. The motion to withdraw is granted by the Appellate Division.

Discussion: In a litigated matter, a lawyer has no absolute right to withdraw. But the ethics rules allow a lawyer to withdraw when a client deliberately disregards a fee agreement. The rules also allow withdrawal when the client makes it unreasonably difficult for the lawyer to carry out the representation. In this case, no "note of issue" had been filed—meaning that the case was not yet ready to go to trial. Thus, defendants will have plenty of time to get a new lawyer, and the plaintiff will not be prejudiced by delay.

## KRIEGSMAN v. KRIEGSMAN
### Superior Court of New Jersey,
### Appellate Division, 1977

Facts: The Rose firm (a law partnership) appealed from an order of the Chancery Division denying their application to be relieved as counsel for the plaintiff in her divorce action. Plaintiff had paid the Rose firm a $2,000 retainer fee. Due to the defendant husband's delaying tactics and efforts to represent himself in the matter, the case dragged on and the Rose firm was required to do more than the ordinary amount of work on plaintiff's behalf. By that time, plaintiff had gone on welfare and was unable to pay additional fees of $7,354.50. Thus, the Rose firm asked to be relieved as her counsel.

Issue: Did the lower court err in refusing to let the Rose firm withdraw?

Holding: The lower court was correct. When a law firm accepts a retainer, it impliedly agrees to prosecute the matter to a conclusion. The firm is not at liberty to abandon the case without reasonable cause. Plaintiff's inability to pay the fee is not reasonable cause.

Discussion: Contrast this case with the *Y.J.A. Realty* case, above. There the defendants apparently had the ability to pay, but simply refused to do so. In *Kriegsman*, the plaintiff convinced the court that she did not have the ability to pay. Further, in *Kriegsman* the plaintiff would have been seriously harmed if she had to switch lawyers after the Rose firm had put so much time and effort into the case. In *Kriegsman* the trial judge set the case for an early trial—an effective way to end the defendant husband's delaying tactics and to limit the Rose firm's further exposure.

# CHAPTER FOUR
# ADVERTISING AND SOLICITATION

## Discussion Problem 1

A] Problem 1 asks you to suppose that you have just opened your law practice in a town where you do not know many people. It then asks you about several possible ways of building your clientele.

## Part (a)

A] Part (a) asks: May you join a social club for the sole purpose of meeting new people and luring them as clients?

B] I understand that this is an age-old, accepted way to build up a law practice. But, of course, the "luring" has to be subtle for two reasons, one practical and one ethical. Practically, I'm not going to get very far if I bounce up to a group of strangers, announce myself, and inform them that I'm a new lawyer in town and would like to become their friend and confidant. Ethically, I must steer clear of the rule against solicitation of legal business. [*See* ABA Model Rule 7.3 and CRPC 1-400(B) and (C).] Comment 4 to ABA Model Rule 7.3 states that the prohibition against in-person solicitation is not intended to prohibit an attorney from participating in social organizations. I think that I can tell club members that I am a lawyer, and what types of legal work I do, and I can discuss legal issues with them, but I cannot ask them to send me fee-paying business.

## Part (b)

A] Part (b) of Problem 1 asks whether you may call on other lawyers at their offices and let them know that you are willing to take on work that they are too busy to handle.

B] ABA Model Rule 7.3 expressly excludes the contacting of lawyers, as contrasted with laypersons, from the prohibitions against in-person solicitation, and comment 4 to that rule observes that "no serious potential for abuse" exists "when the person contacted is a lawyer." The object of the rule against solicitation is to prevent prospective clients from being overreached. [*See* Comment 1 to ABA Model Rule 7.3.] That is not likely to happen when the person on the receiving end is another lawyer. [Cal. State Bar Op. 1981-61 (solicitation of business from another attorney not prohibited).]

A] Could you offer to compensate these other lawyers for referring business to you?

B] No—that would violate ABA Model Rule 7.2(b) and CRPC 2-200(B). But well-established lawyers often have more work than they can handle, and they may be glad to hear about a young beginner to whom clients with small, simple matters can be referred. [CRPC 2-200(A) permits a California lawyer to pay a forwarding or referral fee to another California lawyer under some circumstances; that issue is discussed in Chapter Five.]

## Part (c)

A] Part (c) of Problem 1 asks: May you volunteer to give a seminar on estate planning for the local chapter of Young Businesswomen of America, hoping to get legal business from some of those who attend?

B] In years past, the organized bar put limits on this kind of thing. [*See* ABA Canons of Professional Ethics, Canon 40 (1908) (lawyers must not accept business arising from articles they write on legal topics); California Rule of Professional Conduct 18 (1928) (lawyers must not give specific legal advice in newspaper articles or radio programs); ABA Model Code DR 2-104(A)(4) (lawyers who speak or write for the public on legal topics must not emphasize their own qualifications or give individual legal advice).] The bar's motivation was partly noble and partly selfish. First, a writer or speaker might badly mislead a lay person by trying to answer a legal question without having an opportunity to learn the full facts that prompted the question. Second, the bar feared that some lawyers might use public forums to evade the old rules on advertising and solicitation. Third, the bar doubtless feared that some lay persons would prefer free advice at a seminar, or in a newspaper, or on radio, to paid advice given in a lawyer's office.

A] You spoke of "years past." What are the current constraints on a lawyer who wants to give a seminar like the one in Part (c)?

B] Neither the ABA Model Rules nor the California Rules contain specific restrictions on this kind of client-luring activity. But in giving such a seminar, a lawyer is subject to three general constraints. The first one is the duty of competence. [ABA Model Rule 1.1 and CRPC 3-110.] A lawyer ordinarily cannot give competent legal advice on a specific question without knowing all the relevant facts. A lawyer who tries to give all-purpose answers at a seminar may badly mislead a lay person whose problem sounds similar but is in truth significantly different.

A] What are the other constraints?

B] The second is advertising. To the extent that the lawyer in Part (c) uses the seminar as a forum for touting her own legal services, her statements must be truthful and not misleading, or else she will be subject to discipline. [CRPC 1-400(A).] The California Communications Standards come into play here. For instance if she makes a prediction or guarantee about the outcome of a matter, it will be presumed misleading, and she must bear the burden of proving that it is not. The third constraint is solicitation. Suppose that during a break in the seminar, the lawyer and audience are standing around having refreshments. If the lawyer uses that opportunity to initiate personal contact with an audience member for the purpose of hustling fee-paying legal business, the lawyer is engaged in solicitation. [*See* ABA Model Rule 7.3. and CRPC 1-400(C).]

## **Part (d)**

A] Part (d) asks: May you list your name with the local court as a person who is willing to take court-appointed cases?

B] Sure. That's a common way for young lawyers to get business. Taking court-appointed cases is no way to become rich, but a young lawyer needs experience and also needs exposure to local judges and to other members of the bar. The experience and exposure will help produce higher-paying work down the road.

A] Part (d) also asks whether you may contribute to a local judge's re-election campaign fund, hoping to secure good court appointments from the judge. May you?

B] No—ABA Model Rule 7.6, added in the year 2000, specifically prohibits so-called "pay-to-play" campaign donations.

C] Doesn't that rule infringe on a lawyer's right to participate freely in the election process?

B] No, because the rule proscribes only those contributions that are made for the specific purpose of garnering legal work in exchange. [*See* James Podgers, *A New Ethics No-No,* A.B.A. J. 96 (April 2000).]

## Part (e)

A] Part (e) asks about listing your name with a local lawyer referral service. What are those services, and how do they operate? [*See* ABA Model Rule 7.2(b)(2), and comments 6 and 7; CRPC 1-600; California Communication Standard 10.]

B] A traditional lawyer referral service is non-profit and is operated or approved by a local bar association or similar organization; its object is to help members of the public find lawyers. If I'm willing to take on new clients, I can give my name to the lawyer referral service. They will put it on their list; some services keep various lists on which lawyers are divided by fields of practice.

A] Suppose I'm a lay person who doesn't know any lawyers, but I think I have a legal problem with my landlord, and I want a lawyer's advice. How would the lawyer referral service help me?

B] You'd look in the classified pages of the local phone book, and you would find a listing for the lawyer referral service. You would call them, and they would give you a lawyer's name off their list. (The service has a rotation system so that referrals are spread evenly over all lawyers who participate.) You'd call that lawyer, make an appointment, and then go see him or her. Typically that lawyer gives you an initial appointment for a low fee—perhaps $25-$50 for the first half hour. The lawyer remits part or all of that fee to the lawyer referral service to help cover its operating costs. Often the initial appointment is enough to solve the client's problem. If so, that's that. If not, and if the client wants to hire the lawyer to do further work on the problem, then the two of them reach their own agreement about the lawyer's fee.

A] Earlier you stressed the word <u>traditional</u> when you described a "traditional lawyer referral service." Is there a non-traditional kind?

B] During the 1980's some lawyers banded together to operate "private" lawyer referral services, which were often nothing more than telephone switchboards that referred callers to the lawyers who owned the service. The tradenames and advertising of some of these operations misled consumers, who thought they were getting impartial referrals from a unbiased source. Some states have taken steps to regulate lawyer referral services to prevent that kind of deception. [*See, e.g.*, Rules and Regulations of the State Bar of California Pertaining to Lawyer Referral Services, Including Minimum Standards for Lawyer Referral Services in California, reprinted in West's California Rules of Court (State) 859 (2002).]

## Part (f)

A] Part (f) asks whether you may place advertisements for your legal services. If so, are there restrictions on what media you can use and what you can say?

B] A state can flatly prohibit lawyer advertising that is false or misleading. If advertising is not false or misleading, then the state cannot regulate it without showing a "substantial governmental interest." Further, the regulation must directly and materially advance the substantial government interest, and it must "narrowly tailored" to serve that interest. [*See* Justice O'Connor's analysis in the *Went For It* case, reproduced in the casebook.] Neither the CRPC nor the ABA Model Rules impose limits on the media in which a lawyer may advertise.

A] Can you give us an example of a governmental interest that the Supreme Court has said is "substantial" enough to support a restriction on truthful, non-misleading lawyer advertising?

B] The *Went For It* case provides two examples. One was Florida's interest in protecting the "privacy and tranquility of personal injury victims and their loved ones" against intrusive contacts by lawyers. The second was Florida's interest in "protect[ing] the flagging reputations of Florida lawyers" by stopping them from engaging in intrusive conduct that is "deplorable and beneath common decency."

A] Suppose that you wish to advertise your services in the newspaper. Are there any restrictions on content—other than the obvious ones about statements that are false or misleading?

B] California is alone among the states in regulating content through rebuttable presumptions. [California Communications Standards, printed after CRPC 1-400; *see also* CAL. BUS. & PROF. CODE § 6158.1.] For example, if a lawyer's business-getting communication includes an endorsement or testimonial from a former client, the communication is *presumed* to be misleading. In a disciplinary proceeding, the lawyer would carry the burden of proving that it was not misleading. Query whether the presumption approach places an unduly cramps free speech.

A] How do other states regulate content?

B] Most of them use ABA Model Rule 7.1, which prohibits false or misleading advertising. A communication can be false or misleading by commission or omission—a material misrepresentation of law or fact will violate the rule, as will the omission of a fact which, by virtue of its omission, renders the advertisement misleading. Even truthful statements may nonetheless be misleading—and therefore prohibited under Rule 7.1—under three circumstances:

First, your ad must not create unjustified conclusions about you. For example, you cannot state "Admitted to Practice Before the United States Supreme Court" in your ad, even if true, because the average person would ascribe greater significance to this particular qualification than is warranted. [*See* Comment 2 to ABA Model Rule 7.1.]

Second, your ad must not create unjustified expectations about the results you are likely to achieve. For example, you cannot state that your last five plaintiffs each recovered over a million dollars, even if that's absolutely true. [*See* Comment 3 to ABA Model Rule 7.1.]

Third, you cannot compare your services with those of other lawyers in ways that cannot be factually substantiated. For example, you cannot claim to have the "most efficient probate service in Elm County" unless you can prove it, and proving such a slippery proposition would be quite a feat. [*See* Comment 3 to ABA Model Rule 7.1.]

## Part (g)

A] Part (g) asks whether you may publish a brochure that describes your law practice, states the kinds of matters you handle, and gives a schedule of the fees you charge for a variety of routine legal services.

B] Yes, I could publish such a brochure. Indeed, for many old, conservative firms, a descriptive brochure is the first exploratory step into the world of lawyer advertising. Typically such brochures contain some nice glossy pictures of smiling lawyers looking at books in the law library and of well-scrubbed staff members working at computer terminals. They also often contain biographic descriptions of the lawyers, and they contain a textual description of the law firm and the kinds of services it provides.

A] Could your brochure indicate the fields of law in which you practice?

B] Yes, stating fields of practice is no problem, but claims that one is certified as a "specialist" are subject to some restrictions. [*See* ABA Model Rule 7.4; CRPC 1-400(C)(6).]

A] Could your brochure include a schedule of the fees you charge for routine legal services?

B] Yes; *Bates* itself is direct authority for that proposition, assuming the information is truthful and not misleading. [*See* ABA Model Rule 7.1, 7.2.]

A] May you publish the information on a website?

B] Yes—the same general principles that govern advertising in print or on radio or television also apply to advertising on newer forms of public media. [*See* ABA Model Rule 7.2(a) (expressly including electronic communication and public media).] I couldn't say anything on a website that I couldn't say in a newspaper or television ad, for example. Note also that ABA Model Rule 7.3(a) prohibits the solicitation of a prospective client through a real-time electronic exchange.

A] Could you use www.winbig.com as your site address, assuming it has not already been registered by somebody else?

B] I think the right way to answer that is to decide whether I could say in a newspaper or television ad: "Hire me and win big," or something to that effect. I think that would be an improper statement under ABA Model Rule 7.1, which, under Comment 3, prohibits the creation of unjustified expectations about potential results. [*See generally* Arthur Garwin, *Commentary on Domain Names*, A.B.A. J. 64 (Feb. 2000).]

A] How about advertising yourself as a "Super Lawyer" or "Best Lawyer" when you've been included in a "Super Lawyers" poll for a magazine advertising supplement or in "Best Lawyers in America"?

B] The New Jersey Supreme Court's Committee on Attorney Advertising has concluded that such an advertisement is misleading because it is likely to create unjustified expectations, and is therefore unethical. [See N.J. Comm. on Attorney Advertising, Op. 39 (7/17/06), available at http://www.judiciary.state.nj.us/notices/ethics/CAA_Opinion%2039.pdf.] However, lawyers in New York are permitted to advertise "bona fide professional ratings," which reportedly would allow them to advertise their inclusion in the "American Lawyer Top 100." [See Brooke Masters, *Law Firms Face New Limits on Advertising*, FINANCIAL TIMES, Jan. 5, 2007.]

## Discussion Problem 2

A] Problem 2 is about lawyer Lovette, the plastics workers, and the chemical that causes blood disease.

### Part (a)

A] Part (a) asks whether Lovette may put an ad in the local paper, informing plastics workers of their rights and inviting interested persons to contact her. May she do that?

B] Yes. The *Zauderer* case, mentioned in the text, seems right on point. In that case, the dangerous product was the Dalkon Shield, and the lawyer's newspaper ad informed potential claimants of their rights and invited them to contact the lawyer. So long as the statements are truthful and not misleading, that kind of advertising is protected by the First Amendment.

### Part (b)

A] Part (b) asks whether Lovette may send an informative form letter to each plastics worker, inviting the worker to contact her for further information. May she send such a letter by U.S. Mail?

B] Yes. The *Shapero* case, described in the text, decided that direct-mailed, narrowly-targeted form letters are more like newspaper ads than like face-to-face solicitation. Assuming that the content is not false or misleading, such letters cannot be prohibited. They can, however, be reasonably regulated. [*See*

*Went For It, Inc.*, in the casebook.] Thus, ABA Model Rule 7.3(c) requires them to be marked as "advertising material," so the recipient can easily trash them if she doesn't want to be bothered. [*See also* California Communication Standard 5.]

A] Is your answer the same if Lovette sends the letters by e-mail, using the e-mail addresses published in the town business directory?

B] Yes. [*See* Comment 3 to ABA Model Rule 7.2 (authorizing e-mail communication).]


## **Part (c)**

A] Moving to part (c), would Lovette be allowed to hire a team of telephone callers to phone each plastics worker, briefly describe the DNXP problem, and invite each worker to contact Lovette for more information?

B] No. Both ABA Model Rule 7.3(a) and CRPC 1-400(B) and (C) proscribe solicitation by live telephone call. The same rule applies if the lawyer uses a lay person to make the calls. [ABA Model Rule 8.4(a)(lawyer must not violate a disciplinary rule through the acts of another person); *accord* CRPC 1-120. *See also* CAL. BUS. & PROF. CODE §§ 6151–52 (prohibiting the use of runners or cappers to solicit legal business).]

A] Why is live telephone solicitation prohibited, while postal solicitation is permitted? Does that make any sense? Is it because live telephone sales campaigns are so intrusive, particularly when the ringing phone interrupts us at the dinner table?

B] The intrusiveness of telephone solicitation is part of the reason for the distinction. Justice Brennan's opinion for the majority in *Shapero* does mention invasion of privacy as a relevant consideration. But I'd say the main reason for the distinction is that live telephone solicitation presents a greater risk that the potential client will be badgered, pressured, and perhaps overreached. As Justice Brennan observed, a person who receives a solicitation letter can put it aside to consider later, or can throw it in the trash. In theory, one who receives an unwanted live telephone solicitation can simply hang up, but many people are reluctant to do that. A second reason is that direct mail solicitation is easier for the bar to police than would be live telephone solicitation. [*See* Ohio Ethics Op. 90-2 (1990).]

A] Notice that <u>recorded</u> telephone solicitation messages are allowed under ABA Model Rule 7.3, but not under CRPC 1-400(B) and (C). Are there sound reasons to distinguish between live and recorded calls?

B] The first reason is the relative ease of policing. It takes only one listening to police a recorded phone solicitation that goes to a hundred potential clients. But to police a hundred live phone solicitations would require a hundred listenings. The second reason is that a person who does not want to hear a recorded phone solicitation can hang up without the same sense of rudeness one feels when hanging up on a live caller.

## Part (d)

A] Part (d) asks whether Lovette may pass out her handbills on the public sidewalk outside a plastics factory, and whether she may initiate conversations with the workers about representing them. What do you think?

B] Clearly she would run afoul of the no-solicitation rule if she initiated a conversation in which she offered to represent a worker. The *Ohralik* case, discussed in the text, explains why it is permissible for states to have a blanket ban on face-to-face solicitation. The likelihood of abuse is clear, and the face-to-face solicitation cannot be effectively policed by the bar. Thus, it can be banned outright.

A] Suppose Lovette simply stands silent at the factory gate and passes out her handbills to workers?

B] If she does that, she's likely to become the respondent in a test case. For the lawyer herself to pass out handbills is on the borderline of face-to-face solicitation. Were I a judge, I'd vote for discipline here. If Lovette is standing at the factory gate giving DNXP handbills to potential plaintiffs, the temptation to use the handbills as a prelude to conversation is overwhelming. Once a conversation starts, the dangers of face-to-face solicitation are present—pressuring and over-reaching by the lawyer, with no chance for effective policing by the bar. [*See* Ohio Supreme Court Board of Commissioners on Grievances and Discipline Op. 99-5 (lawyer must not personally pass out brochures).] I think the Ohio opinion goes overboard, however, when it asserts that a lawyer cannot even hire somebody else to hand out the brochures.  The closest contrary authority is Assn. Bar of City of N.Y. Op. 81-94 (1981), which says that a lawyer may hire a non-lawyer to pass out leaflets to passers-by on a public street.  The committee reasoned that using a non-lawyer to pass out the leaflets avoids the risks.  If the non-lawyer simply passes out the printed material, and does not engage in conversation with those who receive it, the non-lawyer seems analogous to the postal worker who delivers a solicitation letter, or a newspaper carrier who delivers a paper containing a lawyer's ad.

A]  One more question—may lawyer Lovette initiate communications in a real-time Internet chatroom, inviting plastics workers to retain her in DNXP cases?

B]  No—that is treated like in-person or live telephone solicitation.  [*See* ABA Model Rule 7.3(a); *see also* Fla. Bar Standing Comm. on Advertising, Op. A-00-1, 12/15/00.]

## Discussion Problem 3

A]  Problem 3 asks whether you may represent the woeful young mother you met in the hallway of the courthouse.  You speak her native language, she has no lawyer, and she's faced with unlawful detainer proceedings brought by her landlord.  May you offer to be her lawyer?

B]  Not if my motive is to earn a legal fee.  [*See* ABA Model Rule 7.3; CRPC 1-400(B) and (C).]  If I offer my services out of the goodness of my heart, rather than for pay, then it would be permissible under ABA Model Rule 7.3 and CRPC 1-400(B) and (C).

A]  Suppose you <u>do</u> want to earn a fee.  I can understand why the bar should discipline a lawyer who habitually hangs around the courthouse halls, offering his services to all and sundry.  [*See, e.g., In re Perrello*, 394 N.E.2d 127 (Ind. 1979).]  But what can possibly be said in favor of a rule that prohibits the kind of useful, warm-hearted offer of help that we find in Problem 3?

C]  The *Ohralik* case points out the risks of face-to-face solicitation.  First, the potential client is often caught in a time of stress when he or she cannot make a thoughtful, well-informed decision about whether to hire a lawyer or what lawyer to hire.  Second, a fast-talking lawyer may overcome the better judgment of a lay person who is facing an unfamiliar problem. Third, face-to-face solicitation is not open to public scrutiny, and it would be impossible for the organized bar to police effectively. Even though some acts of solicitation may not cause these harms, the Supreme Court in *Ohralik* said that a state could have a prophylactic rule to ban all face-to-face solicitation.

A] What can be said for the other side—why should the bar permit the kind of solicitation described in Problem 3?

C] Professor Monroe Freedman points out that the ban on solicitation operates unevenly. Upper-crust lawyers solicit decorously through their social contacts, their country clubs, and their established clientele. [MONROE FREEDMAN & ABBE SMITH, UNDERSTANDING LAWYERS' ETHICS 345 (3d ed. 2004).] But, he argues, lawyers who serve tenants, injury victims, and those on the low end of the social and economic scale are forbidden to initiate personal contact with potential clients for the purpose of luring fee-paying business. [*Id.* at 346.] An injured person is far more likely to receive a prompt visit from a clever insurance adjuster, seeking to induce a quick settlement, than from a tort lawyer who could offer advice about the injured person's legal rights. [*Id.* at 342-43.]

B] So what's the answer to Problem 3? Is the lawyer subject to discipline or not? I realize that as a practical matter the bar is not likely to spend its limited disciplinary resources on cases where the lawyer's conduct was harmless. But in theory, is the lawyer in Problem 3 subject to discipline?

A] Most commentators read *Ohralik* as authorizing a blanket ban on face-to-face solicitation, whether or not it is harmful in the particular case. That is the theory behind ABA Model Rule 7.3. Professor Rhode argues that the blanket ban is too crude, because it bans the worthy solicitation along with the unworthy. [Deborah Rhode, *Solicitation*, 36 J. Legal Educ. 317 (1986); *see also* DEBORAH RHODE, PROFESSIONAL RESPONSIBILITY—ETHICS BY THE PERVASIVE METHOD 112-13 (2d ed. 1998).] She suggests that the present ban could be replaced with a set of carefully drawn time, place, and manner rules that would hit at the real evils of solicitation—coercion, harassment, and overreaching. [*Id.*] She also favors tighter controls on contingent fees and incompetent legal work. [*Id.*]

## BATES v. STATE BAR OF ARIZONA

## United States Supreme Court, 1977

<u>Facts</u>:  Appellants Bates and O'Steen operated a legal clinic to provide legal services for moderate income persons who could not qualify for governmental aid.  They did only "routine" legal work such as uncontested divorces, adoptions, and bankruptcy.  The two lawyers advertised their fees and services, a violation of the Arizona version of ABA Code DR 2-101(B).  The State Bar recommended a one week suspension for each attorney.  Bates and O'Steen sought review in the Arizona Supreme Court.  That court rejected their contentions that the advertising ban violated the Sherman Act and the free speech clause.  They appealed to the United States Supreme Court.

<u>Issues</u>:  Does Arizona's ban on lawyer advertising violate the Sherman Antitrust Act?  Is it an unconstitutional interference with free speech guaranteed by the First and Fourteenth Amendments?

<u>Holding</u>:  Arizona's advertising ban does not violate the Sherman Act because that statute does not reach trade restraints that are conceived and supervised by a state government.  But the advertising ban is an unconstitutional interference with free speech.  Attorney advertisements of prices for routine legal services are protected under the First Amendment.  Such advertising is subject to reasonable restrictions on time, place, and manner.  Lawyer advertising that is false, deceptive, or misleading can be restrained.

<u>Discussion</u>:  The Court considered and rejected several reasons for the ban on advertising:

1)  Adverse Effect on the Profession:

    <u>Claim</u>:  Price advertising will commercialize the profession.  A client may lose trust in his attorney if he perceives that the attorney is motivated by profit and not solely by a commitment to client welfare.

    <u>Response</u>:  Most clients understand that an attorney is working for a fee to make a living.  ABA Code EC 2-19 advises that fees should be established at the outset of the attorney/client relationship.  It seems inconsistent to discipline revelation of fees before a client comes into the office and then require that they be discussed immediately upon arrival.

2)  Inherently Misleading:

Claim: (a) Services are too individualized to be compared informatively through advertisements. (b) Clients cannot determine in advance what services they need. (c) Attorney advertisements might mislead by highlighting irrelevant factors and not skill.

Response: (a) Attorneys are likely to advertise only routine services. Unique services don't lend themselves to advertising and set prices. The Court cited Arizona's own legal services program as an example of possible standardization of legal services. (b) Clients usually contract an attorney only when they have a problem. A client may not know the detail involved in a problem, but the client can doubtless identify the service desired at the level of generality of the advertising. (c) Potential deception is a problem. However, the client may still be better served with some information rather than none. In addition, the state bar retains its power to correct omissions.

3) Increased Litigation:

Claim: Advertising will encourage increased litigation.

Response: Advertising might increase the use of the courts, but that is better than for people to suffer a wrong silently. Many people don't take legal action because of fear of cost or inability to find a suitable attorney. Advertising would help remedy that by educating the public.

4) Adverse Economic Effects:

Claim: Advertising will promote increased fees due to increased overhead and create an entry barrier to beginning attorneys.

Response: Advertising will probably foster competitive pricing, resulting in lower fees. Advertising will aid young attorneys in penetrating the market as contrasted with the traditional method of social contacts to create business.

5) Adverse Effect on Work Quality:

Claim: If lawyers are permitted to advertise, the quality of their work will decline.

Response: Restraining advertising will not deter poor work. Advertising of routine work, fostering clinics in this case, may actually improve quality by reducing the chance for error.

6) Difficulty in Policing Advertising:

Claim: A regulatory agency will be needed to police advertising by lawyers.

Response: The majority of attorneys will continue to behave ethically and they will police the misuse of advertising themselves.

## FLORIDA BAR v. WENT FOR IT, INC.
### United States Supreme Court, 1995

Facts: Florida Bar rules prohibit lawyers from sending targeted, direct-mail solicitation letters to accident victims or their families for 30 days following an accident or disaster. Florida adopted these rules after a two year study of the effects of lawyer advertising on public opinion. The rules were challenged by a Florida lawyer (who was later disbarred for unrelated reasons) and his wholly owned lawyer referral service. The U.S. District Court referred the case to a Magistrate Judge, who recommended that the Florida Bar rules be declared valid. The District Court rejected the Magistrate's advice and held the rules invalid on the authority of *Bates*, above. The Eleventh Circuit affirmed, noting its regret that *Bates* required it to do so.

Issue: Do Florida's rules offend the limited protection granted to commercial speech under the First and Fourteenth Amendments?

Holding: In the circumstances presented in this case, the Florida rules do not offend the First or Fourteenth Amendments.

Discussion: [Justice O'Connor, writing for herself and Chief Justice Rehnquist, and Justices Scalia, Thomas, and Breyer.] Until the mid-1970's, the Supreme Court granted no free-speech protection to pure advertising, but the Court changed course in the mid-70's, first in a case involving price advertising for prescription drugs, and later in *Bates*, involving lawyer advertising. In the following two decades, the Court developed its commercial speech doctrine, centering around an "intermediate scrutiny" analysis stated in *Central Hudson Gas & Electric Corp. v. Public Service Comm'n of N.Y.*, 447 U.S. 557 (1980). *Central Hudson* gives the government a free hand in regulating speech that concerns unlawful activities or that is false or misleading. Commercial speech that does not fall into either of those categories may be regulated if the government meets three requirements: (a) the regulation must serve a substantial governmental interest; (b) the regulation must "directly and

69

materially advance" that interest, and (c) the regulation must be narrowly tailored to achieve a reasonably close fit with the governmental interest. [The *Central Hudson* test apparently survives the Court's ruminations in *44 Liquormart, Inc. v. Rhode Island*, 517 U.S. 484, 116 S.Ct. 1495 (1996), which involved a state's effort to withhold truthful, non-misleading liquor price information from its citizens to promote temperance.]

As for the first requirement, the Florida Bar asserted a substantial interest in protecting accident victims and their families from intrusive, unwelcome contact by lawyers. Moreover, the Florida Bar had a substantial interest in protecting the reputation of the legal profession, and Florida's two year study proved that reputation was seriously tarnished by direct-mail solicitation in the immediate wake of an accident or disaster.

As for the second requirement (that the regulation must "directly and materially advance" the governmental interest) the Court distinguished the present case from *Edenfield v. Fane*, 507 U.S. 761, 113 S.Ct. 1792 (1993), which invalidated a ban on in-person solicitation by certified public accountants. The accountancy board offered no evidence that accountants over-reach, or trick, or unfairly convince potential clients. In contrast, the Florida bar's two year study produced convincing evidence that lawyers' direct-mail advertising is regarded by personal injury victims and their families as intrusive, annoying, invasive, and designed to "take advantage of gullible or unstable people."

As for the third requirement (that the regulation must be narrowly tailored to achieve a reasonably close fit with the governmental objective), the Court echoed earlier holdings that the "least restrictive means" test does not apply to commercial speech. True, the Florida rules do not distinguish between severe injury cases (where victims and their families might wish to be left alone) and minor injury cases (where those concerned might be ready and able to use help from a lawyer). True also, injury victims and their families may be pestered during the 30-day period by fast-talking insurance adjusters and defense lawyers in search of cheap settlements. The Court found those points unpersuasive, stating simply: "The Bar's rule is reasonably well-tailored to its stated objective of eliminating targeted mailings whose type and timing are a source of distress to Floridians, distress that has caused many of them to lose respect for the legal profession." [We have omitted the dissenting opinion by Justice Kennedy, joined by Justices Stevens, Souter, and Ginsburg.]

## CHAPTER FIVE
## ATTORNEY FEES AND FIDUCIARY DUTIES

### Discussion Problem 1

A] Problem 1 asks you about a typical lawyer, Dolores. She's a solo practitioner with three years' experience. She has her office in a mid-sized city. She puts in 60 hours a week at the office, and from that she can bill about 40 hours per week to clients. That's fairly typical. She is approached by a typical client, house painter Leonard, who wants her to handle a $6,000 contract dispute for him. She figures the case will take her about 10 hours, plus another two hours of basic research. Leonard wants her to quote him a flat fee at the outset.

### Part (a)

A] Part (a) asks what you think would be a fair fee, and how you arrive at that figure.

B] I'm sure this is not how lawyers actually go about computing their fees, but I tried to do it in steps, using the information we were provided in the problem. [The method is crude, but it does have modest precedent in the literature. *See* WILLIAM G. ROSS, THE HONEST HOUR: THE ETHICS OF TIME-BASED BILLING BY ATTORNEYS 16, text at n. 64 and authorities there cited (1996).]

Step 1: I figured out how many billable hours a year Dolores works. She bills about 40 hours per week. She works 48 weeks a year (and takes four weeks of vacation). Multiplying 40 times 48, we get 1,920 billable hours per year.

Step 2: I figured out what her yearly overhead cost was. It averages $7,000 per month, and it goes on 12 months a year, whether or not she's away on vacation. Multiplying $7,000 times 12, we get $84,000 per year in overhead.

Step 3: I divided the yearly overhead by the yearly billable hours to find out how much she's going to have to charge per hour just to cover her overhead. $84,000 divided by 1,920 gives us $43.75, which I rounded up to $44. She will have to charge her clients $44 per hour just to cover her expenses—before she makes a dime for herself.

Step 4: The fourth step requires some guess work. I took a guess about how much Dolores ought to be making in yearly pre-tax income. She has three years of

71

experience, and she's a solo practitioner in a middle-sized city. I guessed that lawyers with those characteristics are earning about $80,000 per year, before taxes. Then I divided $80,000 by her yearly billable hours to find out how much she will have to charge per hour to produce that amount of income. That turns out to be $41.66, which I rounded up to $42.

Step 5: I added together the hourly charge to cover overhead and the hourly charge to cover income: $44 + $42 = $86 per hour. Thus, I took $86 per hour as the ordinary hourly rate she should be working with when she computes a client's fee.

Step 6: Next I had to decide how many hours to attribute to Leonard's work. Dolores believes it will take her about 10 hours, plus two more for some basic research that a more experienced lawyer would not have to do. CRPC 4–200(B)(8) and ABA Model Rule 1.5(a) say that the skill and experience of the lawyer can be taken into account in deciding what is a reasonable fee. I think it would be unfair to expect Dolores to give away the two hours of basic research. On the other hand, during those two hours, she is developing a skill that she will be able to charge for when a similar case comes along. Thus, I struck a compromise—halfway between 10 and 12 is 11. If you multiply 11 times $86, you get $946.

A] Is that where you stop? Is that the *only* amount that would be reasonable to charge Leonard?

B] No. In fact, the problem says that other lawyers in the community would charge about $1,500. Time is not the only factor that can be taken into account. The California Rules and the ABA Model Rules list more than half a dozen other factors that can be considered in setting a reasonable fee. The list is not exclusive, and some factors are irrelevant to a given case. My $946 figure is just a baseline from which to work. If Dolores gets the work done promptly, without having to distract Leonard from his job too much, and if she gets a full $6,000 recovery for Leonard, then I think she should feel comfortable charging him $1,500 or so. On the other hand, if she lets the debtor stall the case, and if she frequently has to distract Leonard from his job, and if she gets only a small recovery for Leonard, then I think she should charge him less than the $946 figure.

## Part (b)

A] Moving to part (b) of Problem 1, suppose Dolores agrees to do Leonard's work for a flat fee of $1,750, and suppose they make an oral agreement to that effect. Is Dolores subject to discipline?

B] No. I think $1,750 is within the bounds of reasonableness. Bear in mind this is a flat fee—a fee that is fixed at the outset of the matter. The problem tells us that Leonard insists on having a flat fee. The peace of mind that he gets from that is worth a price, and I don't think $1,750 is too high. After all, Dolores is forced to take a gamble here; the case may turn out to consume much more time than she has predicted. Although other lawyers in the community would be charging $1,750 for ~~$1500~~ this work, the fee "customarily charged in the locality" is only one of the factors to be considered—it is not the sole factor or the determining factor.

C] There's a second issue in part (b). Was it proper for Dolores to make an *oral* fee agreement with Leonard, rather than putting the fee agreement into writing?

A] Would you have used a written agreement in that situation?

C] In California, she'd need a written fee agreement. [CAL. BUS. & PROF. CODE § 6148.] ABA Model Rule 1.5 *recommends* written fee agreements but does not make them mandatory except in contingent fee cases. Common sense suggests that a lawyer should put *all* fee agreements in writing. That helps assure that the lawyer and client will come to a clear understanding about the fee at the outset, and it helps avoid disputes later.

## Part (c)

A] Part (c) asks you to suppose that Leonard wants a contingent fee arrangement. If Dolores agrees to do the work for 35% of the recovery, would that be proper?

B] Yes, it would be proper to use a contingent fee here. ABA Model Rule 1.5(c) requires the fee agreement to be in a writing that is signed by the client. [*Accord* CAL. BUS. & PROF. CODE § 6147.] Further, the written agreement must explain how the expenses of litigation will be treated in computing the lawyer's share, and the ABA rule says it must notify the client of any expenses the client will have to pay even if he loses the case. The California statute requires the agreement to notify the client that the lawyer's share is subject to negotiation. [*Id.*]

A] Would 35% be unreasonably high in these circumstances?

B] I don't think so. Let's suppose that Dolores wins a total victory; she gets a judgment for the entire $6,000 that Leonard claims is due. And suppose there are $1,000 in costs, and that the costs are to be deducted from the recovery before

Dolores' fee is computed. After deducting the costs, you'd multiply $5,000 by .35 and get a fee of $1,750. I think that's within the bounds of reason, bearing in mind the gamble that a contingent fee lawyer has to take.

## Part (d)

A] Part (d) asks whether your estimate of a fair fee would change if the amount in controversy were $60,000 rather than $6,000, and if Leonard were a painter of portraits rather than a painter of houses.

C] Yes, my estimate would go up. The CRPC and ABA Model Rule 1.5(a) say that the amount in controversy is one thing a lawyer may take into consideration in setting the fee. Furthermore, a contract dispute about a portrait is likely to be a lot more difficult than a dispute about house painting. Leonard's customer probably has some reason for not paying the bill. If that reason involves some supposed defect in Leonard's performance, Dolores is far more likely to run into tricky issues of law and fact in a portrait painting case than in a house painting case.

## Discussion Problem 2

> [In preparation for the class discussion of Problem 2, you way wish to read Lisa G. Lerman, *Symposium on Unethical Billing Practices: Scenes from a Law Firm,* 50 RUTGERS L. REV. 2153 (1998) and Douglas R. Richmond, *The New Law Firm Economy, Billable Hours and Professional Responsibility, 29* HOFSTRA L. REV. 207 (2000). The following additional sources are also useful: WILLIAM G. ROSS, THE HONEST HOUR: THE ETHICS OF TIME-BASED BILLING BY ATTORNEYS (1996); Lisa G. Lerman, *Blue-Chip Bilking: Regulation of Billing and Expense Fraud by Lawyers*, 12 GEO. J. LEGAL ETHICS 205 (1999).]

## Part (a)

A] Part (a) of Problem 2 describes how the billing is done in a certain business law firm. What's your reaction to that description?

B] It sounded pretty ordinary to me. Last summer I clerked in a firm rather like this one. The summer clerks had lots of contact with the partners—I guess they were trying to sell us on the firm—so we got to ask a lot of questions. One day four of us were taken out to lunch by a couple of the partners, and they asked us what we wanted to know about the way the firm operates. This billing thing came up, and what they told us sounded much the same as part (a). The big thing they stressed is the importance of every lawyer in the firm keeping accurate time records.

D]  My mother is a partner in a law firm that does mostly insurance defense work. She's always complaining about the auditors mentioned in part (a). In her case it's the insurance company claims managers, who go over her bills hoping to find a nickel or dime to complain about. She says that some claims managers are good and really understand what lawyers do and why it costs what it does. It's the other claims managers that make her sputter. She says they don't really understand the litigation process, and they often try to stop her from spending time on things that she thinks are essential in preparing for trial.

A]  Your mother is not alone—many lawyers have started to speak about bill auditors and claims managers in the same acid terms that physicians use about HMOs. For whatever help it may be, some states have issued ethics opinions reminding lawyers that they must not surrender their own judgment to functionaries who insert themselves into the relationship between the lawyer and the client. [*See* Alabama Op. RO-98-02; Indiana Ethics Op. 3 (1998).]

## Part (b)

A]  Let's move to part (b) of Problem 2. What do you think of associate Albert, who worked 30 hours on a problem and logged only 10 of those hours, fearing his boss would think he's a dolt if he reported the full 30 hours?

C]  Albert isn't the only one to try this trick. I did it myself last summer when I was clerking. The lawyer I was working for asked me to draft some interrogatories in a Lanham Act case involving a deceptive Internet address. When she gave me the assignment, I didn't know the difference between the Lanham Act and a charging rhinoceros. I ended up spending a lot of time on background reading, but I didn't want to let her know how unprepared I was to handle that kind of assignment. I worked very late several nights in a row, and then I logged only about one fourth of the time I actually spent on the project.

A]  What happened?

C]  I don't know how my boss caught on, but she did. She was nice about it though. She called me in and asked me how many hours I'd actually worked, so I had to tell her. She explained that there are three reasons not to do what I did. First, it's the billing partner's job to decide how much of a beginning lawyer's logged time can fairly be charged to the client. The billing partner knows what the task was, what the lawyer's experience and ability were, and approximately how long the task would have taken a more experienced lawyer. If a young lawyer is discounting her time when she fills out her time record, the billing partner doesn't have an accurate base to work from. Second, in firms that use billable hours as part of their criteria for rewarding lawyers, a lawyer who under-reports his time is shooting himself in the foot. Third, a lawyer who under-reports her time is, in one sense, stealing money from the law firm's till. That sounds harsh, but the point is that the billing partner is the best judge of whether a beginning lawyer is spending too much time on a project. That's why it's vital that every lawyer in the firm must log time accurately, reporting no more and no less than the time actually spent on the client's matter.

## Part (c)

A] Part (c) of Problem 2 concerns the number of billable hours the law firm expects from its associates each year. What was your reaction to that situation?

B] The people in our class who have interviewed with lots of firms have concluded that firms are like people—most of them are honest and tell it like it is, but some of them tell you what they think you want to hear. As a young person looking for a job, you have to probe and find out as much as you can about the reality of working for that firm. If you have a chance, it's good to talk with some of the youngest lawyers in the firm; they may tell you things that the recruiting partners will not.

C] I've heard it's pretty common for firms to tell you that they want all their lawyers to be well-rounded people with plenty of time for family and community, but then to pile the work on, to get the most billable hours they can out of you. And it's not just the young people—lots of the middle-age and older partners are slaving away nights and weekends too.

D] From the facts given here, I don't think we can tell whether Tara got lied to, or whether she was gullible and didn't ask the right questions of the right people before she decided to go to work for this firm. What's important for her now is to decide what she's going to do about her situation. If she doesn't want to work as hard as the firm apparently expects, she'd better start looking for a new job that suits her better.

## Part (d)

A] Apparently some of the more experienced associates in the firm have found a way to cope with the firm's high billable hour expectations, as you see in part (d) of

Problem 2. There associate Allison discusses two "survival skills," the first of which involves the firm's policy of billing in minimum units of a tenth of an hour (6 minutes). If you make five phone calls, each two minutes long, is it ethical to log 30 minutes for that 10 minutes worth of work? [*See* WILLIAM G. ROSS, THE HONEST HOUR: THE ETHICS OF TIME-BASED BILLING BY ATTORNEYS 165-69 (1996).]

D] Every firm has to pick some time interval to use as its minimum unit of time for purposes of record keeping. In the old days, most firms used the quarter hour. These days, I understand that most firms use the tenth of an hour (6 minute) interval, because the decimal system is easy to handle. I don't see anything odious about charging a tenth of an hour for a two-minute phone call, so long as the client is told about that policy in advance and consents to it.

A] That's an important point to draw from ABA Formal Op. 93-379, reproduced in your text. Informing the client, and getting the client's consent, is a vital step in fair billing. How would you go about informing the client about billing policies?

D] I think it should be a separate paragraph in the firm's written fee agreement with the client. The paragraph should cover not only phone calls, but also the firm's policy on billing for out-of-town travel expenses, copying, delivery service, and the like. Putting it in the fee agreement helps assure that the client knows about it from the outset.

B] I agree that it's OK to establish something other than one minute as the firm's minimum time unit. The process of recording a lawyer's time is by nature imprecise, and using a fine calibration cannot make the measurement more precise. On the other hand, I'd favor a different response to your question. You asked whether it is ethical to charge a half hour for making five two-minute phone calls. I believe most lawyers would say yes. However, if all five of those two-minute calls were for the same client, I think the lawyer should aggregate them. That would make ten minutes total, which would round upward to .2 hours, not .5 hours.

C] I'd favor another change from the common practice. Lawyers always round upward, but not downward. I like Professor Lerman's idea of rounding in both directions. [Lisa G. Lerman, *Lying to Clients*, 138 U.PA. L. REV. 659, 751 (1990).] If the firm uses a quarter hour as its minimum time interval, then a task that takes half of that interval (7.5 minutes) can be rounded up to a quarter hour, but a task that takes less than half must be rounded down to zero. For example, a ten-minute task can be rounded up to 15 minutes, but a five-minute task must be rounded down to zero.

A] What do you think of associate Allison's second "survival skill," that is to log "think and worry" time, when you are thinking or worrying about a client's problem while you use the restroom, or eat lunch, or clean house, or try to sleep.

D] Get serious! This is fraud. She admits that she mis-describes it on her time record—she doesn't call it "thinking about client's problem while cleaning up baby's room." She calls it "review and analysis of . . ." something or other. That's going to make the client and her boss think that she was at her desk reviewing court papers or research material or the like. This woman should be disbarred.

B] Maybe it's not a clear cut as you think. Suppose she's reading a deposition transcript at her desk, and she continues reading while she walks down the hall, and while she uses the restroom, and while she's washing her hands, and while she walks back to her desk. Shouldn't she be able to log at least some of that time?

D] Well, maybe some of it, but I don't think you can read a deposition transcript and wash your hands at the same time without getting the pages wet. The same goes for the lawyer who thinks about the client's problem while eating a sandwich at the lunch counter. Obviously it is legitimate for a lawyer to log at least part of the time spent talking business over lunch with a client or co-counsel. I think it is also OK to log at least some of the time if a lawyer is reading a deposition transcript while eating a sandwich alone at the lunch counter. But I draw the line at logging time spent "just thinking" about the client's matter while eating that sandwich. One of the reasons lawyers earn a higher hourly wage than taxi drivers is that lawyers are constantly thinking and worrying about some client's problem—it comes with the territory, and it's already reflected in our higher hourly wage.

C] I think the issue here is one of deception. If Allison's time record says "Preparation for deposition of . . ." when in fact she is lying in bed, trying to sleep, but worrying about the questions for the deposition, then I think she is trying to deceive both the law firm and the client. If I were her boss, I'd fire her for that.

## Part (e)

A] Hearing no dissent, let's move on to part (e) about associate Arnold's "survival skills." What do you think of Arnold's first piece of advice—learn to record your time whenever you switch tasks during the day. Is that sound advice?

B] Yes, but it's hard to do that when you are working on several different items for different clients. I had trouble using the time-keeper software where I was clerking last summer, and I ended up making manual entries on a yellow pad beside my telephone and then entering the information into the computer at the end of the day. When I get a real job after graduation, I'll look around for a time-keeper program that is easier to use.

D] The important point in Arnold's advice is not to work along all day without recording your time, thinking that you will be able to remember everything at the end of the day. The longer the interval between the doing and the recording, the less accurate the time record will be.

A] What about Arnold's second piece of advice—learn to avoid re-inventing the wheel. Arnold says he has figured out some patterns in his work, and he has devised some computerized forms that save him a lot of time. He remembers how much time it formerly took him to do the tasks in question, and that's how much time he logs now. How do you react to that?

C] I think we need to consider it from two points of view. Let's consider the client's point of view first. Suppose that the client's fee agreement with the firm says that the client will pay on a strict time basis, and that the fee agreement prices Arnold's time at $200 per hour. Suppose, further, that Arnold spends 30 minutes doing a task for the client and that it would have taken Arnold two hours to do that same task before he developed his present skill and his computer forms. How much time should Arnold log—30 minutes, or two hours?

B] He should log 30 minutes only. [*Cf.* ABA Formal Op. 93-379 (if lawyer charges strictly on time basis, and is lucky enough to be asked the same question twice, lawyer must pass the savings on to the second client).]

C] What if the $200 price tag on Arnold's services is out of date—the fee agreement was made several years ago, before Arnold developed his present skill and his computerized forms. Shouldn't Arnold log two hours?

B] No, he should still log the actual time spent—30 minutes. The law firm, of course, ought to renegotiate the fee agreement with the client, to bring the hourly prices up to date. Until that happens, however, I think would be deceptive for the firm to charge the client for more than 30 minutes of Arnold's time.

C] What if the client's fee agreement with the firm is *not* strictly on a time basis? For example, what if it's a "task based" fee agreement, in which the client agrees to pay $X for the task that Arnold completed in 30 minutes?

B]  If that's the deal, then the firm will bill the client for $X—the amount of time Arnold spent will be irrelevant to that billing transaction.

C]  But Arnold's time log will still be relevant as between Arnold and the firm, and that brings us to the second point of view—the firm's point of view. How should the firm react if Arnold completes a task in 30 minutes, but logs two hours because that is the amount of time it would have taken him earlier in his career, before he developed his present skill and his computerized forms?

B]  The firm ought to tell him not to do that. The firm needs to have an *accurate* record of Arnold's time for at least two reasons. First, the firm needs to know how to price Arnold's time—if he can now complete in 30 minutes a task that used to take him two hours, then his hourly billing rate needs to be raised. Second, the firm needs to know how many hours Arnold is really working so that it can reward him fairly in comparison with the other lawyers in the firm.

## Discussion Problem 3

A]  Problem 3 concerns attorney Welch and some funds and property she handled in a collection case for Seaboard Marine Supply. Did she handle the funds and property correctly?

B]  No, she really fouled it up. First, she let that check sit around for two weeks before she deposited it. The Comments to ABA Model Rule 1.15 begin by stating that a lawyer should hold property of others "with the care required of a professional fiduciary." Welch's delayed deposit was certainly below that standard of care. [*See also* CRPC 4-100(B)(1) and ABA Model Rule 1.15(d), which require a lawyer to *notify the client promptly* after receiving funds on the client's behalf.]

A]  Why? What's the possible harm?

B]  First, the money was lying fallow for two weeks. Second, there's some chance that the check might be mislaid if it's not cashed promptly. Third, and most important, the person who issued the check, Dringle, is a deadbeat—the kind of guy who buys two fancy boats and doesn't pay for them. Dringle's checking account may have contained enough to cover this check the day he wrote it, but who knows what it will contain two weeks later? I think Welch put her client's funds unnecessarily at risk by letting the check sit around that long.

A] You're being awfully harsh on Welch. The problem says she was in trial and working 16 hours a day. What do you expect from her?

B] Sixteen hours and five minutes. That's all it would take to tell her secretary or some other lawyer in the office to get this matter taken care of. A heavy workload for one client should not allow her to put another client at risk of loss.

A] What do you think of the way she handled the other part of the transaction—the part about the motorboat?

B] She fouled that up too. Dringle the Deadbeat leaves a note saying the motorboat is tied up at the dock. Is he telling the truth? Who knows? Welch surely doesn't; she's too busy to find out. But assume Dringle is telling the truth. Did he chain and lock the boat to the dock? If not, it's long since been stolen. Did he have permission to leave it at the dock? If not, it's long since been towed away by the Harbor Patrol. When he tied it up, did he cover it? If not, who knows what it's full of now. And what about last week's heavy storms—perhaps we will find it smashed against the rocks. All of those interesting possibilities could have been avoided if Welch had simply taken the extra five minutes to have someone in her office telephone Seaboard so they could come over to pick up the keys and put the boat in a safe place. Welch is subject to discipline under CRPC 4-100(B) and ABA Model Rule 1.15(a) and (d), and she should be civilly liable for any loss Seaboard suffers because of her negligence.

## Discussion Problem 4

A] Problem 6 asks about attorney Arner who represented one Corman in a lawsuit. Did Arner handle the money properly?

B] No, in two respects. First, he signed Corman's name to the check. The problem makes no mention of Arner's having a power of attorney to sign Corman's name to checks. It looks like plain old forgery to me.

A] And what's the second way?

B] I didn't like the way Arner sneaked his fee out before even bothering to notify Corman about the check or consulting with Corman about the fee. His fee agreement with Corman did give him the right to deduct the fee from the proceeds before paying the remainder to Corman. But that did not give Arner the unilateral power to decide what fee Corman should pay. The $50,000 should have initially gone into Arner's trust account because both Corman and Arner had an interest the $50,000. ABA

Model Rule 1.15(e) says that when an attorney and another person both claim an interest in property possessed by the attorney, that property must be kept separate until the dispute is resolved. [*See also* CRPC 4-100(A)(2).] I think Arner should have sent Corman an itemized bill, showing what was done and how many hours were spent on the case. Then, if Corman expressed no objection to the bill, Arner could withdraw his share from the client trust account. That would comply with ABA Model Rule 1.15(c), which states that an attorney can withdraw his or her share from the trust account "as fees are earned."

## ROBERT L. WHEELER, INC. v. SCOTT
### Supreme Court of Oklahoma, 1989

Facts: Robert L. Scott (client/appellant) hired Robert Wheeler (lawyer/appellee) to represent him in a loan collection and foreclosure proceeding instituted by mortgagee United Oklahoma Bank. Over a ten month period, Wheeler billed Scott $140,116.87 for 1,295.9 hours of work. Scott paid $54,275.37 of that amount but failed to pay the remaining $85,841.50. Just prior to the hearing on mortgagee's motion for summary judgment, Wheeler threatened to withdraw from the case if Scott did not pay the attorney fees. Scott did not pay and Wheeler did not withdraw. Instead, a first year associate appeared at the hearing at which summary judgment was granted for the mortgagee. Wheeler then withdrew from the case and sought attorney fees. The firm representing the mortgagee charged the bank $75,534.10 for 850 hours of work by seasoned attorneys. According to the bank's attorneys, the foreclosure was a simple case even though it involved a large amount of money and property. The trial court reduced the total attorney fees from $140,116.87 to $125,723.00. The appellate court affirmed and Scott appeals that decision.

Issue: After summary judgment was entered against appellant Scott in a mortgage foreclosure proceeding, and after the trial court subsequently reduced Wheeler's fees, was the fee still excessive?

Holding: Yes, the fee was still excessive.

Discussion: In a thorough and detailed manner, the Oklahoma Supreme Court analyzes the fee under 12 factors that are reflected within ABA Model Rule 1.5. The trial court had focused on the time spent on the case instead of balancing all of the factors—an approach that was particularly problematic because once all of the factors were considered, it became obvious that the number of hours claimed was excessive for such a relatively straightforward matter, requiring no specialized knowledge and precluding no other employment, the lack of restrictive time limitations, the resolution of the matter through summary judgment, and the fact that the primary attorney was an inexperienced first- year associate.

# CHAPTER SIX
## COMPETENCE, DILIGENCE AND
## UNAUTHORIZED PRACTICE

### Discussion Problem 1

A] Problem 1 concerns lawyer Layton's adventures on the Internet. She's an Arizona lawyer who responded by e-mail to a Rhode Islander's Internet request for advice on Rhode Island legal malpractice law. Layton's response included incorrect advice about the malpractice statute of limitations. The Rhode Islander relied on the bad advice and lost her cause of action as a consequence.

### Part (a)

A] Part (a) of the question asks whether Layton is guilty of practicing law in Rhode Island without a license.

B] The term "guilty" suggests that we are being asked about criminal liability rather than professional discipline. To avoid being like lawyer Layton, I rushed to the Rhode Island statute books. Like most states, Rhode Island makes it a crime (punishable by a year in jail) to practice law in the state without being a member of the state's bar. [General Laws of Rhode Island §§ 11-27-1 through 11-27-19. The California equivalent is CAL. BUS. & PROF. CODE §§ 6125-26.] I have never seen a definition of "practice of law" that is not circular, and Rhode Island's is no exception. It says that the "practice of law" is the "doing of any act for another person usually done by attorneys at law in the course of their profession . . . ." [General Laws of Rhode Island § 11-27-2.] Since that doesn't help much, the definition goes on to provide four non-limiting examples: 1) appearing as somebody's representative in a court or similar tribunal; 2) giving somebody advice on a question of law; 3) acting as somebody's representative in bringing or settling a civil claim or criminal case; and 4) drafting a legal document for somebody, such as a will or articles of incorporation.

A] Do lawyer Layton's acts fit one of those four examples?

B] Sure—Layton gave the Rhode Island woman "advice on a question of law," namely advice about how legal malpractice law applied to a certain set of facts, and advice (which turned out to be wrong) about the malpractice statute of limitations.

A] Do you think Rhode Island's criminal statute would be invoked against an attorney from another state?

B] As a practical matter, it seems unlikely, because the culprit in our case is far, far away in Arizona, is not profiting from practice in Rhode Island, and is not holding herself out as a lawyer in Rhode Island. I suspect Rhode Island prosecutors have better things to do with their time and budgets. Moreover, the Rhode Island unauthorized practice statutes have a tricky limitation: they do not apply to "visiting attorneys at law" who are licensed to practice in another state and who are temporarily in Rhode Island on legal business or who are in Rhode Island to conduct a case *pro hac vice*. [*Id.* § 11-27-13.] If a prosecutor asserts that one practices law in Rhode Island simply by sending an e-mail to a Rhode Islander, then perhaps Layton could respond that she was "just visiting" via cyberspace.

A] Let's assume that Layton is not likely to be criminally prosecuted in Rhode Island. Could she be subject to professional discipline for unauthorized practice?

B] ABA Model Rule 5.5(a) makes a lawyer subject to discipline if she practices in a jurisdiction where she is not admitted to practice. [*Accord* CRPC 1-300(b).] ABA Model Rule 8.5(a) allows her to be disciplined by the Arizona bar, even though her unauthorized practice took place in Rhode Island, but it implies that she could not be disciplined by the Rhode Island bar because she is not admitted in Rhode Island. The choice of law provision in 8.5(b)(2) indicates that if the Arizona bar disciplines her, the applicable ethics rules would be the Arizona rules.

## Part (b)

A] Part (b) of Problem 1 asks whether Layton would be subject to discipline for incompetence. What do you think?

B] ABA Model Rule 1.1, the very first rule, makes a lawyer subject to discipline for failing to provide competent representation to a client. [*Cf.* CRPC 3-110(A).] That means that the lawyer must use "the legal knowledge, skill, thoroughness, and preparation reasonably necessary for the representation." [ABA Model Rule 1.1; CRPC 3-110(B).]

A] You talk about "representation of a client." How did the Rhode Island woman get to be one of Layton's "clients"?

B] It doesn't take a fancy ceremony to become a "client" for legal ethics purposes. It doesn't require the payment of a fee, and it doesn't require a retainer agreement. One can argue that the Rhode Island woman became Layton's client when Layton responded by e-mail to her legal inquiry. [*See* Joan Rogers, *Ethics, Malpractice Concerns Cloud E-Mail, On-Line Advice*, 12 ABA/BNA LAWYER'S MANUAL ON PROFESSIONAL CONDUCT 59 (1996).]

A] What if Layton had put a disclaimer provision in her e-mail communication, saying something like this: "This letter does not contain a legal opinion or legal advice, and it does not create a lawyer-client relationship between us. Your fact situation may be different from the facts assumed here. You should not rely on this letter, and you should not act without consulting an attorney." Would the disclaimer accomplish anything?

B] Legally, perhaps not. A judge or disciplinary panel might well ignore it. However, it might help as a practical matter: the layperson who receives a message with a clear disclaimer might pay attention to it and thus not rely on the message. [*Id.* at 69.]

A] Since you are speaking of practical matters, is it likely that Arizona will discipline Layton for giving incorrect legal advice to the woman from Rhode Island?

B] It's not likely if this was Layton's only misadventure. I have never seen a lawyer discipline case in which a lawyer was charged with a single act of incompetence and nothing else. In most cases, the lawyer has acted incompetently time after time, or else the lawyer has violated other disciplinary rules along with the competence rule. The organized bar has only a limited amount to spend on discipline cases, and it puts its money where it will do the most good. Further, for isolated acts of incompetence, there's always the possibility of a civil action for legal malpractice.

## Part (c)

A] That brings us to part (c) of Problem 1: is Layton liable to Cushing for legal malpractice?

B] In the subsequent Discussion Problems we will talk about malpractice liability in more detail. As a short answer here, I'd say that Cushing has a tenable malpractice claim against Layton. Layton dispensed legal advice about the statute of limitations—in an unfamiliar jurisdiction—without doing any legal research. That is a particularly dangerous kind of advice to dispense off the seat of your pants, and to me it seems clearly below the standard of care. Because of Layton's faulty advice, Cushing lost her cause of action. In a malpractice case against Layton, Cushing will have to prove that she in fact had a sound claim against the divorce lawyer, and she will have to prove the value of that claim. Cushing will also have to prove actual causation, but that shouldn't be hard on these facts. Finally, Cushing will have to prove proximate causation—that sound policy favors protecting a person in her position who suffers this kind of injury. To me, that's an easy policy choice because I can't think of any reason to immunize lawyers who dispense dangerously defective legal advice, off the seat of their pants, over the Internet.

## Discussion Problem 2

A] Problem 2 concerns client Cameron who took her case to a law firm, paid them a $5,000 advance on attorney fees, and then became the victim of delay. The question asks whether professional discipline or malpractice liability is a possibility in this situation. Let's consider malpractice first; will Cameron be able to recover for legal malpractice here?

B] As a practical matter, a malpractice action seems out of the question here because her damages are probably too small to justify the effort. We are not told what kind of case she had, nor what kind of harm (if any) she suffered because her case was delayed. If she eventually won a money judgment in the main case, perhaps she can argue that she was damaged because her use of that money was delayed. Likewise, she might argue loss of use for the $5,000 fee advance. But she's got proof problems concerning actual causation. Judge Jergins was responsible for part of the delay here, but a litigant can't sue a judge for "judicial malpractice" for being slow in deciding cases. [Concerning judicial immunity *see Stump v. Sparkman*, 435 U.S. 349, 98 S.Ct. 1099, 55 L.Ed.2d 331 (1978).] Perhaps Judge Jergins would have acted faster if lawyer Benson had prodded him along, but how would one prove *how much* faster? In short, on the facts we are given in the problem, malpractice recovery seems unlikely.

A] What about professional discipline? Who could be subject to discipline here?

B] First, Judge Jergins is subject to discipline. ABA Code of Judicial Conduct, Rule 2.5 and Comment 3, are right on point: "A judge shall perform judicial and administrative duties competently and diligently." Comment 3 explains, "Prompt disposition of the court's business requires a judge to devote adequate time to judicial duties, to be punctual in attending court and expeditious in determining matters under submission, and to take reasonable measures to ensure that court officials, litigants, and their lawyers cooperate with the judge to that end."

A] Are any of the lawyers at Alarcon & Brown subject to discipline for the delay Cameron suffered?

B] Associate Anson is not, at least on the facts given in the problem. He was assigned to work on the case, but he left the firm before doing significant work on it.

A] What about Benson—he sat on the case for 10 months without even filing a complaint. Isn't that gross neglect?

B] Perhaps. The problem says Benson had a heavy workload, and that's why he took 10 months to get the complaint on file. If Benson was suffering in silence, and his superiors were unaware of his heavy workload, Benson certainly bears responsibility for his inability to manage his work. [*See* Comment 2 to ABA Model Rule 1.3 (noting that lawyers must control their workload so that each matter can be handled competently); *see also* ABA Model Rule 5.2(a) (noting that subordinate lawyers are bound by the Rules of Professional Conduct even if acting at the direction of another person).] Here, however, a "management committee" assigned Cameron's case to Benson. I assume the management committee is a group of partners. If the management committee knew—or should have known—about Benson's workload, it seems these partners should be disciplined. The case should not have been assigned to an associate whose workload was so heavy that it took him 10 months to file the complaint.

A] *Could* the members of the management committee be disciplined?

B] ABA Model Rule 5.1 says that the partners, managers, and supervisory lawyers in a law firm must make reasonable efforts to ensure that all lawyers in the firm act ethically. Furthermore, if Benson's 10-month delay violated ABA Model Rule 1.3 (duty to act diligently and promptly), then the management committee members should be subject to discipline under ABA Model Rule 5.1(c)(2). They either knew or should have known what Benson's workload was when the case was assigned to him. In a sense, they *caused* the whole problem, or at the very least they failed to mitigate the consequences.

## Discussion Problem 3

A] In Problem 3 we have attorney Adams who let the statute of limitations run on client Chandler's claim against the airline company. Do we have the beginnings of a malpractice case here?

B] Absolutely. A reasonably prudent lawyer simply does not miss statutes of limitations. In the small firm where I clerked last summer, they had a "tickler" system. Every case that came into the office was routed through a woman who had been at the firm since the landing at Plymouth Rock. She "calendared" the case, meaning that she recorded all the important deadlines the firm would have to meet in the case. All court papers were routed through her so she could record response dates. For instance, she knew what date you had to file the answers to the plaintiff's interrogatories in *Grutz v. Frap*, and she knew what date had been set for Mr. Grutz's deposition, and when you had to complete discovery in the case, and when you had to file the pretrial conference memos, and so forth.

A] What did she do with all that information?

B] Two things. First, for each department in the firm, she prepared a weekly calendar of things that had to be done that week, plus everything that would be coming up in the week that followed. All the lawyers kept their own calendars as well, but hers was the failsafe device. Second, everything that was sent out of the firm also had to be routed through her. Thus, if you had not filed the answers to the *Grutz* case interrogatories by the 18th, and if they were due on the 19th, she'd give you a cranky phone call to find out what was going on.

A] I'd think you'd have to be a saint to hold that job.

B] My supervising attorney said they'd thought about replacing her with the kind of computer system they use in large law firms, but when they priced the system and the monthly input costs, they decided it was cheaper to pay her salary and put up with her phone calls.

A] Getting back to where you started: reasonably prudent lawyers simply do not miss statutes of limitations. Adams has acted negligently here, and if Chandler could prove the other elements, she'd have a good malpractice claim. Is Adams also likely to get disciplined?

B] Probably not for simply missing the statute of limitations, assuming it was not intentional, and assuming it was an isolated incident. But I think he certainly ought to be disciplined for the way he compromised the claim with Chandler.

A] What more could you expect of the poor man? He paid Chandler $6,500 out of his own pocket—that was $2,000 more than her medical costs. And Chandler obviously understood the deal and agreed to it; she signed both a release and an endorsement on the back of his check that explained the situation.

B] But I think Adams violated ABA Model Rule 1.8(h). [*Accord* CRPC 3-400(B).]

A] Does that rule make it unethical for a lawyer to settle a potential malpractice claim?

B] No, of course not—settlement of disputes is always favored in the law. However, in this situation, the lawyer is in a position potentially to dupe the client by rushing the client into a quick settlement when the client may not even realize the strength of her claim for legal malpractice. In this case, Adams should have advised Chandler in writing of the desirability of independent counsel and given an opportunity to consult such counsel before settling the claim. [*See* ABA Model Rule 1.8(h)(2); *see also* RESTATEMENT (THIRD) OF THE LAW GOVERNING LAWYERS § 54(3) and (4) (2000).]

## Discussion Problem 4

A] In Problem 4, attorney Arlene agrees to represent client Crampton in a medical malpractice case. She tells him that she has never handled such a case before, but that she will do her best. Let's stop there; has she committed malpractice simply by taking on the case?

B] No, of course not. Otherwise, how could you ever take on your first case? Or move into a new field of law? [*See* Comment 2 to ABA Model Rule 1.1; CRPC 3-110(C).]

A] O.K., then let's consider the four alleged mistakes she made.

## Part (a)

A] Part (a) says that Arlene failed to consult an expert on hospital administration; with an expert's help, she could have shown that the hospital was understaffed.

B] That seems like an obvious point that a reasonably prudent lawyer ought to have tracked down. If the nurse was frazzled from overwork, that will be a big step toward proving liability. The failure to conduct a reasonable fact investigation is malpractice.

## Part (b)

A]  Part (b) says that Arlene used only one medical expert at trial.  Is that malpractice?

B]  The problem says that the jury "might have been more impressed" had several experts testified.  Then again, the jury might have been bored stiff by dull, repetitive expert testimony.  This seems to me to be a tactical choice typically left to the lawyer's good judgment.  [*See* Comment 2 to ABA Model Rule 1.2.]  If Arlene's decision to use only one expert was well-informed and thoughtful, I don't think she should be second-guessed in a malpractice case.

## Part (c)

A]  Part (c) says she failed to find out whether there were eyewitnesses around when the plaintiff received the improper medication.  Is that malpractice?

B]  That sounds like another instance of failure to perform a reasonably competent fact investigation.  I'd say that's malpractice.

## Part (d)

A]  Part (d) says she failed to find the State Department of Health regulation that sets the proper staff/patient ratio in hospitals.  Is that malpractice?

B] The hospital's failure to follow a statute or regulation could be very potent evidence of negligence.  If a reasonably prudent lawyer would have tracked down that regulation, then this is another instance of malpractice.  Proper legal research is part of a lawyer's duty of competence.  Lawyers are not expected to know every rule of law, but they are expected to look up the ones they don't know.  If the answer is there to be found by standard legal research techniques, and a lawyer doesn't find it (or doesn't even look for it), that's malpractice.

**Discussion Problem 5**

A] Problem 5 illustrates the topic discussed in the casebook's note entitled "The Ethics of Second-Rate Legal Service." Here lawyer Levitt is being asked to defend a corporation in a consumer protection case under some severe restrictions. Huffington (the corporation's house counsel) tells Levitt that the corporation has set a budget of $125,000 for *everything* connected with the case (attorney fees and all), that Huffington will give Levitt virtually everything Levitt needs in the way of discovery and legal research, and that Levitt is expected to handle the case in accordance with a pattern dictated by Huffington. Let's begin with something we should already know. Suppose Levitt doesn't want to defend Infoscope in this case unless he can do it his own way—he doesn't want to become a robot lawyer on Infoscope's assembly line. Does he have an ethical duty to represent Infoscope?

B] No, of course not. We learned about that back in Chapter Three. The problem tells us that Levitt has previously represented Infoscope in several matters. That past work may make him personally reluctant to turn down Infoscope now. He might have a hard choice to make, but his constraints are personal rather than ethical. He has no ethical obligation to undertake Infoscope's defense.

A] Would it be ethically proper for Levitt to try to convince Huffington to let him do the defense, but on his own terms? For example, he could offer to do the work for a specified hourly fee, or a fixed fee, and he could agree to study the papers from past cases and to recycle whatever he can in an effort to keep the price down. Would that be ethically proper?

B] Sure, Levitt can certainly propose that to Huffington, but it sounds like Huffington and the board of directors have already decided what they want.

A] All right, let's assume that Huffington won't budge. Would it be ethical for Levitt to undertake the defense on Huffington's terms?

B] I hate to be wishy-washy, but I think Levitt should take a careful look at the files in two or three of those prior cases before making up his mind. The summary judgment memos and affidavits ought to lead him pretty quickly to the possible trouble spots.

A] What do you mean possible trouble spots?

B] The note in the textbook about "Second-Rate Legal Service" flags them. If Levitt handles the defense using Huffington's cookie-cutter method, will the $125,000 budget be enough to allow him to handle the matter competently, and yet earn a reasonable fee? If not, Levitt's business sense should tell him to reject the case. Will Huffington's cookie-cutter method require him to do anything that he thinks is illegal or unethical? If so, he *must* reject the case. [*See* ABA Model Rule 1.16(a)(1); *cf.* CRPC 3-700(B).] Will it require him to do anything that he thinks is foolhardy or obnoxious? If so, that would certainly be a good reason to exercise his freedom to reject the case. [*See* ABA Model Rule 1.16(b)(4); *cf.* CRPC 3-700(C)(1)(e).]

A] Would it be ethically proper for Levitt to agree to represent Infoscope, but then totally ignore Huffington's instructions and handle the case however he sees fit?

B] No. If he is going to take the case, then he has to obey the client's instructions—so long as the instructions are within the bounds of the law and are consistent with the lawyer's ethical obligations. [*See* ABA Model Rule 1.2; *see also* RESTATEMENT OF THE LAW OF LAWYERING § 21, comment d (2000).]

A] Can you see any way for Levitt to take this case and follow Huffington's instructions without running the risk of a legal malpractice judgment?

B] Yes—use the device suggested by ABA Model Rule 1.2, and set forth with more specificity in the Restatement § 19—an agreement that limits Levitt's duties to Infoscope. It should probably be a part of the fee agreement between Levitt and Infoscope. If Infoscope is adequately informed and agrees to those limits, then the agreement should satisfy Rule 1.2 and § 19, thus insulating Levitt from a malpractice claim by Infoscope. [*Id.* § 19, comment a.]

A] Haven't you ignored a key element of Rule 1.2 and § 19—the limits must be *reasonable*.

B] Yes, that's important. But reasonableness seems likely in this situation. Infoscope would not want to impose limits on Levitt that would cause Infoscope to lose the case.

A] If you were Levitt, would you take this case and agree to follow Huffington's instructions?

B] That might depend on how hungry my family is. I don't think I'd be happy with law practice if all I'm doing is processing cases according to a pattern dictated by some in-house counsel.

## Discussion Problem 6

A] Problem 6 asks about hardworking Daley, a non-lawyer who appears to do about everything that needs doing around the Ames, Bell, and Chen law firm.

## Part (a)

A] Part (a) asks if Daley can do some basic legal work for her brother and sister-in-law, provided that lawyer Chen looks over her work. Would that be satisfactory?

B] No, I think there's a better way to come to much the same result. [*See* ABA Model Rule 5.5(b) and the Comment thereto; CRPC 1-300.] If Daley appears to be in charge here, somebody may accuse her of the unauthorized practice of law. Further, if Chen has assisted her by looking over her work, he too could be in trouble under the rules just cited.

A] So how should the arrangement be structured?

B] I think Daley's brother and sister-in-law should come into the office for an appointment with Chen, and they should clearly understand that Chen is in charge of their matter. (Since they are relatives of a valued employee, Chen probably won't charge them.) Then, if the matter involves some tasks that Chen can delegate to Daley (such as legal research or preparing drafts of routine legal documents), Daley can do those tasks under Chen's supervision. Finally, Chen should take responsibility for the entire matter, including Daley's work. Doing it this way avoids unauthorized practice problems, and it also helps assure that the brother and sister-in-law will get competent legal service.

## Part (b)

A] Part (b) of Problem 6 asks whether the law firm can pay Daley a bonus equal to 10% of the fees the firm earns from a client who came to the firm because of his friendship with Daley. Is that permissible?

B] No. I think that would violate CRPC 1-320(A) and ABA Model Rule 5.4(a), which prohibit sharing fees with a non-lawyer. I suppose the fear here is that lawyers will employ a squad of "investigators" or "representatives" who will earn their livelihood soliciting business for their lawyer employers.

## Part (c)

A] Part (c) asks whether Daley can be included in the law firm's new retirement program if the program is funded in part by fees earned by the lawyers. May Daley participate?

B] Yes, Daley can participate. There's a special exception to the fee splitting rule that permits non-lawyer employees to participate in law firm compensation and retirement plans. [ABA Model Rule 5.4(a)(3); CRPC 1-320(A)(3).]

## Part (d)

A] Part (d) asks whether Daley may purchase a token number of shares in the law firm, simply so that she will be qualified to serve as the treasurer of the professional corporation. Is this allowed?

B] No, she can't do that. A non-lawyer must not hold stock in a law firm, and a non-lawyer must not be a corporate officer or director or the equivalent of a law firm. [ABA Model Rule 5.4(d); CAL. BUS. & PROF. CODE § 6161; CAL. CORP. CODE § 13406.]

# CHAPTER SEVEN
## CONFIDENTIAL INFORMATION

## Discussion Problem 1

### Part (a)

A]  Chapter Seven concerns the lawyer's ethical duty to protect the client's confidential information.  Problem 1 asks you to compare the ethical duty with a related body of law, the attorney-client privilege.  Part (a) asks you to suppose that lawyer L, attending a P.T.A. potluck supper, has gossiped with a friend about the reasons one of L's clients wants to divorce her husband.  Does the attorney-client privilege apply at P.T.A. potluck suppers?

B]  No.  The attorney-client privilege applies in governmental proceedings, where the government has the powers of subpoena and contempt to compel the giving of evidence.  Court proceedings are the most obvious example.  The privilege is a <u>limit</u> on that governmental power—the government cannot compel the revelation of a communication that is protected by the privilege.  [*See* RESTATEMENT (THIRD) OF THE LAW GOVERNING LAWYERS §§ 68-72 (2000).]  The P.T.A. potluck supper is not an occasion where the government has the power to compel the giving of evidence, and therefore the attorney-client privilege does not apply there.

A]  Why does the attorney-client privilege exist in the law of evidence?

B]  The traditional argument is a utilitarian one: the attorney-client privilege helps assure that justice is done.  A lawyer cannot effectively protect a client's rights unless the lawyer knows the client's side of the story, and the privilege helps insure that the client will speak candidly with the lawyer.  Professor Louisell argued for a different, rights-based view of the privilege.  [*See* David Louisell, *Confidentiality, Conformity and Confusion: Privileges in Federal Court Today*, 31 TUL. L. REV. 101 (1956).]  He argued that the common law privileges (attorney-client, husband-wife, and penitent-clergy) are part of a citizen's "right to be left alone," free from governmental interference in certain important human relationships.

A]   So your answer to the first question in part (a) is "no"—the attorney-client privilege does not apply at P.T.A. potluck suppers.  What about the second question: Does the attorney's ethical duty to preserve confidential information apply at P.T.A. potluck suppers?

B] Of course it does. And everywhere else, save only those situations in which the attorney-client privilege takes over. When L gossiped with his friend about his client's reasons for wanting a divorce, L breached his ethical duty to his client.

A] What could be the consequence of that?

B] First, L could be disciplined by the bar. [ABA Model Rule 1.6(a).]

A] Anything else?

B] If the client was harmed by L's gossip, she would have a good civil claim against L. [*See* RESTATEMENT (THIRD) OF THE LAW GOVERNING LAWYERS § 60, comment a (2000).] L has breached his duty of fidelity as her agent. The law of agency prohibits an agent from revealing or misusing information that the principal gives the agent in confidence. [*See* RESTATEMENT OF AGENCY 2d § 395 (1958).] At the very least, the client should be able to sue L to recover whatever damages she suffers because of L's gossip. [*Id.* § 399.]

## **Part (b)**

A] Part (b) of Problem 1 concerns lawyer L who is defending client X in a drunk driving case. L learns from a talkative bartender that X drinks heavily every night after work. The first question is whether the attorney-client privilege applies to what L learned from the bartender.

B] No, it does not. The attorney-client privilege covers communications between the attorney and client (including, in certain circumstances, communications with their respective agents). We have no reason to suppose that the bartender here is acting as some kind of agent for either the attorney or the client; apparently he's just a person who has observed the client's behavior. So the attorney-client privilege does not cover the communication.

A] Part (b) next asks whether L is free to reveal the bartender's information to whomever she wishes. Is she?

B] No. Even though this is not the kind of "confidential communication" that would be protected by the attorney-client privilege, it is nevertheless protected by L's ethical duty to her client because it is information that is related to the representation. [*See* ABA Model Rule 1.6(a).]

## Part (c)

A] Part (c) asks about lawyer L who uses an agent to buy up Blackacre for his own account after learning that his client Y wants to buy it to build a shopping center. L hopes to turn a profit by having the agent re-sell Blackacre to Y. Has L violated the attorney-client privilege?

B] Again, the privilege is irrelevant to this problem. The privilege limits the government's power to compel the giving of evidence in a governmental proceeding. There's no governmental proceeding here, and there is no compulsion. Rather, L is simply taking private advantage of what he learned in confidence from Y.

A] Has L breached any ethical duty when he uses the agent to buy up Blackacre?

B] Certainly. He has breached ABA Model Rule 1.8(b), which says that a lawyer must not use information relating to the representation of a client to the client's disadvantage.

## Part (d)

A] Part (d) asks you to suppose that L buys up an adjoining parcel, Greenacre, knowing that it will triple in value when Y puts the shopping center on Blackacre. Has L violated an ethical duty?

B] This is an example of an attorney trading for his own advantage on confidential information of his client. The predecessor to the ABA Model Rules made that conduct a disciplinary violation [ABA Model Code of Professional Responsibility DR 4-101(B)(3)], but the ABA Model Rules have no parallel provision.

A] If L could not be disciplined by the bar, is there any other kind of trouble he might get in when he personally profits by trading on a client's confidences?

C] Yes—L can be forced to disgorge his profits to the client, unless he got properly informed consent from the client before buying Greenacre. That's a standard remedy against a self-dealing agent, and it's equally applicable to self-dealing lawyers. [RESTATEMENT OF AGENCY § 388, comment c (restitutionary remedy in the form of disgorgement of profits); RESTATEMENT (THIRD) OF THE LAW GOVERNING LAWYERS § 60(2) and comment j (2000).]

A] That's correct. Moreover, it makes no difference whether the client was or was not harmed by the lawyer's personal use of the confidential information. Comment j to § 60(2) points out that a lawyer's interest in turning a personal profit may interfere with the quality of the legal advice the lawyer gives the client. Moreover, there is no social value in letting lawyers enrich themselves  by trading on clients' confidences without getting the clients' informed consent.

## Part (e)

A]  Part (e) concerns client Z, the man who intentionally burned down his own barn and now wants to collect on his fire insurance policy. Lawyer L is on the witness stand and is asked what Z told L about burning the barn. Should the court sustain Z's claim of the attorney-client privilege?

B]  No.  Z sought L's legal services for the purpose of defrauding the insurance company.  The attorney-client privilege does not apply when the lawyer's services were "sought or obtained to enable or aid anyone to commit or plan to commit what the client knew or reasonably should have known to be a crime or fraud." [Uniform Rule of Evidence 502(d)(1); *Standard Fire Ins. Co. v. Smithart*, 211 S.W. 441 (Ky. 1919).]

A]  Suppose that the court correctly overrules Z's claim of privilege because of the crime-fraud exception.  Suppose that L then refuses to testify in response  to the question, stating:  "Even though the privilege does not apply, I still have an ethical duty not to reveal my client's confidential information.  Therefore I refuse to answer the question."

C]  If L takes that position, he had better be prepared to go to jail for contempt. In a court proceeding, the applicable body of law is the privilege. If the privilege does not protect the information, then L must answer the question—even though in other contexts he would have an ethical duty not to reveal it voluntarily. [*See, e.g.,* CAL. EVID. CODE § 911 (absent a statutory or constitutional privilege, a witness cannot refuse to answer); ABA Model Rule 1.6, Comment 3 (explains relationship between the privilege, the work product rule, and the ethical duty of confidentiality).]

A] The second question in Part (e) asks whether lawyer L should have warned the fire insurance company that Z was planning to file a fraudulent claim. For the sake of the argument, let us make two assumptions:

- First, assume that to make such a fraudulent claim would be a crime in this jurisdiction;

- Second, assume that L is quite certain that Z will in fact carry out his plan and make the fraudulent claim.

C] The *old* view, reflected in the predecessor to the ABA Model Rules, would permit—but not require—L to warn the insurance company. [*See* ABA Model Code of Professional Responsibility DR 4-101(C)(3).] That view allowed an attorney to reveal the client's intent to commit any future crime, and the information necessary to prevent that crime. In applying that old view, a lawyer would want to consider the likelihood that the client would change his mind and not carry out the crime, the nature and degree of potential harm to the victim of the crime, and the chances that the client's criminal plan will be stopped in some other way if the lawyer does not act.

A] You call it an *old* view. Is there a *new* view?

C] There is a progression of views. The former version of ABA Model Rule 1.6(b)(1) permitted a lawyer to reveal a client's confidential information to prevent "reasonably certain death or substantial bodily harm," but didn't permit a lawyer to reveal confidential information to prevent any other type of crime or fraud. Thus, under the former version, lawyer L could not warn the insurance company.

A] You said the *former* version. What is the current version?

C] Amendments to ABA Model Rule 1.6 in 2003 created additional exceptions to the duty of confidentiality similar to those expressed in Restatement § 67, which permits a lawyer to reveal a client's confidentially expressed intent to commit a crime or fraud that will cause future substantial financial injury, but only if the client has employed, or is employing, the lawyer's services in the matter. In Problem 1(e), however, lawyer L never agreed to represent Z, so I don't think it could be said that Z was employing L's services in the fire insurance matter. Therefore, under either ABA Model Rule 1.6 or Restatement § 67, lawyer L could not warn the insurance company. [And a reminder, of course, that the fraud exception within ABA Model Rule 1.6 does not exist in the California Rules.]

## Discussion Problem 2

A] Problem 2 concerns Anthony, the court-appointed defense lawyer for Dorman. Dorman is charged with the first-degree murder of a young girl. Dorman tells Anthony in confidence that he killed that girl and two others as well. The parents of the other two girls are still searching for them as runaway children. What should Anthony do?

B] I think he should first advise Dorman about the benefits of clearing his conscience of all of it. Perhaps these other two murders form the basis for an insanity defense. Or perhaps they open up a possibility for a plea bargain. Or perhaps confession and contrition will work in Dorman's favor at sentencing time.

A] Suppose he understands but rejects that sound advice. What then?

B] I see no way to bring this within the "prevent death or bodily harm" exception to the confidentiality rule [ABA Model Rule 1.6(b)(1)] because Dorman's victims are already dead. And I don't see any other exception that would work. Therefore, Anthony must respect Dorman's confidence. He cannot reveal what Dorman told him—he can't tell the police or the girls' families. This is like the *Belge* case, cited and discussed in the *Meredith* opinion in the casebook. Keeping quiet would be morally repugnant for a lay person, but Anthony's role as a lawyer demands that his lips be sealed in this situation.

A] Suppose that when Anthony goes out to check the hiding place that Dorman has described, he discovers that one of the girls is still alive, though badly beaten and in a coma. What then?

B] He must call the ambulance.

A]   If the ambulance comes, the police will be close behind—wouldn't Anthony be harming Dorman by calling the ambulance?

B] If one girl is still alive, Anthony can use the "prevent death or bodily harm" exception to the confidentiality rule [ABA Model Rule 1.6(b)(1)], because quick medical attention may save the girl's life.  Moreover, it could benefit Dorman to have the confidence revealed, because if the girl lives, he will face one less murder count.

A] A moment ago you said that Anthony *must* call the ambulance.  Would he be subject to professional discipline if he did not call the ambulance?

B] No, he wouldn't be subject to professional discipline, but he would be a rotten human being.  ABA Model Rule 1.6(b) says an attorney *may* reveal confidential information in certain circumstances, not that he *must* do so.  [*See also* ABA Model Rule 1.6, Comment 15; *accord* CRPC 3-100.]  However, I think Kant's categorical imperative, as well as the golden rule and the utilitarian analysis would all impel Anthony to call the ambulance.

**Discussion Problem 3**

A] Problem 3 concerns the hit and run driver who has revealed her identity to you in confidence.  Now you are having your deposition taken, and you are asked for the names of all persons who consulted you on the day in question.  What should you do?

B]   Since a deposition is an adjunct of a court proceeding, the applicable body of law is the attorney-client privilege.  The law of privilege requires me, as attorney, to claim the privilege on behalf of my client.  [Uniform Rule of Evid. 502(c).]

A]   What about the hornbook law that the privilege generally does not protect the client's identity, the fact that the client consulted the attorney, or information about attorney fees?

C]   That's the general rule, but the general rule doesn't apply to this situation.  If revealing the client's identity would also reveal the essence of the communication between the client and the attorney, then the privilege protects  the client's identity. [*See* CHRISTOPHER B. MUELLER AND LAIRD C. KIRKPATRICK, EVIDENCE § 519 (2d ed. 1999); RESTATEMENT OF THE

LAW GOVERNING LAWYERS § 69, comment g (2000); the seminal case is *Baird v. Koerner*, 279 F.2d 623 (9th Cir. 1960).]

A] In what sense would revealing the client's identity reveal the essence of the communication?

C] Here is an example in simpler form. Suppose the plaintiff's lawyer in this case takes my deposition and asks me: "State the name of each person who consulted you on the afternoon of August 11th concerning a hit and run accident." If I answered that question, I would in essence reveal that my client told me that she was the hit and run driver. The problem is the same in substance when the plaintiff's lawyer asks for the name of every client who consulted me that afternoon on whatever topic. The inquiry is subject to a two-part objection: (a) the name of the hit and run client is privileged, and (b) the names of the other clients are not relevant.

A] You have reached the same conclusion as the court in *Baltes v. Doe*, 4 ABA/BNA Lawyer's Manual on Professional Conduct 356 (Fla. Cir. Ct. 1988), the case on which Discussion Problem 3 is based. [*See* Hazard & Hodes §9.11 (discussing *Baltes* and other cases on client identity under the privilege).]

## Discussion Problem 4

A] Problem 4 concerns the pistol-packing client who shot his probation officer. He does not want you to surrender him to the authorities, and he has just laid his pistol on your desk and is about to walk out. What will you do about the pistol? Let me suggest some possible choices for your consideration. ABA Model Rule 1.15 says that when you receive property that belongs to your client, you must label it and put it in a safe place, such as a safe deposit box. Do you think that would be a good idea here?

B] No! ABA Model Rule 3.4(a) and various penal statutes about obstruction of justice prohibit me from obstructing another party's access to evidence and from unlawfully altering, destroying or concealing material that has potential evidentiary value.

A] Then suppose you tell the client to remove the pistol from your office?

B] I have two problems with that. First, I don't like the idea of putting a pistol back in the hands of a murderer. Second, I think he'd be perplexed by the legal advice I'd have to give him.

A] What would that advice be?

B] First, I'd have to advise him that if he keeps the pistol in his possession, and if the police find it in his possession, that fact will be powerful evidence against him at his murder trial. Second, I'd have to advise him that if he hides or destroys the pistol, and if the prosecutor can prove that he did so, that will be powerful evidence against him at his murder trial. That's what Wigmore called "spoliation" evidence, and it creates a strong inference that he's guilty of the murder. Furthermore, if I were to advise him to hide or destroy the pistol, that advice would not be protected by the attorney-client privilege and might even make me an accessory to the crime of murder. [*Clark v. State*, 159 Tex. Cr. R. 187, 261 S.W.2d 339, *cert. denied*, 346 U.S. 855 (1953) (advice to dispose of murder weapon held not privileged); *see, e.g.*, CAL. PENAL CODE § 32 (defines accessory).] In short, I'd have to tell him that he's damned if he keeps the pistol, and he's damned if he hides or destroys it. I don't think he'd find my advice very consoling.

A] Let's think further about what would happen if he left the pistol in your office. First, would the pistol be protected from discovery by the attorney-client privilege?

B] No. If this client had the pistol at his house, the police could search for it and seize it, assuming they do so in a way that complies with the Fourth Amendment. Likewise, the police could search for it and seize it in my law office, again assuming they comply with the Fourth Amendment. The attorney-client privilege would not protect the pistol from the search and seizure.

A] If the attorney-client privilege does not protect the pistol itself, then is the privilege totally irrelevant to our discussion?

B] No, the privilege is relevant because it protects *communications* between the client and the attorney *about* the pistol, even though it does not protect the pistol itself. [*See Olwell* and *Meredith* in the casebook.] Further, it protects what I, as attorney, learn or observe about the pistol as a result of communications with my client. [*Id.*] In *Olwell*, the coroner tried to obtain a knife by serving a subpoena duces tecum on the lawyer, requiring him to come to a hearing and bring all knives in his possession belonging to his client. The court said that was tantamount to requiring the lawyer to reveal his privileged communications with the client about the knife.

A] Is *Olwell* of any assistance to you in deciding what to do if your client decides to leave the pistol on your desk?

B] According to the dictum in *Olwell*, I could retain the pistol briefly if that were necessary to help me prepare the defense (for instance, if I needed to have it tested in some way). After that I'd have a duty to turn it over to the prosecutor. But when the prosecutor introduces the pistol in evidence at trial, the prosecutor cannot let the jury know that the pistol came from me. That's the compromise the *Olwell* court strikes between protecting privileged communications and protecting the prosecutor's access to evidence.

A] Does that suggest any legal advice you would want to give your client before he decides whether to leave the pistol on your desk?

B] Yes—I'd advise him that, should he decide to leave the pistol with me, I'll have to turn it over to the prosecutor, but that the prosecutor could not let the jury know that I was the one who turned it over. My client needs to know that before he makes up his mind what to do. [*See* ABA Model Rule 1.4(b).]

A] When you give the pistol to the prosecutor, may you provide the prosecutor with additional details, such as your client's name and the crime committed?

B] No. You learned that information through communications protected by the attorney-client privilege.

A] Suppose your client suggests this course of action. He will leave the pistol with you. Then, after you have had it tested, or whatever else you need to do to prepare the defense, you will turn it over to the prosecutor. But, before you turn it over, you will wipe it off thoroughly with a soft cloth, and you will mail it to the prosecutor in a plain brown box with no identification and no return address.

B]  No way.  I'd be destroying evidence.  [ABA Model Rule 3.4(a).]  That's similar to the *Meredith* case, where the client told the lawyer that he'd thrown  a stolen wallet into the trash can behind his house.  That was a privileged communication.  The lawyer sent his investigator to find the wallet.  The court said that if the investigator had simply observed the wallet in the trash can and left it there, the attorney-client privilege would protect the observation.  The investigator could not be required to testify about what he saw.  However, the investigator in fact removed the wallet from the trash and took it back to the lawyer's office.  Then the lawyer turned it over to the prosecutor.  The court said that the *peculiar location* of the wallet, in the trash can behind the client's house, was itself a valuable piece of evidence tending to connect the client with the crime.  By removing the wallet, the investigator had, in a sense, "destroyed" that piece of evidence.  Thus, the court said, the attorney-client privilege could not be invoked to prevent the investigator from testifying where he obtained the wallet.  The court's final footnote is a vital and easily overlooked part of the decision.  It adopts a compromise similar to the one in the *Olwell* case.  The prosecutor is entitled to have the jury know where the wallet was found, but the prosecutor must take all reasonable steps to prevent the jury from learning that the source of the evidence was the client's lawyer.  For instance, the prosecutor and defense counsel could simply stipulate that  the jury may be told that the wallet was found in the trash can behind the client's house—without revealing who found it or how it came to be in the prosecutor's possession.

A]  How do you relate the teachings of *Meredith* to your client's problem with the pistol?

B]  My client's possession of the pistol is analogous to the location of the wallet in the trash can.  The prosecutor is entitled to inform the jury that the pistol was in my client's possession shortly after the murder.  But the prosecutor could not let the jury know that I am the source of that information. Again, I've got a duty to advise my client that this will be the consequence if  he decides to leave the pistol on my desk.

A]  Let's see if we can sum up your client's predicament.  First, you have advised him that if he takes the pistol back, and if the police find it in his possession, that will be damning evidence against him.

B]  Right.

A] Second, you've advised him that if he takes the pistol away and hides it or destroys it, and if the prosecutor can prove that he did so, then that will be damning evidence against him.

B] Right.

A] Third, you've advised him that if he leaves the pistol with you, you will turn it over to the prosecutor, who will then inform the jury that the pistol was in your client's possession shortly after the murder—and that, too, will be damning evidence against him.

B] Right.

A] These are not very attractive choices you are offering your client, are they?

B] Right. But the point is, that's *his* problem. He's the one who committed murder. *He* must bear the moral and legal consequences of what he did. I suppose he would appreciate it if I offered to take the pistol out to the wrecking yard and have it mashed to oblivion inside an old Ford. But that would make it *my* problem, and that I will not do.

**Discussion Problem 5**

A] In Problem 5, your client, Enos Furman, has come to you with some very bad news. You have represented him over the past two years in a series of lease-loan transactions. Now he has told you in confidence that he forged some of the documents used in those transactions. In short, he has defrauded banks into lending him money that he cannot now repay. He has solemnly promised you never to do that again, and he has asked you to represent him in a new series of lease-loan transactions. What will you do?

B] First, I'd want to find out if Furman's story is truthful and accurate. I'd want to make sure of the facts. Maybe Furman is suffering some kind of mental breakdown. Maybe he thinks he has done something wrong when in fact he has not. Further, he hasn't given me the full story. He's said "some" of the transactions involved forged documents. How many? Which ones? How much money is involved? What did he do with the money, and can he get it back? I couldn't give him sensible advice until I find out the facts.

A] Good. Often some good hard lawyering will moot what appears to be a sticky ethics problem. Let's assume your investigation of the facts turned up a gloomy picture. Suppose that Furman forged the documents in five of the ten transactions, and suppose that he has defrauded the banks of five million dollars. Further, suppose he has spent every dime of it on wild living and hasn't a thing to show for it. But let's assume one cheerful fact. Throughout the entire affair, you neither knew, nor had any reason to know, that he was doing anything wrong. The only thing you did in those prior transactions was prepare some legal papers. What advice should you now give Furman?

B] I should advise Furman of the legal consequences of what he has done. In each of the five transactions, he has obtained money by false pretenses, a crime. He has also committed forgery, another crime. Moreover, he is civilly liable to the banks for their losses. Thus, I'd need to advise Furman of his legal rights and of the kind of criminal and civil proceedings he can expect to face.

A] What next?

B] Common sense suggests that I should urge Furman to rectify his fraud on the banks. Nothing in the ABA Model Rules mandates that, but sound tactics would require it in any event. I should be trying to figure out a way to have Furman come clean and make a deal with the banks and prosecutor.

A] What if he refuses to rectify the fraud? Or, what if he points out the obvious: he *cannot* rectify the fraud because he has already frittered away the money?

B] He must have a *few* assets left, and I assume he can get an honest job. If he is willing to repent, we may be able to work out an appropriate arrangement with the prosecutor and the banks.

A] Suppose repentance isn't what he had in mind. He is simply seeking your sound legal advice about his situation. Now that he has obtained your advice, he reminds you that everything you have learned from him was in absolute confidence. Is this situation any different from the one we faced in Problem 2? There the client told the lawyer about two other girls he murdered, and the lawyer was ethically bound to keep quiet.

C] It seems different to me. In Problem 2, the villain had been caught and was going to stand trial for murder. For him I could muster some civil liberties enthusiasm—assure him a fair trial and so forth. In Problem 5, Enos Furman is sitting in my office, laying out his sins, and hoping not to get caught. Furthermore, the lawyer in Problem 2 doubtless had nothing to do with the client's murders, and nobody would think otherwise. But in Problem 5, people may think that I, as Furman's lawyer, knew about the forged documents or even helped Furman defraud the banks.

A] Under the former version of ABA Model Rule 1.6, there was no exception to the duty of confidentiality that would apply to this situation, and note that there is no applicable exception under CRPC 3-100. Is there anything available to us under the current version of ABA Model Rule 1.6?

B] ABA Model Rule 1.6(b)(3) permits a lawyer to reveal confidential information "to prevent, mitigate or rectify" substantial financial injury due to a client's crime or fraud "in furtherance of which the client has used the lawyer's services." Seems a perfect fit.

A] Furman has also asked you to represent him in a series of new lease-loan transactions. How would you respond to that invitation?

C] I'd tell him no!

A] Why? Furman has solemnly promised you that he will never again defraud anyone. The man is trying to turn over a new leaf. Isn't forgiveness a divine virtue?

C] Yes, but even God makes contrition a condition precedent to redemption. Furman is not contrite. On the contrary, he sits in my office, commanding my silence about his past frauds, and asking me to represent him in a series of new transactions, which he *assures* me will be lawful. If I were to represent him in the new transactions, I'd have to spend countless hours checking, double-checking, and triple-checking Furman's operations to make sure he isn't smuggling more fraudulent documents under my nose! [*See* ABA Model Rule 1.2 (assisting a client in a crime or fraud).] If Furman won't come clean about the past transactions, then as a matter of personal choice I won't represent him in future transactions. Life is too short to put up with guys like Furman.

A]  You are not telling me that you think the rules of legal ethics require you not to represent Furman in the future, are you?

C]  No, of course not.  If I believed that Furman is telling me the truth and that all of his future dealings will be clean, then I could represent him in those future dealings.  I'm just telling you that I don't trust him, and as a matter of personal preference, I do not want to represent somebody that I do not trust.

## WASHINGTON v. OLWELL
### Supreme Court of the State of Washington, 1964

Facts:  On September 7, 1962, Henry Gray and John Warren were in a fight that resulted in Warren's being mortally injured by knife wounds.  On September 8th, Gray was taken into custody and admitted stabbing Warren.  Gray was not sure what became of the knife.

On September 10th, David Olwell, appellant, was retained as Gray's attorney.  After his first conference with Gray, Olwell came into possession of the knife thought to be the murder weapon.  The coroner then issued a subpoena duces tecum commanding Olwell to appear and produce the knife.

Olwell appeared at the coroner's inquest and refused to turn over the knife, claiming the attorney-client privilege.  The Superior Court found him in contempt.  Olwell appeals from the trial court's contempt order.

Issue:  Was the subpoena duces tecum invalid because it required the attorney to give testimony concerning information he received in confidence from his client?

Holding:  The subpoena was invalid; the contempt order is reversed.

Discussion:  An attorney should not be a depository for a murder weapon, but he may retain it for a reasonable time to prepare for the client's defense.  After a reasonable period, the attorney should, on his own motion, turn the weapon over to the prosecutor.

The prosecutor, when attempting to introduce the weapon at trial, cannot disclose its source.  By thus allowing the prosecution to recover the weapon, the public interest is served, and by prohibiting the prosecution from disclosing the source, the client's privilege is preserved. Hence, a balance is reached between conflicting interests.

Here the subpoena duces tecum is invalid because it required the attorney to testify, without the client's consent, regarding matters arising out of the attorney-client relationship. Therefore, the trial court's order finding Olwell in contempt is reversed and the proceedings are dismissed.

## PEOPLE v. MEREDITH
### Supreme Court of California, 1981

Facts: On April 3, 1976, Wade (the victim) and a friend went to a nightclub. Defendant Meredith, planning to rob Wade, sent defendant Scott into the club to find Wade. When Wade came out, Meredith attacked him. Two shots were fired, and Meredith ran away.

Scott went over to the body; he picked up and hid a bag containing beer. He later returned for the bag. One month later, after being charged with first degree murder and robbery, Scott told his attorney, Schenk, that he had seen a wallet near Wade's body. Scott said he picked it up and put it in the bag with the beer. Later Scott split the money in the wallet with Meredith. After trying to burn the wallet, Scott threw it in a trash barrel behind his house.

Schenk hired investigator Frick to find the wallet. Frick found it, Schenk examined it and then turned it over to the police. The prosecution subpoenaed Schenk and Frick to testify at the preliminary hearing. At the hearing, Schenk said he received the wallet from Frick, but refused to answer further questions because he learned of the wallet through privileged communications. On a threat of contempt, Schenk said contact with his client led to disclosure of the wallet's location. Frick was questioned about finding the wallet. Over objection, Frick testified that he found the wallet in the trash can behind Scott's house.

Issue: Under California law, does the attorney-client privilege extend to observations that are the product of privileged communications? If so, is the privilege lost when defense conduct frustrates prosecution discovery?

Holding: The attorney-client privilege extends to observations made as a consequence of protected communications, but if the defense counsel removes or alters evidence, the location or condition of the evidence is no longer protected by the privilege.

Discussion: California Evidence Code § 954 states: "The client . . . has a privilege to refuse to disclose, and to prevent another from disclosing, a confidential communication between the client and lawyer." Here, Scott's statements to Schenk about the wallet were protected by the attorney-client privilege. Schenk's statements to Frick were also within the privilege. California Evidence Code § 912(d) states that a disclosure that is "reasonably necessary" to accomplish the purpose for which the attorney has been consulted does not constitute a waiver of the privilege. In order for Frick to perform the investigative services for which Schenk hired him, it was reasonably necessary for Schenk to tell Frick about the wallet.

The attorney-client privilege also protects observations made as a consequence of privileged communications. Because the purpose of the privilege is to encourage open communication, a client must be free to confide in an attorney without fear of disclosure. For example, in *Olwell*, above, the securing of the knife was a direct result of information given to Olwell by his client. The attorney-client privilege is not strictly limited to communications; to hold otherwise would impinge on the flow of information between attorney and client and would frustrate the purpose of the privilege.

When the defense removes or alters evidence, it interferes with the prosecution's opportunity to discover that evidence. To extend the attorney-client privilege to a case in which the defense removed evidence might encourage defense counsel to race the police to seize critical evidence. Therefore, an exception to the attorney-client privilege is made where defense counsel has removed or altered evidence.

If defense counsel leaves the evidence where it was discovered, his observations are protected by the privilege. If, however, counsel removes the evidence, the location and condition of the evidence are not protected by the privilege. Here, because Frick removed the wallet, testimony as to its location is admissible. The court did not err in admitting this testimony. However, the prosecutor must take reasonable steps to insure that the jury does <u>not</u> learn that the source of the evidence was the defense counsel. [N.B. Make sure that students do not overlook the critically important final footnote to the court's opinion.]

# CHAPTER EIGHT
## CANDOR IN LITIGATION

### Discussion Problem 1

A] Chapter Eight deals with the attorney's duty to be candid in conducting litigation on behalf of the client. Problem 1 concerns candor about the law in a case in which adversary counsel (and apparently the judge as well) are unaware of a recent decision that would support your adversary's position.

### Part (a)

A] Part (a) asks whether you would have a duty to tell the judge about the decision if it were a decision of the New York Court of Appeals in a veterinary malpractice case.

B] The answer would be Yes. Under ABA Model Rule 3.3(a)(2), you must disclose a legal authority that is from the controlling jurisdiction and that is directly adverse to your position. Our case is pending in the federal district court in New York City, and federal jurisdiction is based on diversity of citizenship. Under the *Erie* doctrine, that means that the law of the State of New York will supply the rule of decision on a substantive issue, such as the appropriate standard of care in a professional malpractice case. [*See Erie R. Co. v. Tompkins*, 304 U.S. 64 (1938).] Thus, the New York Court of Appeals' decision would be from the "controlling jurisdiction." Further, it is a veterinary malpractice case, just like the case at bar. You'd be hard pressed to argue that it is not "directly adverse." Having once disclosed it, you could then argue that it is an unsound decision, or that there are sixteen reasons why your case is distinguishable from that case.

### Part (b)

A] Part (b) asks whether you would have to disclose it if it had been rendered by the Arizona Supreme Court in a veterinary malpractice case.

B] No—that's not the "controlling jurisdiction."

## Part (c)

A]  Part (c) asks whether you would have to disclose it if it were from the New York Court of Appeals in a legal malpractice case.

B]  No—that's not "directly adverse."  I realize one can draw an analogy between a veterinarian who claims to be a specialist in an arcane medical field (like ruminant epidemiology) and a lawyer who claims to be a specialist in an arcane legal field (like price discrimination under the Robinson-Patman Act).   But if the word "directly" is to be given any meaning at all, then I think the disclosure rule would not apply to a case that is against you only by analogy.

A]  The last sentence in Problem 1 asks if there are any tactical reasons to go beyond what the ethics rules require as respects disclosure of adverse authority?

B]  Yes, sound tactics may suggest disclosing adverse material even where it is not required. The trial judge wants to be able to trust what you say and to put some faith in your legal analysis. Suppose that the judge eventually stumbles across the Arizona decision, or the New York decision in the legal malpractice case.  And suppose the judge somehow finds out that you knew about those cases all along.  If the judge thinks that those two cases are reasonably pertinent to the legal issues he or she has to decide, how will the judge be likely to feel about you and your client?  The judge may know, intellectually, that you had no ethical duty to disclose those cases and that you were simply following the letter of the law.  But isn't that judge likely to be less trusting of your arguments on other legal points that come up later in the case?  Further, if *you* disclose the adverse authorities, rather than let the judge or your adversary find them, that may help you take the sting out of them.  It can put you in a more credible light when you argue that they are unpersuasive or should not be followed. Finally, if the trial judge has considered all of the relevant legal authorities, you lessen your adversary's chances of taking a successful appeal.

### Discussion Problem 2

A]  In Problem 2 you are representing the defendant in a negligence case, and you have a chance to move for a directed verdict at the close of the plaintiff's evidence. The plaintiff has failed to discover the existence of a key eyewitness. Do you have a duty to disclose the existence of that eyewitness?

B]   No.   Assuming you have been forthright in carrying out your own automatic disclosure obligations [*See, e.g.,* Fed. R. Civ. P. 26(a)(1), as amended in 2000] and in responding to the plaintiff's discovery requests, you do not have a duty to disclose.  Our system of justice is premised on the notion that each side will bring out the facts that help that side.  That's the basis for Comment 1 to ABA Model Rule 3.4 which states: "The procedure of the adversary system contemplates that the evidence in a case is to be marshaled competitively by the contending parties."  It is also the basis for Comment 1 to ABA Model Rule 4.1, which states: "A lawyer is required to be truthful when dealing with others on a client's behalf, but generally has no affirmative duty  to inform an opposing party of relevant facts."  [*See also* RESTATEMENT (THIRD) OF THE LAW GOVERNING LAWYERS § 120, comment b.]  ABA Model Rules 3.3 and 4.1 specify certain things you must do and not do.  You must not knowingly make false statements of law or fact.  You must not knowingly offer false evidence.  Further, ABA Model Rule 3.4 says you must not unlawfully obstruct your adversary's access to evidence.  None of those rules  contemplates a duty to *volunteer* a harmful fact when you are in an adversary context.  The lack of any such duty is further apparent from ABA Model Rule 3.3(d).   When you appear *ex parte*—that is, without the adversary being present to bring out the facts on the other side—then you *do* have a duty to bring out *all* of the material facts that are necessary to an informed decision. [*Accord* RESTATEMENT (THIRD) OF THE LAW GOVERNING LAWYERS § 112(2) (2000).]

A]   How does all this apply to the facts stated in Problem 2?

B]   In Problem 2, your adversary has had access to the facts, just as you have.   Indeed, the problem states that she has engaged in extensive discovery.  Most competent lawyers, at an early stage of the case, would pose an interrogatory asking you to identify anyone you know of who has knowledge of this or that disputed fact. Had your adversary done that, she would have unearthed this  key eyewitness, but she apparently failed  to do it.   Her client will suffer an injustice, but that's the way the adversary system works. [*Accord* N.Y. County Bar Op. 309 (1933).]

**Discussion Problem 3**

A] In Problem 3, you are the in-house counsel for a drug company. You have hired an outside lawyer, Adney, to defend the company in a products liability case that involves a baldness remedy that allegedly causes stomach ulcers. While searching for items responsive to plaintiff's document demand, Adney's paralegals have found a set of "smoking gun" documents in the company's files. Adney plans not to produce the documents, arguing that they are not called for by the plaintiff's demand. The documents in question do not mention the baldness remedy; they relate to a different drug that contains the same active ingredient as the baldness remedy. Plaintiff asked for "all documents relating to Luxair (the baldness remedy) and the risk of stomach ulcers." Do you agree with Adney's decision not to produce the document?

C] The problem tells us that this is a "state court products liability case," but it doesn't tell us what kind of document discovery rule applies in this state. If this state has a traditional discovery rule [*see, e.g.,* Fed. R. Civ. P. 34], then the party seeking the documents takes the initiative by writing up a document demand, stating with extraordinary care and particularity the kinds of documents he wants to see. The party who responds to the demand is entitled to read the demand with the same degree of care and particularity. For instance, if the demanding party asks for all 2009 and 2010 documents that concern X and Y, the responding party would *not* be required to produce a 2008 document that concerns X and Y.

A] You speak of a "traditional" rule; is there some *other* kind of document discovery rule?

C] Between 1993 and 2000, some federal district courts followed a rule that required the parties to automatically produce—without waiting for a demand by the adversary—all documents in their control that were *"relevant to disputed facts alleged with particularity in the pleadings."* [Former Fed. R. Civ. P. 26(a)(1)(B).] Under that rule, you had to automatically produce documents that would help your adversary's case as well as documents that would help your own case. However, individual federal district courts were allowed to "opt out" of that rule. Many did opt out, which produced a serious lack of national uniformity, causing confusion for lawyers who practice in more than one federal judicial district.

A] What happened in 2000?

C] Effective December 1, 2000, Fed. R. Civ. P. 26(a)(1) no longer contains an "opt out" clause, and it requires you to automatically produce—without waiting for a demand by your adversary—all documents in your control that *you* may use to support *your* claims or defenses. In other words, you must automatically cough up the stuff that helps your case, but not the stuff that helps the other side's case. The other side can, of course, file a traditional demand under Fed. R. Civ. P. 34 to force you to produce the documents that will help their side of the case.

A] O.K., let's assume that the "smoking gun" reports in Problem 3 do not fall within the automatic production rule, and that the plaintiff has filed a traditional demand for document production under a state law equivalent of Fed. R. Civ. P. 34. Do you think that the outside lawyer, Adney, is acting unethically if he reads the plaintiff's demand literally and with the same precision one would exercise in construing a metes and bounds description of a piece of real property?

C] No, I do not think that is unethical. Our prior discussion on Problem 2 applies here as well. We work in an adversary system. We turn square corners, and we are entitled to assume that the lawyer on the other side is doing the same. Mind you, I'm talking about ethics here; I'm <u>not</u> talking about wise tactics.

A] Yes, I understand. However, ABA Formal Opinion 93-376 puts a heavy burden on the lawyer whose client lies in a discovery response. If the drug company does not produce the "smoking gun" documents in response to the plaintiff's document demand, hasn't the drug company lied? Isn't the drug company telling the plaintiff in essence: "We don't have any additional documents that are relevant to our baldness drug and your bleeding ulcers"?

C] No, the drug company isn't saying that at all. What the drug company is telling the plaintiff is: "We don't have any additional documents that are covered by your document demand." I think that's the representation being made, either expressly or by implication, when a party hands over a box of documents in response to a document demand.

A] I'm having a hard time understanding why you think the "smoking gun" documents are not called for by the document demand. What would plaintiff have had to ask for in his demand in order to get those documents?

C] If he had asked for "all documents relating to the risk of stomach ulcers and to Luxair or its active ingredients," that would have gotten the documents. I once worked for a wise old litigator who explained it this way. "In civil discovery, the lawyer seeking the discovery is like a piano player. The lawyer responding to the discovery request is like a piano. If the piano player strikes the wrong notes, the piano has no duty to play the right tune. If, however, the piano player strikes the right notes, the piano has no choice—it must play the right tune."

A] You mentioned a few minutes ago that you were addressing my ethics question, not talking about sound tactics. Does anybody want to talk about sound tactics?

B] Yes. I agree with C about the ethics of it, but I think this drug company's in-house counsel may want to have a conversation with outside lawyer Adney about tactics. They need to think together about whether it would be a good idea to produce the "smoking gun" documents at this stage of the litigation, even if they are not technically called for by the document demand.

A] What should the house counsel and Adney be considering as they make that tactical decision?

B] We have already decided, I think, that it would be *ethical* to decide not to produce these documents in response to the present document demand. On the *tactics* question, we need to think about: (a) the advantages and disadvantages of producing the documents now, and (b) the chances that we will have to produce them later.

A] Sometimes a poor tactical decision early in the case can keep coming back to haunt the lawyers who made it. In a drug injury case like this one, the plaintiff will undoubtedly conduct discovery about the ingredients of the drug. It won't be long before the plaintiff learns that phlogestin is the active ingredient in Luxair, and the plaintiff will almost certainly ask the company to produce whatever documents it has on phlogestin and stomach ulcers. It may save money and time for everyone to get these "smoking gun" documents out on the table early in the case. More important, the drug company may be able to minimize the harm if it produces the documents when and how it wishes, rather than giving the plaintiff the pleasure of extracting them.

B] Absolutely. Further, I think the in-house counsel in this problem is acting wisely in trying not to second guess the decisions made by outside litigators. But that doesn't mean that the in-house counsel should sit back and be a mute observer. In-house counsel has a lot to contribute to the relationship. In a sense, she is "the client" in the relationship, or at least she is the one through whom the client speaks to the outside litigators. It's her job to think about such things as the company's reputation, the morale of its employees and officers, the possible effects of bad publicity on future product offerings, future stock offerings, the company's ability to hire good people, and the like.

**Discussion Problem 4**

A] Problem 4 raises the so-called "trilemma" issue. You have read about it at length in the text. You will recall that the three horns of the trilemma are these:

First, as a lawyer you are told to seek your client's trust and to find out everything the client knows about the case so that you can represent the client effectively.

Second, you are told to preserve your client's confidential information (with few exceptions).

Third, you are told to act with candor, to refrain from presenting evidence that you know is false, and (sometimes) to reveal your client's frauds.

In Problem 4, you are defending one Decker in a murder case. He has an excellent alibi and three friends to back him up. All is looking good, but then some hypothetical disasters occur:

## Part (a)

A] Part (a) asks you to suppose that ten weeks before trial you get information that shows beyond doubt that Decker and his friends are lying about the alibi and that Decker did commit the murder. When you confront Decker, he reminds you that you are his lawyer, not his jury. He wants you to call him and his three friends as witnesses and to let the jury decide his guilt or innocence. What should you do?

B] ABA Model Rule 3.3(a)(3) tells me that I must not offer evidence that I *know* is false. How can I ever *know* for sure that the information my investigator brings me is the true version and that the story told by Decker and his friends is false? It really is the jury's job, not my job, to decide what is true for purposes of this case. (ABA Model Rule 3.3(a)(3) also says that I *may* refuse to offer evidence that I *reasonably believe* is false, but that rule doesn't apply to the testimony of a criminal defendant.)

A] What will happen if I let go of this casebook?

B] It will hit the floor.

A] Do you know that it will?

B] Yes.

A] Are you certain?

B] Unless you have some trick in mind, yes, I am certain it will hit the floor.

A] What makes you certain?

B] My everyday experience with gravity. My common sense. I fell off the garage roof and broke my leg when I was seven. I studied gravity in basic science courses.

A] Can you not be equally certain of other propositions, such as: X is lying, or X killed Y?

B] Yes, I guess so. But you are ignoring my basic point. As lawyer in the case, it is not my job to decide whether my client is lying or telling the truth, or is guilty or innocent. That is for the trier of fact, the jury in this case. I have no role as fact finder.

A] Look again at ABA Model Rule 3.3(a)(3). It speaks of "evidence that the lawyer *knows* to be false." Doesn't that ethics rule necessarily mean that a lawyer *does* know some things? Doesn't that ethics rule command the lawyer to be, in part, a finder of fact?

B] Okay, I guess so. But when there's room for doubt about a fact proposition, shouldn't a trial lawyer resolve that doubt in favor of the client?

A] Absolutely. [*See People v. Riel*, 22 Cal.4th 1153, 998 P.2d 969 (2000), *cert. denied,* 531 U.S. 1087 (2001) (attorneys must not present evidence they know to be false, but they may present evidence that they suspect, but do not personally know, is false).] It is one thing to say that you must resolve doubts in favor of your client, and quite a different thing to say that a lawyer must be an ignoramus, a person who "knows" nothing and passes no judgments. In Part (a) of Problem 4, we are asked to assume that your investigator's information shows "beyond any fleeting whiff of doubt" that Decker and his friends are lying and that Decker committed the murder. So let's assume that you *know* that the story told by Decker and his friends is false. What now?

B] Here's another place where good hard lawyering may avoid a sticky ethics issue. First, I'd advise Decker of the likely consequences of presenting a false defense, including the consequences it would have on my role as his defense counsel. Decker himself has a constitutional right to take the witness stand. [*See Rock v. Arkansas*, 483 U.S. 44, 49-53 (1987).] But I *must not* call his friends to the stand to back up his story if I *know* that they will lie. [ABA Model Rule 3.3(a)(3).] Further, if I *reasonably believe* his friends will lie, then I *may* refuse to call them. [*See also* RESTATEMENT (THIRD) OF THE LAW GOVERNING LAWYERS § 120, comment i (criminal defense lawyer has authority not to call perjurious third party to witness stand and must exercise that authority).]

A] So if Decker testifies to his fake alibi, he will be dangling out there all by himself, with nobody to confirm the alibi?

B] Right. Finally, I'd advise him that we ought to start from scratch on his defense. Doubtless there are many lines of defense that we haven't even considered yet because we assumed up to now that we would be using the alibi defense. My object in giving him this advice would be to convince him that committing perjury would be both wrong and stupid.

A] What if he *insists* on having you call him as a witness to testify to the alibi?

B] Then I'd consider withdrawing as Decker's defense counsel. Part (a) hypothesizes that it is ten weeks before trial. I suspect the judge would let me withdraw that far in advance of trial. [The local rules of most courts require a lawyer to get the court's permission before withdrawing from a litigated case. *See* ABA Model Rule 1.16(c).]

A] Do the ABA Model Rules *force* you to try to withdraw in this situation?

B] No, unless the perjury issue has created such a gulf between Decker and me that I could not competently defend him. [Comment 15 to ABA Model Rule 3.3.]

A] Even though the Model Rules do not *force* you to try to withdraw, do you think that withdrawal would be desirable in this case?

B] As Professor Freedman has pointed out, my withdrawal would be in one sense futile. Decker will get a new lawyer, and this time he will be more cautious about revealing information that might lead the new lawyer's investigator to the truth. If the new lawyer never discovers the truth, then Decker and his friends will present their same false evidence, and a miscarriage of justice may result.

A] If your withdrawal would be futile, why do it?

B] First, my withdrawal would remove me personally from the wrongdoing. Second, Decker's new lawyer would not be personally involved in wrongdoing because (by the hypothesis) she would not know that the testimony of Decker and his friends is false. Thus, even though my withdrawal would not produce justice in Decker's murder case, it would keep lawyers out of the circle of wrongdoers.

123

## Part (b)

A]  Part (b) asks you to assume that you get the information from your investigator ten minutes before you are to begin presenting the defense case-in-chief. What will you do now?

B]  Ask for a recess.

A]  Right! The longer the better. Suppose the judge gives you the rest of the day. What will you do during that time off?

B]  Am I certain that my investigator's information is correct? If there's room for doubt, I should resolve it in Decker's favor and proceed with the defense as planned. [ABA Model Rule 3.3, Comment 8.]

A]  As in Part (a), let's assume there's no room for doubt—you <u>know</u> Decker and his friends will be lying on the witness stand.

B]  Let's see if we agree on the initial steps. First, I should counsel Decker about the consequences of presenting false evidence, in the hope that he will change his mind. If that doesn't work, I should think about withdrawal, but the judge probably won't let me withdraw at this point in the case.

A]  Suppose that you cannot withdraw and that Decker insists that you call him and his friends as witnesses. What will you do?

B]  As to Decker's friends, clearly I must not present their testimony if I know that it is false. [ABA Model Rule 3.3(a)(3).] After *Nix v. Whiteside*, this surely wouldn't be regarded as ineffective assistance of counsel. If Decker wants to fire me as his counsel, he'll have to take that up with the judge.

A]  And what about Decker's own testimony?

B]  ABA Model Rule 3.3, Comments 7 and 9, note that some jurisdictions have ruled that, in some situations, the Fifth and Sixth Amendments require counsel for a criminal defendant to allow the defendant to testify, even if counsel knows that the testimony will be false. Comment 7 goes on to say that in those jurisdictions, the obligation of the advocate under the ABA Model Rules is subordinate to such a constitutional requirement.

A]  What do you understand to be the California approach to this subject?

B]  *People v. Johnson*, reproduced in Chapter 8, approves a procedure much like the one recommended in ABA Standard for the Defense Function 4-7.7: if you can't talk the defendant out of perjury,  then you may call the defendant to the witness stand and let him tell his story in narrative fashion. *Johnson* doesn't mention the point, but other authorities are uniform in stating that you *must not rely* on the false parts of his story in your closing argument. [*People v. Guzman*, 45 Cal.3d 915, 248 Cal.Rptr. 467, 755 P.2d 917 (1988), *cert. denied*, 488 U.S. 1050 (1989).]

## Part (c)

A]   Part (c) asks you to suppose that you did not get the investigator's information until ten minutes *after* you have presented Decker's and his friends' false testimony.  How does that change the situation?

B]  Part (c) is easier than Parts (a) and (b) in one way, but it is harder in another way.  Part (c) is easier because it tells us that Decker has now admitted that the investigator's information is correct and that he did murder the victim.  That helps to sooth my qualms about regarding Decker and his friends as perjurers.  But Part (c) is harder than (a) or (b) in a different way—the evil deed has already been done, and as lawyer I don't have many options about what to do. [*See* Justice Stevens' concurring opinion in *Nix v. Whiteside*, 475 U.S. at 191, 106 S.Ct. at 1007 (1986).]

A]  What ought to be your first response to the perjury?

B]  First, I should urge Decker (and separately his friends) to recant their perjury and set the record straight. [*See* Comment 10 to ABA Model Rule 3.3.] If they refuse, I should consider asking the court's permission to withdraw.  As we discussed above, ABA Model Rule 3.3, comment 15, does not *force* me to try to withdraw unless I could no longer competently represent Decker.  Moreover, the trial judge is very unlikely to let me withdraw during the trial.

A] Assuming that withdrawal is not an option, what next?

B] ABA Model Rule 3.3(a)(3) says that I must take "reasonable remedial measures." Comment 10 to Rule 3.3 explains that I must disclose the perjury to the judge, even if that requires me to reveal client confidences that would otherwise be protected by Rule 1.6. It's then up to the judge to decide what to do—explain the matter to the jury, or declare a mistrial, or perhaps do nothing.

A] What should a California lawyer do in the circumstances posed in Part (c)?

B] Extrapolating from the *Johnson* case, I'd guess that the criminal defense lawyer should keep quiet about the perjury, but should not rely on the perjurious story in closing argument.

A] What's the jury going to think if the defense lawyer's closing doesn't rely on Decker's testimony?

B] A sensible juror would conclude that Decker lied and that the defense lawyer wants no part of it.

A] That's going to hurt Decker's case, isn't it?

B] Yes, but what's the alternative? Should the legal ethics rules permit or even require the defense counsel to participate in Decker's effort to mislead the court?

A] No, certainly not. But there's no denying that Decker's case will suffer if the defense lawyer doesn't rely on Decker's testimony in closing argument.

B] Alas, poor Decker must now face the consequences of his own conduct—first, committing murder, and second, lying about it.

### Part (d)

A] Part (d) asks you to suppose that you do not discover the perjury committed by Decker and his friends until ten weeks after the jury has acquitted Decker. How is that ten weeks different from the ten minute time lapse in Part (c)?

B] Under ABA Model Rule 3.3(c), my duty to take the remedial measures we have discussed comes to an end at the "conclusion of the proceeding." Comment 13 to Model Rule 3.3 explains that the proceeding comes to a conclusion "when a final judgment . . . has been affirmed on appeal or the time for review has passed."

A] Part (d) says that ten weeks have passed since Decker was acquitted by the jury. Will there be any appeal in this case?

B] Obviously Decker won't appeal, and in the United States a prosecutor's ability to appeal is narrowly circumscribed. [*See, e.g.,* CAL. PENAL CODE § 1238 (lists situations in which prosecutor can appeal).] Even if the prosecutor could appeal in Decker's case, ten weeks would be beyond the appeal deadline in most jurisdictions. [*See, e.g.,* Fed. R. App. Proc. 4(b)(1)(B) (notice of appeal must be filed within 30 days after entry of judgment); Cal. R. App. Proc. 31(a) (notice of appeal must be filed within 60 days after entry of judgment).] It seems safe to say that my duty to reveal the perjury to the court has ended.

## Part (e)

A] I think we have already covered the main issues raised in Part (e). If there is doubt about your investigator's information and about whether Decker and his friends are telling the truth, then you should resolve the doubt in Decker's favor. [*See* ABA Model Rule 3.3, comment 8.]

B] ABA Formal Op. 87-353 notes that some lawyers make themselves intentionally ignorant by failing to question the client about the facts of the case, thus enabling them to claim that they did not "know" the client was testifying falsely. The opinion warns against that approach. Intentional ignorance may not avoid the disclosure mandate of ABA Model Rule 3.3, and it may also constitute incompetence under ABA Model Rule 1.1.

## PEOPLE v. JOHNSON
### California Court of Appeal for the Fourth District

<u>Facts</u>:   Defendant Johnson was convicted of numerous violent sexual offenses, kidnapings and robberies.   At an *in camera* hearing after the prosecution closed its case in chief,  the defense counsel told the trial judge that he had an ethical problem and could not call the defendant to testify, despite the defendant's desire to testify.  The trial judge noted for the record that the defendant wanted to testify, but that the defense counsel would not let him.  The defendant did not testify, was convicted, and received multiple life sentences.  On appeal, defendant claimed that he had been deprived of his federal constitutional right to testify on his own behalf.

<u>Issue</u>:  Did the trial court err in denying defendant the right to testify on his own behalf?

<u>Holding</u>:  Yes, the trial court did err.  It should have allowed the defendant to take the witness stand and tell his story in narrative fashion.  However, the error was harmless, because the direct and circumstantial evidence against the defendant was so overwhelming that it could not have been countered by the defendant's testimony.

<u>Discussion</u>:

1.    The Court of Appeal reviewed the history behind the criminal defendant's constitutional right to testify on his own behalf.  In olden times in England, the parties to civil cases and the defendants in criminal cases were not competent to testify as witnesses, because their obvious bias made their testimony worthless.  The English competency law was transplanted to the American colonies.  Gradually the competency law changed, first in civil cases, and later in criminal cases.  Georgia was the last of the U.S. jurisdictions to have a law making criminal defendants incompetent to testify, and in 1960 the United States Supreme Court declared the Georgia law unconstitutional.   Later still, the Supreme Court held, in *Rock v. Arkansas*, that the Fifth and Sixth Amendments, in combination with the due process clause guarantee that a criminal defendant may testify on his own behalf if he wishes to do so.

2. The Court of Appeal then worked its way through Monroe Freedman's trilemma analysis, discussing each of the possible courses of action:

- requiring the defense lawyer to try to talk the defendant out of testifying falsely;
- requiring the defense lawyer to ask permission to withdraw;
- refusing to let the defendant testify;
- allowing the defendant to testify in narrative form, but not using the false parts of the story in closing argument;
- allowing the defendant to testify in the ordinary manner, and using the false parts of the story in closing argument.
- telling the court about the defendant's intent to commit perjury, and letting the court decide what to do about it.

3. Trying to talk the defendant out of committing perjury is everyone's first choice, the Court of Appeal said. But what if the defendant insists on testifying and insists on telling a story that the lawyer knows—because of confidential information—is false?

4. Other authorities have asserted that if the client cannot be talked out of perjury, the lawyer must try to withdraw. The Court of Appeal did not impose that requirement, noting that even if the trial judge allows withdrawal, it merely passes along the problem to a new lawyer.

5. Refusing to let the client testify has several drawbacks. It turns the lawyer into a judge of the client's veracity. Further, it may require a mini-hearing at which the lawyer will be pitted against his own client. Finally, it completely denies the client's constitutional right to testify.

6. Disclosing the planned perjury to the court also has drawbacks. It negates the chance that the defendant might have changed his mind and testified truthfully. Further, it may require the same mini-hearing mentioned in 5, above.

7. The narrative approach is not perfect, but at least it makes an effort to compromise between the defendant's right to testify and the lawyer's obligation not to present evidence he knows is false. The Court of Appeal was not impressed by the argument that the narrative approach tips off the jury to the falsity of defendant's story—the jurors may well think that some

special rule applies to the defendant and allows him to testify without being questioned like other witnesses. Further, the prosecutor can cross-examine and introduce impeachment evidence and contrary evidence on the merits—those tools will reduce the chances of successful perjury.

# CHAPTER NINE
# FAIRNESS IN LITIGATION

## Discussion Problem 1

A] Here you represent the plaintiffs in a race discrimination action against Monolith Consolidated Industries.

## Part (a)

A] Part (a) of Problem 1 asks whether you may hire a private investigator to hunt up information about the attitudes toward race discrimination held by individual members of the panel from which the jury will be chosen. Would that be proper?

B] The only help I could find in the ABA Model Rules is Rule 4.4 (a general admonition against abusing the rights and interests of third persons) and ABA Model Rule 3.5(b) (prohibiting *ex parte* contact with jurors and jury panel members "unless authorized to do so by law or court order"). [*See also* RESTATEMENT (THIRD) OF THE LAW GOVERNING LAWYERS § 115 (2000), which says that, except where the local law allows it, a lawyer must not communicate with or try to influence a member of the jury pool, or a member of the jury once it is chosen.] CRPC 5-320(A) and (E), however, are right on point. Part (A) says that I must not communicate either directly or indirectly with a member of the jury pool. Further, part (E) says that I must not conduct an investigation of potential jurors in a way that may influence that person's state of mind concerning present or future jury service.

A] So what is your answer to Problem 1(a)?

B] I don't see how an investigator could develop specific, useful information about a person's attitude toward race discrimination without actually talking to the person, or at least to the person's close associates. As for interviewing the jury panel members' close associates, that itself could degenerate into a kind of harassment. Furthermore, just imagine the expense of gathering information in that manner about 150 jury panel members! Given the normal constraints of time and money, the problem is purely academic.

## Part (b)

A]  Part (b) asks whether you may send your paralegal around to search public records to find out what you can about the jury panel members' voter registration and property ownership.

B]  Yes, I could do that.  Those are public records, available to anyone who wants to take a look at them.  I see no problem of harassment here.  On the other hand, I understand that there's considerable disagreement among skilled trial lawyers about the usefulness of this kind of information.  It depends in part on how much faith you place in stereotypes.  Who is more likely to favor the plaintiff in a race discrimination case?  A registered Republican who owns no real property in the county, or a registered Democrat who owns her own home and two pieces of income property besides?

## Part (c)

A]  Part (c) asks how lawyers generally gather information about jury panel members in the jurisdiction where you plan to practice.  Does anybody know?  [*See* Molly McDonough, *Private Lives*, A.B.A.J., May 2006, at 14.]

C]  Yes.  Some of the large cities in California have commercial "jury services."  They are in the business of investigating the backgrounds of people on jury panels.  They compile "jury books" that state all the information they have been able to gather about each panel member.  A lawyer who has a case set for trial can gain access to that information by paying a fee to the jury service.  The lawyer can then use the information during jury selection.  Reputable jury services take great care to avoid harassment of prospective jurors; they limit their investigations to material that is available to the general public—for instance, county land records, voter registration records, records of vital statistics, motor vehicle records, court records, business directories,  credit reports, computer databases that cover newspaper stories, and the like.  Their circumspection is a product of self-interest.  An investigation service would lose its lawyer customers if it vexed or harassed potential jurors.

A]  What happens if no jury service is available?

B]   The California Judicial Council has approved an optional jury questionnaire for use in civil cases.  [*See* II West's California Judicial Council Forms MC-001 (2000).]  The members of the jury pool to fill out an extensive questionnaire that asks about their education, occupation, family, affiliation with organizations, prior experience with the law and the court system, prior jury service, and the like.  Copies of the questionnaires are made available to the lawyers when it comes time to select the jury.  Lawyers seem to like the questionnaires because it speeds up *voir dire* and gives lawyers a lot of useful information at little or no cost.

## Discussion Problem 2

### Part (a)

A]   Part (a) of Problem 2 asks what you should do if you are riding in an elevator with a juror who asks you whether you have some red-hot testimony to keep the jury awake today.

B]   ABA Model Rule 3.5(b) prohibits *ex parte* contact with jurors absent authorization in the local law or a court order.  Restatement § 115 says that I "must not communicate" with a member of the jury.  CRPC 5-320(B) is to the same effect—I must not communicate directly or indirectly with a member of the jury.

A]   Surely that rule is limited to communications about the merits of the case itself, isn't it?

B]   No.   Section 115 and CRPC 5-320(B) say a lawyer must not communicate, period.  It apparently means exactly what it says.  If it had been intended to proscribe only communications about the case, it would have said so.

### Part (b)

A]   Let's test your theory by looking at part (b) of Problem 2.  There the juror in the elevator simply turns to you and asks you what you thought of last night's ball game on television.  Are you telling us that you cannot even respond to that harmless question?

B]  I don't think the rule requires you to humiliate the juror by standing there in icy silence.  Perhaps you should respond with something like this: "I'm very sorry, but I am not permitted to talk with jurors during the trial." If you say more than that, and engage in friendly small talk in the elevator, you are looking for trouble.  For example, in *Florida Bar v. Peterson*, 418 So.2d 246 (Fla. 1982), a lawyer and one of his expert witnesses went to the local delicatessen during the noon trial recess.  They allowed themselves to be  seated at a table that was also occupied by two of the jurors.  This fact was observed by two secretaries who worked for the adversary law firm. They reported what they had seen, and the court granted the adversary's motion for a mistrial.  Later a referee was appointed to determine what, if any, communications passed between the lawyer and the jurors at the lunch table.   The referee concluded that there had been some form of communication, but it was not clear exactly what was said.  The evidence did *not* demonstrate that  the lawyer was trying to gain any unfair advantage in the litigation.  Nevertheless, the lawyer was disciplined.  He was publicly reprimanded, put  on probation for one year, and required to pass the Multistate Professional Responsibility Examination.   The opinion makes clear that the lawyer was disciplined not because of *what* he said, but because he said *something*.

**Discussion Problem 3**

A]  Problem 3 asks what you should do about the adversary's paralegal who was seen during lunch talking in hushed tones with one of the jurors.

B]  Again the ABA Model Rules provide no specific guidance.  Comment (a) to Restatement § 115 notes that several jurisdictions require a lawyer to report to the court any improper conduct by or to a juror.  California is one of those jurisdictions—CRPC 5-320(G) states the rule.

A]   What makes you think the conversation between the juror and the paralegal is improper?

B]  Nothing, really.  Perhaps these two are good friends and are discussing Seventeenth Century Spanish poetry.  On the other hand, there are two reasons to be suspicious.  First, the juror may be discussing the case with the paralegal. That would violate the instruction the trial judge undoubtedly gave the jurors not to discuss the case with anybody.  Second, the adversary law firm may be trying to pull something sneaky by using the paralegal to communicate information to a juror.

A] So what would you do about it?

B] One thing I clearly would *not* do is walk up to them in the cafe and demand an explanation. A confrontation at that point could alienate the juror and make a mistrial all the more likely. Besides, I might end up with a broken nose. I think I'd grab a quick lunch and then head back early to the courthouse. If I have developed a good working relationship with the lead trial counsel for the adversary, I'd hunt up that person before court reconvened. I'd tell lead counsel candidly what I'd observed and remind lead counsel of my ethical duty to report any impropriety to the judge. Then I'd invite lead counsel to accompany me to seek a word with the judge in chambers before court begins for the afternoon. We would talk with judge and let the judge decide what to do from there.

A] Why would you get lead counsel for the adversary involved? Do the rules require you to do that?

B] No, but it's a good idea anyway. First, there's much to be said for avoiding unnecessary *ex parte* communication with the judge, even on matters unrelated to the merits of the case. Second, courtesy requires me to let adversary counsel know what I'm about to do. Third, if I'm winning the case, the last thing I want is a mistrial. Chances are good that the lunch time conversation between the paralegal and the juror was wholly innocent. Nobody can find that out quicker than lead counsel for the adversary.

**Discussion Problem 4**

## Part (a)

A] Part (a) of Problem 4 asks whether you may talk with a member of the jury, after the case is over, to get her comments on the way you presented evidence and on your closing argument.

B] Assuming there's no local law or court rule against it, then it would be permissible. ABA Model Rule 3.5(c) would prohibit the communication if it involved misrepresentation, coercion, duress, or harassment, or if the juror had informed the attorney that she did not wish to talk. Restatement § 115, comment d, notes that some jurisdictions prohibit all post-trial communication with the former jurors. Other jurisdictions, including California, permit post-trial communication with a former juror, provided that the lawyer does not try to harass the former juror or influence his or her actions in a future case. [*See* CRPC 5-320(D).] The lawyer in the *Lind* case in the casebook got into trouble for his attempt to influence discharged jurors in the *present* case (by trying to stop them from talking with opposing counsel) and for conduct that could cause jurors in future cases to fear sharp investigative practices by lawyers who seek to overturn jury verdicts.

## Part (b)

A] In Part (b) of Problem 4, you have reason to suspect that the bailiff delivered some material not in evidence to the jury room during the deliberations. May you inquire of some of the jurors to find out whether that's true?

B] I don't know.

A] Good—that's the right answer. It depends entirely on the local law and local court rules, and there's considerable variation from place to place. You've heard the old common law rubric that "a juror cannot impeach his own verdict." The policy behind that rubric is that litigation should come to an end sometime, that jury verdicts should be stable, and that jurors should be protected from annoyance and embarrassment. But there's a countervailing policy: if a jury's verdict is defective because of improper influence or consideration of inadmissible material, then sealing the jurors' mouths can only promote irregularity and injustice. The dominant modern view is the one expressed in Federal Rule of Evidence 606(b): when a jury verdict is questioned, a juror will <u>not</u> be allowed to give evidence (by testimony, or affidavit, or otherwise) about any statement made during the jury deliberations, nor about the effect that anything had on the mind of any juror, nor about the juror's mental processes during the deliberations. However, a juror <u>will</u> be allowed to testify about any "extraneous information" that was improperly brought to the jury's attention, and about any "outside influence" that was improperly brought to bear on any juror. The line drawn in Federal Rule 606(b) is also a sensible line for attorneys to follow in post-trial communications with jurors. [*Elisovsky v. Alaska*, 592 P.2d 1221, 1229 (Alaska 1979) (adopts the evidence rule standard for post-trial communications).] In short, in a post-trial interview with a juror, you could not ask what anybody said during the deliberations, nor what impact a piece of evidence had on the jurors, nor what thought processes led this juror to conclude as she did. You could, however, ask whether the bailiff delivered the entire deposition transcript to the jury room. The unadmitted parts of the transcript may well have been prejudicial.

## Discussion Problem 5

A] Problem 5 asks whether it was proper to talk to former and current Monolith Consolidated employees without consulting counsel for Monolith. You were inquiring about any information they may have had that would be helpful to your claims against Monolith.

B] Under ABA Model Rules 4.2 and 4.3 and CRPC 2-100, the first question you should have asked is whether these employees were "represented" by Monolith's counsel or had counsel of their own. Monolith's lawyers may claim to represent, and may even have offered representation to, all current employees. [This could create conflict of interest problems that we'll discuss in a later chapter.] Furthermore, CRPC 2-100 and Comment 7 to Rule 4.2 cover communications with a person (i) who "supervises, directs, or regularly consults with the organization's lawyer concerning the matter"; (ii) who has "authority to obligate" Monolith with respect to the matter; and (iii) whose "act or omission in connection with the matter may be imputed" to Monolith for purposes of civil or criminal liability. [*But see* RESTATEMENT (THIRD) OF THE LAW GOVERNING LAWYERS § 100 (2000) (using narrower definitions).]

A] It sounds like a lawyer should be pretty careful about getting adversary counsel's consent before talking with current employees of an adversary. The problem is compounded because some of the characteristics of employees who should *not* be contacted will not be known to the inquiring lawyer in advance of the contact (for example, were they involved in the events that may create liability). This doesn't mean you won't be able to take their depositions and won't be allowed to inquire into what they know that may help with your case as part of discovery. When you are talking with an unrepresented person, ABA Model Rule 4.3 requires you to be careful not to be deceitful, and not state or imply that you are disinterested or permit the unrepresented person to make that assumption.

A] What about former employees? Are the rules different for them?

B] Ordinarily the plaintiff's lawyer would not need consent of Monolith's counsel before talking with a *former* agent or employee of Monolith. [*See* ABA Model Rule 4.2, comment 7 ("Consent of the organization's lawyer is not required for communication with a former constituent."); RESTATEMENT (THIRD) OF THE LAW GOVERNING LAWYERS § 100, comment g (2000).] It would be different, however, if the former employee were still working regularly with Monolith's counsel on the defense of the case.

## Discussion Problem 6

### Part (a)

A] Part (a) of Problem 6 asks about certain payments you agreed to make to one of your witnesses, Edgar Taylor. First, did Edgar testify as an expert witness or a lay witness?

B] As a lay witness. Apparently he testified about a conversation he'd overheard. There's nothing in Problem 6 to suggest that he was used as an expert witness.

A] Why does it make a difference whether he was used as an expert or a lay witness?

B] I'm allowed to compensate expert witnesses for professional services rendered in preparing to testify and in giving the testimony but the expert's fee cannot be contingent, either on the outcome of the case or on the content of the testimony. [*See* ABA Model Rule 3.4, comment 3; CRPC 5-310(B)(3).]

A] Please explain the part about "content of the testimony."

B] Suppose I hire a skidmark expert. I agree to pay her $500 if she concludes that the adversary's car was traveling 35 miles per hour before the crash. But if the car was traveling 50 m.p.h., I will pay $1,000. And if it was traveling 70 m.p.h., I will pay $2,000.

A] We get your point. In any event, Edgar was not testifying as an expert. He was a lay witness who simply testified about what he saw and heard. Was it proper for you to promise to pay for his hotel, meal, travel, and incidental expenses?

B] Surely. [*See* ABA Model Rule 3.4, comment 3; CRPC 5-310.] Further, in some jurisdictions there is a modest statutory fee for witnesses who appear pursuant to subpoena; if you subpoena a witness, you must send along a check for the witness fee.

A] Was it proper for you to promise to pay Edgar's lost wages, due to time away from his job?

B] Yes. [*See* CRPC 5-310(B)(2); RESTATEMENT (THIRD) OF THE LAW GOVERNING LAWYERS § 117(1) (2000); Annotated Model Rules of Professional Conduct 329-330 (3d ed. 1996).]

A] Was it proper for you to promise Edgar $100 per day as compensation for his time and trouble in coming to testify?

B] By paying Edgar for his time lost from the job, I have already made him whole for his "time and trouble." I think the extra $100 per day would be improper. [*See* ABA Model Rule 3.4, comment 3.]

A] Aren't you being too hardnosed? With prices as they are these days, $100 per day is not enough to buy perjury. By taking off from his new job, Edgar is probably going to annoy his shop foreman and disrupt his family plans. Shouldn't we at least allow him to come out a bit ahead financially?

B] Aside from whatever ethics problem it raises, it could be poor tactics. Edgar may be asked on cross-examination whether he's being paid anything for his testimony. The extra $100 a day could be grounds for an argument that he's a biased witness, and Edgar could come away from the experience feeling insulted, used, and soiled. On the other hand, if I explain to him that all I can do is reimburse him for expenses and time lost from the job, he will come away from the experience feeling like a good citizen who has done his civic duty in giving testimony when it was needed.

**Part (b)**

A] Part (b) of Problem 6 asks: Should I have notified Monolith's counsel before I spoke to Edgar, the former Monolith assembly line employee, at all?

B] Barring some special continuing role as part of Monolith's defense of this action, or inquiry into privileged Monolith communications, Edgar should be fair game for plaintiffs' lawyers. [*See* ABA Model Rule 4.2, comment 7.]

**Discussion Problem 7**

A] Problem 7 concerns a "dirty trick" pulled on you by adversary counsel. In response to a request for documents, counsel has provided you with copies that are legible but so light as to be extremely tedious to read. We all know that copying machines are perverse creatures with minds of their own, but here it appears that the defective copies were not the machine's fault. Adversary counsel told the machine operator to make the copies hard to read. What should you do in that situation?

B] First, I would make *very* sure of my information. Before confronting adversary counsel, I'd want to be positive that the machine operator was instructed to sabotage my copies.

A] What ethical rules seem to apply here?

B] ABA Model Rule 3.4(a) says that a lawyer must not unlawfully obstruct the adversary's access to evidence or unlawfully alter documentary evidence. Further ABA Model Rule 3.4(d) says that a lawyer must make a "reasonably diligent effort" to comply with discovery requests. CRPC 3-200 prohibits lawyers from continuing employment if the objective is to assert a position for the purpose of harassing another person. CRPC 5-220 says a lawyer must not suppress evidence the member or the member's client has a legal obligation to reveal or produce.

A] Have the adversaries in Problem 7 violated any of those provisions?

B] I think they were harassing me, not making a "diligent effort" to comply with my discovery request.

A] So what would you do about it?

B] I'd telephone adversary counsel and politely ask for new copies at their expense.

A] What if adversary counsel says, "Oh bunk," and hangs up the phone?

B] Then I would write them a polite letter, restating my request, recounting the telephone conversation, and asking for prompt delivery of the new copies, at their expense, without further ado.

A] And if you get no response?

B] I would move for sanctions under Federal Rules of Civil Procedure 26(g) and 37(b) (or the equivalent state rules, if this is a state court case). Even if the court decides that sanctions are not appropriate, I should at least be able to get some new copies of the documents. [*See Roadway Express, Inc. v. Piper*, 447 U.S. 752 (1980); *Litton Systems, Inc. v. American Tel. & Tel. Co.*, 700 F.2d 785 (2d Cir. 1983) ($10 million in costs and attorney fees denied because of counsel's misconduct during discovery). For an entertaining discussion of the world of discovery dirty tricks, *see* Charles Yablon, *Stupid Lawyer Tricks: An Essay on Discovery Abuse*, 96 COLUM. L. REV. 1618 (1996).]

## Discussion Problem 8

A] Problem 8 asks what is the proper way to call the judge's attention to a new appellate decision that bears on a point you were arguing in connection with pretrial rulings on admissibility of evidence.

B] ABA Model Rule 3.5(b) says I must not communicate *ex parte* with the judge, except when the local law permits. CRPC 5-300(B) is to the same effect.

A] So tell us how you will call the new decision to the judge's attention.

B] First, I will consult the local rules to see if there is a procedure for filing a supplemental memorandum, after oral argument, on an issue that the court has taken under advisement. If there is such a procedure, then I'd file a very short memo, explaining why the new decision is relevant and attaching a copy of it. Of course I would serve copies of the memo and the decision on adversary counsel, just as with any other court paper.

A]   Suppose the local rules do not provide for filing a supplemental memorandum of this sort?

B]   Then I would speak with the clerk of the court and ask what procedure this particular judge prefers to follow when counsel wants to call attention to a new decision that will help the judge in a pending matter.

A]   Why wouldn't you just write the judge a formal letter, enclosing a copy of the new decision and sending a copy of the letter and decision to adversary counsel?

B]   Because I've heard that some judges are allergic to mail about pending matters.  They take the view that if lawyers can't say it in a properly filed court document, then it shouldn't be said at all.  I understand that some judges even throw such letters in the trash without reading them.  That's why it's better to check with the court clerk first.

**Discussion Problem 9**

A]   Problem 9 asks how you will respond to the wave of news reporters who surround you on the courthouse steps.  You have serious doubt about the credibility of the key adversary witness, and tomorrow morning you will get your chance to cross examine him.  What will you say this evening to the reporters?

B]   I'd smile, and be pleasant, and tell them that I have no comment.

A]   Why wouldn't you tell them a bit about what they could expect tomorrow morning?

B]   In some situations, my client's interest might well be served if I use the news reporters to help get my client's story across to the public.  But this is not that kind of situation.  ABA Model Rule 3.6 and CRPC 5-120 prohibit me from making prejudicial statements—I think that would include commenting  to the reporters about the credibility of the adversary's key witness or about what  I expect the witness to say on cross-examination.  Furthermore, common sense and good tactics suggest that I should not make any remarks about my intended cross-examination.  I'd rather keep that a complete surprise.  For example, at his press  conference lawyer Gentile [when introduced at a bar meeting, his name was pronounced "Genteal" (like the duck or color)] declined to answer specific questions about the prosecution's witnesses' backgrounds, although he apparently believed in good faith that he had to counteract the widely-reported prosecution views on the case.

A] Gentile might find some shelter in the amendments to ABA Model Rules 3.6 and 3.8 following his "victory." Rule 3.6(c) would allow him to make a statement to protect his client from "the substantial undue prejudicial effect of recent publicity" not initiated by him or his client. Further, amended Rule 3.8(f) requires prosecutors to refrain from making extrajudicial statements that heighten "public condemnation of the accused.")

C] Still, the *Gentile* decision worries me. Gentile did what he thought was right for his client, and he even took care to limit his comments to what he believed the ethical rules allowed. His client was acquitted. Yet, both the Nevada bar and the Nevada Supreme Court found he violated the rules and disciplined him. Only after he took his case to the U.S. Supreme Court was the discipline overturned, and by a slim majority and on narrow grounds at that. But occasionally on the television news, the screen is full of reporters talking to lawyers (and most lawyers answering the questions) about their clients and their cases. Even some judges make comments about their cases and their rulings. What gives?

B] In part, the rules against public statements concerning litigation have been overtaken by the increasingly public nature of litigation and its attendant media coverage. We have come to expect lawyers to comment on high profile litigation. At the same time, the Supreme Court, as reflected in the *Gentile* opinions, has given state disciplinary authorities considerable latitude in restricting comment about pending litigation. It does leave lawyers in a difficult spot. If I am firmly convinced that I must comment to protect my client—that my *only* chance to obtain a fair trial for my client is to comment on the pervasive and unfair pretrial publicity from the prosecution—I do so (as Gentile did) at the risk of my own career and pocketbook. Maybe it is just a reminder that conflicts of interest occur between lawyer and client as well as among clients.

A] You might be interested in these comments by Justice Kennedy in a part of the *Gentile* opinion not reproduced in the text:

An attorney's duties do not begin inside the courtroom door. He or she cannot ignore the practical implications of a legal proceeding for the client. Just as an attorney may recommend a plea bargain or civil settlement to avoid the adverse consequences of a possible loss after trial, so too an attorney may take reasonable steps to defend a client's reputation and reduce the adverse consequences of indictment, especially in the face of a prosecution deemed unjust or commenced with improper motives. A defense attorney may pursue lawful strategies to obtain dismissal of an indictment or reduction of charges, including an attempt to demonstrate in the court of public opinion that the client does not deserve to be tried. [111 S.Ct. At 2728-20]

## Discussion Problem 10

A] Problem 10 asks what you should do, as a young Assistant District Attorney, when you learn that five years ago your boss, the D.A., convicted the wrong man for burning down a church. What's your reaction?

B] It sounds like D.A. Lubeman wants me to cover up the fact that he convicted the wrong man for arson of the church. I can't do that for a couple of reasons. First, I'd find it personally repugnant to stay quiet while Randy Coots is rotting away in prison for something he didn't do. Second, ABA Model Rule 3.8(g) and (h) (added in 2008) would make it a disciplinary violation for me – or for my boss – to stay quiet after receiving this "new, credible and material evidence" that creates a "reasonable likelihood" that Coots was convicted in error.

A] Does California have a counterpart to ABA Model Rule 3.8(g) and (h)?

B] Not yet, but the committee that is drafting the proposed California revised rules may recommend a counterpart. Furthermore, common decency ought to suffice. If a prosecutor tries to cover up an unjustified conviction, that ought to be regarded as an act of moral turpitude in violation of Cal. Bus. & Prof. C. § 6106.

A] True. But how are you going to convince Lubeman not to try the cover-up?

B] That would be a delicate task. I wouldn't want to make Lubeman lose face.

A] Why not? Doesn't he deserve to lose face?

B] Yes, but I have to work for him. Life will be smoother for both of us if I help him discover that covering-up is not an option.

A] Why not an option?

B] For starters, it won't work. I'm not the only person who knows what Emmet Stubbs said. Stubbs's lawyer knows, and the interrogating police officer knows. Our investigator knows that she discovered the chalice and sweatshirt in the Dutton's tractor shed. And the chalice and sweatshirt are physical evidence that confirms what Stubbs said. Even if the cover up would work, it's unethical.

A] How could you raise the legal ethics issue with Lubeman without causing him to lose face?

B] It's quite possible that Lubeman might be unaware of ABA Model Rule 3.8(g) and (h) because they weren't added to the rules until 2008. So I would call them to his attention by asking how we will comply with them.

A] What if that doesn't wake him up?

B] Then I would have to put subtlety aside and remind him that ABA Model Rules 5.1 and 5.2 require him to make sure that I follow the disciplinary rules and require me to not to follow my supervisor's order to do something that is undebatably a disciplinary violation.

## LIND v. MEDEVAC, INC.
### California Court of Appeal, First District, 1990

Facts: Respondent Lind through his conservator filed a complaint for personal injuries against appellants, Medevac and its employees. A jury returned a judgment in favor of appellants. Respondents filed a motion for a new trial or, in the alternative, a motion for judgment notwithstanding the verdict (JNOV). The respondents based their motions on jury misconduct. Appellants opposed the motion because respondents had not submitted juror affidavits which section 658 of the Code of Civil Procedure requires. Respondents complained that they could not obtain the affidavits due to a letter appellant's attorney sent the jurors instructing them that they did not have to respond to any questions asked by the respondent's investigator about the trial.

The trial court denied the JNOV motion due to substantial evidence that supported the verdict. The trial court denied the new trial motion due to the lack of juror affidavits. The trial judge also ordered appellants to show cause why they should not be sanctioned for interfering with respondent's right to obtain juror affidavits. After hearing the arguments, the court imposed $20,000 in sanctions against appellants, holding that they violated the California Rules of Professional Conduct by adversely influencing the jurors in their present and future service as jurors.

Issue: Did the trial court properly sanction appellants for sending a letter to the jurors before the time expired for respondents to file a motion for a new trial?

Holding: Yes. According to the Rules of Professional Conduct, counsel cannot ask questions of or make comments to a jury member intended to harass or embarrass the juror or to influence the juror's future actions in jury service. The Rule applies from the time of jury discharge until the time expires for filing a motion for new trial. However, the trial court erred in imposing sanctions under Code of Civil Procedure section 128. Instead, on remand, the court must determine whether appellants should be sanctioned under section 128.5.

Discussion: Appellants argue that they properly sent the letter to the jurors. In addition, they argue that the trial court lacked the authority to impose sanctions in the way it did. Rule 7-106 of the Rules of Professional Conduct [currently Rule 5-320] provides that, "After discharge of the jury from further consideration of a case with which the member of the State Bar was connected, the member . . . shall not ask questions of or make comments to a member of the jury that are intended to harass or embarrass the juror or to influence the juror's actions in future jury service." The trial court correctly found that Rule 7-106 applies in the period from jury discharge to expiration of the time for filing a new trial motion in the case in which the jurors served.

The letter the appellants sent violated former rule 7-106. The letter easily could influence a juror in present or future jury service. Attorneys can contact jurors post trial in order to request notification by the juror of any post-trial contact with the opposing side.

The trial court erred in awarding sanctions in the form of attorney fees under section 128. The California Supreme Court has held that the court has to base monetary sanctions upon express statutory authority, not judicial discretion as the trial court did here. However, the trial judge suggested in his ruling that he could impose sanctions under section 128.5. Therefore, the trial court can reconsider an award of sanctions under section 128.5 on remand.

## MATTER OF VINCENTI
### Supreme Court of New Jersey, 1983

Facts: Attorney Vincenti represented a defendant in a child abuse case. In court, Vincenti was sarcastic, disrespectful, and occasionally irrational. In open court, he called the deputy attorney general a "bald-faced liar" and a "thief, liar, and a cheat." Out of court he called her by cruder names. He wrote a smarmy letter to the trial judge, essentially accusing the judge of incompetence or corruption or both. Finally, he was rude and obscene to witnesses, potential witnesses, opposing counsel, and other attorneys around the courthouse.

Issue: Was Vincenti's conduct merely an excusable excess of zeal in advocacy on behalf of his client, or was his conduct so bizarre and outrageous as to warrant discipline?

Holding: Vincenti's conduct warrants strong discipline. He is suspended from practice for a year and until further order of the court.

Discussion: The *Vincenti* case makes a useful contrast with the *Gentile* case. Reasonable persons might differ about whether lawyer Gentile's conduct warranted discipline, but could reasonable persons disagree about Vincenti? [For another example, see Grievance Administrator v. Fieger, 729 N.W.2d 451 (Mich. 2006) (attorney, speaking on a radio show about appellate judges who reversed his client's $15 million verdict, called judges "jackasses" and said they deserved to be anally violated).]

## CHAPTER TEN
## BIAS IN (AND OUT OF) THE COURTROOM

This Chapter aims to raise students' awareness of various forms of bias and prejudice in the legal workplace. You may find some students resistant to this material, for a variety of reasons. Some students will recognize their own bias and prejudice, and this discovery will make them uncomfortable. Other students will wish to believe that bias and prejudice existed years ago, but have been eradicated and no longer exist today. Still others will view complaints about bias in the workplace as "whining," and will have no tolerance for how those subjected to such bias may feel.

It is our hope that open discussion of these very real biases and prejudices will help to prepare and enlighten our students, and that the increased sensitivity they will bring to law practice will reduce the incidence of such bias in the legal profession.

### Discussion Problem 1

A] In Discussion Problem 1, the client has suggested to the supervising partner that he would prefer to have a male associate conduct an upcoming deposition, rather than the female associate assigned to the case. Does the client's request reflect bias?

B] It certainly sounds that way. The client's reasons, as provided in the problem, were that the deposition was "important" and that the client desired an "aggressive" approach. The problem does *not* state that the client had worked with a particular male associate whose work he preferred. Instead, the client is asking for a male, rather than female, associate for traditionally sexist reasons—the perception that men are "better" and are more aggressive.

A] What should Dan do?

B] This is the tougher question. Even if the client's reasoning is sexist, it's the client who is paying for the legal services. Doesn't the client have the right to demand a male associate if that's his preference?

A] Doesn't that add an even more unpleasant connotation to the description of lawyers as "hired guns"? And couldn't the law firm potentially be held liable for discrimination? [*See* CRPC 2–400.]

B] Well, what can Dan really do? If the client demands a male associate and Dan refuses, isn't the client likely to pull his business and find another law firm?

C] I wouldn't want to work for a law firm that didn't have any principles—and a law firm that would "cave" to a sexist client without even discussing the issue is, to my mind, unprincipled.

B] But that takes me back to my previous question: If the client is paying hundreds of dollars an hour for legal services, isn't the client entitled to make his preferences known and have those preferences followed?

A] That is, in fact, one of the proffered excuses for acceding to such requests—that the firm would otherwise lose the business because the client would walk.

C] Clients are human and some will be prejudiced. There will be those who prefer men over women, who prefer whites over African-Americans, who prefer Christians over Jews, who prefer heterosexuals over gays or lesbians. But if a lawyer or law firm acquiesces in those prejudices, then the lawyer/law firm is behaving in a prejudiced fashion as well. I don't think the lawyer/law firm can—or should—be able to hide behind "the client made me do it."

A] Is there a potential resolution short of Dan simply acceding to—or denying—George's request on the spot?

B] You mean have Dan accuse the client of being prejudiced? That doesn't sound good for keeping the client's business either.

C] Perhaps there's a more tactful response. Maybe Dan could talk to George about Beth's qualifications—her length of time with the firm, her prior deposition experience, expressions of satisfaction by other clients about Beth's work. Maybe George would be satisfied if he received assurances about her ability. And this ties in with the last question regarding what Beth should do if she learns of George's concerns. Beth might be able to talk directly to George about her qualifications, or alternatively, she might be able to give Dan specific information about her experience that he could pass along to George.

## Discussion Problem 2

A] Discussion Problem 2 involves 73-year-old Ethan who was involved in an automobile accident. There are three questions here: Does Cathy's attorney's questioning reflect bias? Is Cathy's attorney's questioning appropriate? What about her comment?

B] I think Cathy's attorney would be liable for malpractice if she *hadn't* asked questions about Ethan's age, vision, and last driving test. The problem states that whether Ethan was negligent is disputed. Cathy's lawyer *had* to ask about potential eyesight and driving issues.

C] I agree. I suppose the questioning may have reflected some bias because elderly drivers are sometimes presumed to be poor drivers. But I think the same questions likely would be asked of drivers of any age under these circumstances, where negligence is disputed. Where Cathy's attorney crossed the line was in her closing argument, in which she referred to "old coots." That reference was insulting and derogatory—and unnecessary. It likely would present the very real possibility of a mistrial!

B] It was both biased and unwise. The reference to "old coots" reflected back on her entire line of questioning, tainting it with her prejudice. It also risked potentially offending the trier of fact, whether a judge or jury. Even if the judge and jury consisted of younger people, any of them might well have an older friend or relative who is an excellent driver.

A] Okay, so it was biased and unwise. But does Cathy's attorney's behavior implicate any of the ethical rules?

B] Yes. For starters, ABA Model Rule 3.4(e) prohibits a lawyer from alluding to any matter during trial that the lawyer doesn't reasonably believe is relevant. In addition, comment 3 to ABA Model Rule 8.4 states, "A lawyer who, in the course of representing a client, knowingly manifests by words or conduct, bias or prejudice based upon . . . age . . ., violates [this Rule] when such actions are prejudicial to the administration of justice." The issue was whether Ethan was negligent, and his age is not determinative of that issue. The "old coots" reference was biased, unwise, and prohibited by the ethical rules.

## Discussion Problem 3

A] Discussion Problem 3 involved the deputy district attorney's decision to indict a Mexican-American for an alleged assault on what was apparently conflicting evidence. When questioned, the deputy D.A. stated that "those people always have an alibi—they stick together." Does this reply reflect bias?

B] I suppose he might have meant that all accused defendants always have an alibi, but the listener would certainly wonder if he specifically meant Mexican-Americans. So yes, I think his response reflects bias.

C] It seems that the phrase "those people" is regularly used in a context reflecting bias or prejudice.

A] Does the deputy D.A.'s reply raise any ethical concerns?

B] Sure. If he is disregarding the conflicting evidence on the basis of a supposition that the guy must be guilty because he's Mexican-American, he's not living up to his ethical responsibilities as a prosecutor. A prosecutor has a special duty to seek justice, and can't base indictment decisions on racial or ethnic prejudices. This again implicates comment 3 to ABA Model Rule 8.4, because it reflects racial or ethnic bias that is prejudicial to the administration of justice.

## Discussion Problem 4

A] Discussion Problem 4 involves the 28-year-old female associate who is regularly mistaken for a secretary, paralegal, or court reporter. This problem asks three questions: Does this mistaken identity reflect bias? Why would this mistaken identity occur? What steps could be taken to avoid such misapprehensions in the future?

B] I think those first two questions are interrelated. The mistaken identity occurs because many people associate "lawyers" with being male and "secretaries" with being female. This means that, for many people, when they encounter someone without a full introduction, they will make assumptions based on their previous experiences and reflecting their own biases and prejudices.

C] And that suggests a potential solution. When Jennifer introduces herself to someone, she should include both her name and her position. It would be easy for her to introduce herself as Jennifer Holden, a second-year associate at the firm.

A] What if Sam Baker, the partner in his mid-fifties, is the one introducing Jennifer?

C] Seems like Jennifer could still mention her position—"So nice to meet you. I'm a second-year associate here at the firm and I'm looking forward to working with you."

B] She could also mention the issue to Sam and ask him to clarify her position in future introductions.

## Discussion Problem 5

A] Discussion Problem 5 poses questions involving state court trial judge Richard Jenkins.

## Part (a)

A] Part (a) says that Judge Jenkins belongs to a local private club whose bylaws prohibit extending membership to women and minorities. Must he resign?

B] I think so, because Rule 3.6(A) of the ABA Model Code of Judicial Conduct expressly states, "A judge shall not hold membership in any organization that practices invidious discrimination on the basis of race, sex, gender, religion, national origin, ethnicity, or sexual orientation."

A] Does the answer change if the bylaws don't contain an express prohibition, but there are no women or minority members, and the club has rejected all membership applications from women and minorities?

B] I think this implicates Comment 2 to Rule 3.6. The comment says that discrimination can be a "complex question" and offers some factors for consideration. One of the factors is "how the organization selects members" and whether it "arbitrarily excludes" protected groups from membership. Unless the organization "is dedicated to the preservation of religious, ethnic or cultural values of legitimate common concern to its members," or is truly "an intimate, purely private organization" that would be exempt from anti-discrimination laws, the fact that an organization arbitrarily excludes protected groups from membership will generally be determinative.

## Part (b)

A] In Part (b), Judge Jenkins is repeatedly referring to the female defense counsel as "Missy" during a criminal jury trial. Is he subject to discipline?

B] Rule 2.3(B) says that a judge cannot use "words or conduct" that manifest bias or prejudice, including gender bias. Referring to defense counsel as "Missy" would seem to come within this prohibition, and is similar to some of the examples provided in the reading in the text. This one seems pretty clear.

A] Would the answer change if the context was a pretrial civil hearing rather than a criminal jury trial?

B] No. The Rule prohibits such bias or prejudice "in the performance of judicial duties," which clearly would encompass pretrial civil proceedings as well.

## Part (c)

A] In Part (c), Judge Jenkins overheard the bailiff using a racial slur to refer to a Latino lawyer, but did nothing. Is Judge Jenkins subject to discipline?

B] Yes. Rule 2.3(B) imposes an affirmative duty upon judges to avoid bias or prejudice, and extends that duty to court personnel. The question said that the actor was "the bailiff for Judge Jenkins' courtroom," and thereby would clearly be someone "subject to the judge's direction and control" within the meaning of the rule. In addition, Rule 2.12(A) states that judges must require staff and court officials to "act in a manner consistent with the judge's obligations under this Code."

A] Part (c) says that the Latino lawyer didn't hear the comment. Does that matter?

B] No! Would it really be appropriate for court personnel to make whatever insulting and prejudiced comments they wanted, so long as the subject of their comments didn't hear them? Of course not. Insulting and prejudiced comments set the tone in the workplace, which here is a courtroom—a place where people come to seek justice. A judge cannot tolerate such comments by court personnel.

## Part (d)

A] Part (d) reports a conversation where only the lawyers and Judge Jenkins were present. The male prosecutor said he "wouldn't mind dating" the female defense attorney if he "were only twenty years younger." Judge Jenkins simply laughed in response. Is Judge Jenkins subject to discipline?

B] This would seem to come within Rule 2.3(C), which says, "A judge shall require lawyers in proceedings before the court to refrain from manifesting bias or prejudice, or engaging in harassment, based upon attributes including but not limited to . . . gender . . . against parties, witnesses, lawyers, or others."

C] I don't see the problem. Isn't the prosecutor paying defense counsel a compliment?

B] The facts say that the prosecutor and Judge Jenkins *laughed*. That doesn't sound like any compliment to me. Under these circumstances, there's a real risk that the defense counsel viewed the comment as something more akin to sexual harassment.

C] What would you have Judge Jenkins do?

B] The judge should have said something, so that the impropriety of the prosecutor's comment was clearly communicated. Here, the judge merely laughed in response, which acts to condone the comment.

## IN RE CHARGES OF UNPROFESSIONAL CONDUCT
## CONTAINED IN PANEL FILE 98-26
### Minnesota Supreme Court, 1999

Facts: The attorney who is the subject of this disciplinary proceeding filed a motion seeking a court order to prohibit defense counsel from adding "a person of color as co-counsel," asserting that such co-counsel would serve "the sole purpose of playing upon the emotions of the jury." The original disciplinary panel issued a private admonition, finding the conduct was unprofessional, but of an isolated and non-serious nature.

Issue: Did the requested court order constitute a "non-serious" offense?

Holding: No. Race-based misconduct is, by its very nature, a serious offense, and cannot be deemed non-serious.

Discussion: The court emphasized that the attorney's apology, remorse, and lack of malice did not render her behavior non-serious. The court noted that race-based misconduct undermines both confidence in the justice system and the ideals of our society.

## IN RE PLAZA HOTEL CORPORATION
### United States Bankruptcy Court, 1990

Facts: The bankruptcy debtor's counsel repeatedly referred to the female counsel for the United States Trustee as "office help," despite knowing that she was an attorney. He also exhibited a condescending attitude toward the female attorney.

Issue: Is gender-based bias against female counsel grounds for disqualification?

Holding: Yes. Gender-biased remarks constitute grounds for disqualification.

Discussion: Gender-biased remarks are offensive, interfere with equal justice, and are fully sanctionable. Such comments reflect an unwillingness to cooperate with the trustee, and therefore disqualification from representing the debtor is an appropriate sanction.

## IN RE VINCENTI
### Supreme Court of New Jersey, 1998

<u>Facts</u>:   Attorney Vincenti engaged in a number of behaviors, including harassment and intimidation on the basis of sexual orientation.

<u>Issue</u>:   Can harassment and intimidation on the basis of sexual orientation constitute a basis for disbarment?

<u>Holding</u>:   Yes.  Vincenti had engaged in a number of behaviors constituting inexcusable conduct, and the only appropriate sanction was disbarment.

<u>Discussion</u>:   Vincenti's misconduct included ridiculing, harassing, and intimidating a witness who was a social worker.  He had also engaged in a variety of other forms of misconduct, prompting the court to conclude that it could "no longer expose judges, lawyers, litigants, witnesses, and the public to the inexcusable conduct of a renegade attorney."

## IN RE KIRBY
### Minnesota Supreme Court, 1984

<u>Facts</u>: Judge Kirby engaged in a number of inappropriate behaviors, including public intoxication and habitual tardiness.  He also engaged in instances of discourtesy to women lawyers, referring to one as a "lawyerette" and another as an "attorney generalette."  With respect to the allegations of discourtesy,  the referee had concluded that Judge Kirby's apology in open court was a sufficient penalty.

<u>Issue</u>:  Was Judge Kirby's apology a sufficient penalty for his gender-biased remarks?

<u>Holding</u>:   No.  The appropriate penalty was public censure for conduct prejudicial to the administration of justice.

<u>Discussion</u>: Judge Kirby's use of the terms "lawyerette" and "attorney generalette" was offensive, demeaning, and placed women lawyers on less

than an equal footing with male lawyers. Accordingly, public censure is a more appropriate penalty.

## CHAPTER ELEVEN
## CONFLICTS OF INTEREST--
## LAWYERS, CLIENTS, AND THIRD PARTIES

Chapter Eleven concerns the first two of three types of conflicts of interest. The first type is where a third party attempts to interfere in the relationship between an attorney and a client. The second type of conflict of interest occurs when the lawyer has a personal interest that is in conflict with the interests of the client.

The ethics rule on the first type of conflict of interest is clear and simple: The lawyer owes loyalty only to the client, not to any third party. The attorney must therefore resist any effort by a third party to interfere in the attorney-client relationship. [*See* ABA Model Rules 1.7(a)(2), 1.8(b) and (f); CRPC 3-310 (A) and (F).] To apply that simple rule to particular cases sometimes becomes tricky, as we will see in Problem 1.

## Discussion Problem 1

A] Problem 1 asks about attorney Wharton's ethical obligations when faced with an offer to settle that has different implications for the party paying his fee and the party he represents in a negligence case. Let's begin with a much simpler case. Suppose you have agreed to represent an impoverished client—Corrinne—in a child custody case. You are doing the work for a token fee because Corrinne is in strained financial circumstances. Corrinne's father wants her to have the best legal service possible, so he urges you to let him pay your regular hourly fee, and he asks you not to disclose the arrangement to Corrinne, to avoid injuring her pride. What should you do?

B] I should say no. There's an old saying that he who pays the piper gets to call the tune. If Corrinne's father pays her fee, he may think he has some right to direct what I do on Corrinne's behalf. Or at least it might appear that way to Corrinne. She would have every right to be angry at both me and her father if we made that deal behind her back.

A] What's the authority for your answer?

B] ABA Model Rule 1.8(f) and CRPC 3-310(F). I cannot do this unless I tell Corrinne all about it and get her consent. Even then, Corrinne's father cannot tell me what to do in representing Corrinne. [*See* ABA Model Rules 1.8(f)(2) and 5.4(c); CRPC 3-310(F)(1).]

A] Does this help any with Wharton's problems?

B] It does if we assume that Wharton has only one client—Combs—and that Hamilton Casualty is simply a third party that is paying the bills.

A] How's that?

B] If attorney Wharton's client is Combs and only Combs, then Wharton owes her entire loyalty to Combs and must ignore Hamilton's interests. Wharton would carefully and completely explain the settlement offer to Combs, along with the alternatives of trial, counteroffers and the like, and Combs would then choose whether or not to accept the offer. [*See* ABA Model Rule 1.2.] Very likely, Combs will be happy to settle for $90,000. It will all come out of the insurance company's pocket. Of course, the arrangement to have Hamilton pay for Combs' representation must meet all the ABA Rule 1.8(f) conditions, but it most likely will, since this is exactly why Combs purchased an insurance policy from Hamilton. If Wharton allowed Hamilton's interests to affect her representation, then she would have to withdraw from the representation. [*See* ABA Model Rules 1.8(f), 5.4(c), and 1.16(a)(1); CRPC 3-700(B)(2).]

C] But that misses the whole point. Wharton really has two clients, or at least one hybrid client. The role of the lawyer employed by an insurance carrier to provide representation to its insured has been called "the eternal triangle" because it is impossible to simplify without distorting the varying interests and unique contractually-based role of the insurance defense lawyer. [*See* Hazard & Hodes § 12.14. A summary of the customary rules that apply to insurance defense counsel can be found in RESTATEMENT (THIRD) OF THE LAW GOVERNING LAWYERS § 134(2), comments d and f (2000).] Here in California, the Discussion section following CRPC 3-310 specifically states that the "no-third-party-influence" rule does "not abrogate existing relationships between insurers and insureds whereby the insurer has the contractual right to unilaterally select counsel for the insured, where there is no conflict of interest." The *Wausau* case in the casebook notes that, under California law, counsel retained by an insurer to defend an insured has fiduciary duties to both the insurer and the insured.

A] So where does that leave attorney Wharton?

C] Under California law, Wharton appears to have two clients—Combs and Hamilton Casualty—and she has to make sure that neither Combs nor the insurance company is disadvantaged. [*See* Guiding Principles of ABA National Conference of Lawyers and Liability Insurers, 20 Fed. of Ins. Counsel Q. No. 4, 93-100 (1970).] This won't be easy. Although they both share the goal of defeating plaintiff's claim, they are likely to have differing interests regarding their willingness to settle, trial tactics, and the like. [*See* Hazard & Hodes § 12.14, at 12-36.] For example, although Combs may be happy to settle for the $90,000 plaintiff has offered, Hamilton may take a dim view of such a settlement. That's only $10,000 under the policy limit, and Hamilton may believe there is an excellent chance of winning the case at trial. It's hard to see how Wharton can fully satisfy them both. Even if Wharton sees herself as Combs' attorney only, she may well be influenced by the hope that Hamilton will hire her in the future. This places Wharton, and all attorneys hired by insurers to defend insureds, between her "clients" in the "eternal triangle." If the conflict becomes too great, for example, if Hamilton wants to claim its policy coverage excludes the plaintiff's claim, Hamilton will have to hire separate counsel, at Hamilton's expense, to protect Combs' interests. [CAL. CIV. CODE § 2860; *Purdy v. Pacific Auto Ins. Co.*, 157 Cal. App.3d 59, 203 Cal. Rptr. 524 (1984).] According to the *Wausau* case, the *Cumis* counsel may owe some duties to Hamilton—after all, they are paying for the representation—but not enough to constitute a full-fledged attorney-client relationship.

A] Just one other question. Suppose that the insurance company is negligent, or that it acts in bad faith, and that it rejects the plaintiff's offer to settle for $90,000. Six weeks later, the case goes to trial and results in a judgment for the plaintiff in the amount of $125,000. As a matter of insurance law, what does that mean for the insurance company?

B] It means that the insurance company will have to pick up the whole tab.

161

The price of negligence or bad faith in rejecting a settlement offer is the duty to pay the excess judgment—that is, the difference between the judgment and the liability limit stated in the policy. [*See, e.g., Kabatoff v. Safeco Ins. Co. of America,* 627 F.2d 207 (9th Cir. 1980); *Crisci v. Security Ins. Co.,* 66 Cal.2d 425, 426 P.2d 173, 58 Cal. Rptr. 13 (1967).]

## Discussion Problem 2

A] The Sarbanes-Oxley Act applies to lawyers "appearing and practicing before the [Securities and Exchange] Commission"—but as explained in Problem 2, defines this broadly. How do the Sarbanes-Oxley Act provisions compare with ABA Model Rule 1.13?

B] ABA Model Rule 1.13 tells lawyers what to do when representing an organization. In particular, an attorney representing an organization has a responsibility to the organization itself and may not simply rely on the organization's contact person. If the contact person is behaving in a manner inconsistent with the organization's interests and the attorney cannot convince the contact person to change his or her behavior, ABA Model Rule 1.13(b)(3) requires the attorney to take the matter up with the "highest authority that can act on behalf of the organization as determined by applicable law." Comment 5 to Rule 1.13 explains that ordinarily that means the board of directors, but that in some situations the applicable law may place the highest authority elsewhere—for example, in the independent directors.

## Discussion Problem 3

A] The remaining problems in this chapter deal with a second main kind of conflict—situations in which the lawyer has a personal interest that is in conflict with the interests of the client.

## Part (a)

A] Part (a) asks about attorney Sarah who is helping her client Willis get out of some financial problems. One of his few solid assets is a lovely beach cottage. He has been unable to pay the taxes on the cottage, and Sarah has advised him to put it up for public auction. The object, of course, is to have the buyer pay off the back taxes and also pay Willis the remainder in hard cash so that Willis can pay some of his other creditors. The question asks whether at the auction Sarah may have her brother bid for her as undisclosed principal.

B] At first blush, one would think that Willis would be delighted. The more bidders, the higher the price Willis is likely to get.

A] What about at second blush?

B] Why is Sarah using her brother to bid for her? And why will she be an undisclosed principal? Is she not going to tell Willis what she's up to? Suppose that Sarah is successful in buying the beach cottage through her brother as intermediary; how is Willis likely to feel when he discovers what happened? I think Willis might wonder whether Sarah's longing for a beach cottage might have influenced the advice she gave him. Perhaps she would have suggested other, better ways for him to get out of his financial mess had she not been so interested in getting the cottage for herself.

A] Has Sarah offended any disciplinary provision in this situation?

B] ABA Model Rule 1.7(a)(2) says that, absent full disclosure and consent of the client, a lawyer must not represent a client if her professional judgment may be affected by her own interests. Also relevant here is ABA Model Rule 1.8(a), which concerns entering into a business transaction with your own client. In essence, Sarah has entered into a business transaction with Willis, through two intermediaries: the auctioneer and her brother. In this situation ABA Model Rule 1.8(a) requires the following: (a) the terms must be fair to the client; (b) the terms must be spelled out in writing, in clear language that the client can understand; (c) the lawyer must advise the client in writing of the desirability of seeking independent counsel (and provide a reasonable opportunity to do so); and (d) the client must give written consent. The California rules are to the same effect. [*See* CRPC 3-300, 3-310(B)(4), and 4-300.]

## Part (b)

A] Part (b) asks whether Sarah could simply buy the cottage directly from Willis, subject to the tax debt. Would that be proper?

B] This is a clearer example of a lawyer entering into a business transaction with a client. Under ABA Model Rule 1.8(a), Sarah would have to meet the strict requirements we just discussed—terms that are fair to the client, a writing that spells out the terms in clear language, a chance for the client to consult with outside counsel, and written consent by the client. [*Accord* CRPC 3-300.]

## Part (c)

A] Part (c) asks if Sarah could simply lend Willis enough money to pay off the back taxes on the cottage. Would that be proper?

B] Once again, it would be a business transaction with the client, so it would be governed by the rule we have just discussed. Further, if she takes some kind of security interest to secure repayment of the loan, she will have to comply with those same rules. Further, there's the question whether it would be proper for Sarah to lend Willis money at all. As we saw in Chapter Five, there's a general rule about not lending money to a client in the context of pending or impending litigation. [ABA Model Rule 1.8(e); ABA Code DR 5-103(B).] Since it does not appear that there is any litigation pending or impending in Willis' matter, I assume that Sarah is not barred from lending him some money to pay off the taxes. In California, CRPC 4-210 and 3-300 would allow Sarah to make the loan under the conditions stated in those rules. Personally, however, I would not wish to become involved in a client's financial affairs by making such a loan. I think I could do a better job as his lawyer if I were not also his creditor.

## Discussion Problem 4

A] Problem 4 concerns a boundary line dispute between Jefferson and Herchberger. Lawyer Lennihan represents Herchberger.

## Part (a)

A] Part (a) asks: May Lennihan may purchase from Jefferson a 30% interest in the disputed twelve acres?

B] Certainly not. If Lennihan did that, it would be in Lennihan's personal interest to "take a dive" and let Jefferson win the suit.

A] What if Herchberger consents after full disclosure? [*See* ABA Model Rules 1.7(b) and 1.8(a); CRPC 3-300 and 3-310(B).]

B] No client who understood what was going on could conceivably consent to that arrangement. Even if Lennihan obtained such consent from Herchberger, the consent should not be valid. Comment 14 to ABA Model Rule 1.7 notes that some conflicts are nonconsentable, meaning that the lawyer involved cannot properly ask for such agreement or provide representation on the basis of the client's consent. The Discussion following CRPC 3-310 states that for non-discipline purposes, some kinds of conflicts cannot be solved by client consent.

## Part (b)

A] Part (b) asks whether Lennihan may purchase from Herchberger a 30% interest in the disputed twelve acres. May he?

B] No, Lennihan can't do that either. Lennihan's personal interest and Herchberger's interest would be parallel and harmonious in that situation, but nevertheless Lennihan cannot make the purchase from Herchberger. ABA Model Rule 1.8(i) prohibits a lawyer from acquiring a proprietary interest in the "subject matter of litigation" the lawyer is conducting for the client. Here the twelve acres is the subject of the litigation.

A] What's the sense of a rule like that? If Lennihan's interest and Herchberger's interest would be consistent and harmonious, what harm could come from the transaction?

B] If Lennihan has a personal financial stake in Herchberger's victory in the lawsuit, that may affect Lennihan's judgment about how to handle the lawsuit. It may make Lennihan more willing to take risks. Or it may make him less willing to take risks. Client Herchberger is entitled to detached, impartial, objective legal advice. If Lennihan has a personal stake in the case, Herchberger may not get what he's paying for. California has no prohibition parallel to ABA Model Rule 1.8(i), but CRPC 3-310(B)(4) would require full disclosure to Herchberger in order to continue the representation.

# **Part (c)**

A] Part (c) asks whether Lennihan may agree to do the legal work in exchange for a 30% interest in the twelve acres if Herchberger wins. Would that be proper?

B] It certainly offends the policy that I've just explained. This is essentially the same transaction as we discussed in Part (b), but now it is dressed up as a contingent fee agreement. ABA Model Rule 1.8(i) contains two exceptions to the general rule about not acquiring a personal interest in the subject of litigation. One of the exceptions allows a lawyer to accept a contingent fee— even though that gives the lawyer an obvious personal stake in the litigation. Usually contingent fees are payable in money, but they can be paid in property also. [*See* Comment 4 to ABA Model Rule 1.5.] California, of course, allows contingent fees as well.

A] If I understand your answer, under most states' ethics rules, the transaction in Part (b) would be improper, but the transaction in Part (c) would be proper. And you point out that the two transactions are identical in substance. Does that make any sense to you?

B] I suppose that the contingent fee exception is a necessary compromise between policy and practicality. Contingent fees have long been permitted in the United States. (In some other parts of the common law world they are regarded as unethical.) If you allow contingent fees, then you must create an exception to the general rule against acquiring a personal interest in the subject of litigation. The same can be said of the other exception to the general rule— allowing lawyers to secure payment of their fees and expenses by a statutory, common law, or contractual lien on the proceeds of a case. [ABA Model Rule 1.8(i)(1).] In California, contractual liens and other security agreements for fees and costs are subject to CRPC 3-300.

## **Discussion Problem 5**

A] In Problem 5, attorney Annette was present as Curt's lawyer during some business negotiations with Danforth Corporation. Later, Danforth sued Curt. A key issue will be whether Curt made a certain statement during the negotiations. Curt wants Annette to be his trial counsel. May she do it?

B] The analysis is different under the CRPC than under the ABA Model Rules. Let's do the ABA Model Rules first. Under ABA Model Rule 3.7, it makes a difference whether she'd be called as a witness by Danforth, or whether she would be testifying on behalf of her own client, Curt.

A] Suppose, first, that she would likely be called as a witness by Danforth and that her testimony would be against Curt's position in the case. What result under the Model Rules?

B] She would have to decide whether serving both as Curt's trial lawyer and as Danforth's witness would violate the general conflict of interest rule set out in ABA Model Rule 1.7(a). I think that it would. Naturally, she wants to earn a fee by representing Curt at trial, but it may harm his case to use her as his trial lawyer. She owes her loyalty to Curt, but she has to tell the truth on the witness stand. Her role as Curt's lawyer will increase the adverse impact of her testimony against Curt. I think that the "disinterested lawyer" mentioned in the Comment to ABA Model Rule 1.7 would have to conclude that Annette could not in good conscience ask for Curt's consent on this one.

A] O.K, suppose that Annette would be barred from serving as Curt's trial counsel under Rule 1.7. Could her law partner, Elmwood, be Curt's trial lawyer?

B] No, he'd be barred also, because of the vicarious disqualification provision in ABA Model Rule 1.10.

A] Now go back and suppose that Annette's testimony would be *favorable* to Curt's position. She was present at those business negotiations, she remembers everything that was said, and she will swear under oath that he never made the disputed statement. How would that situation be handled under the ABA Model Rules?

B] Here's where it gets complicated. First, Annette would have to decide whether she's got a conflict of interest that violates ABA Model Rule 1.7. She has a personal interest in earning a fee as Curt's trial lawyer. The value of her testimony on his behalf will be decreased by her role as trial lawyer, because of her obvious bias. On the other hand, her testimony will be impeachable for bias even if she does not serve as Curt's trial lawyer—she was representing him during the negotiations, and that fact alone gives her a bias. Furthermore, her good working relationship with Curt, and her familiarity with the facts and law involved in the case create sound reasons why Curt might want to have her as his trial lawyer, despite the possible additional bias. Thus, if Curt is fully advised of the problems, he ought to be able to consent under ABA Model Rule 1.7(b). [*See* Comment to ABA Model Rule 1.7.] If Curt does consent, but Danforth moves to disqualify Annette as trial counsel, then ABA Model Rule 3.7 comes into play. Annette is a "necessary" witness because she is the only person who can back up Curt's side of the story. However, the "substantial hardship" exception in ABA Model Rule 3.7(a)(3) may save her from disqualification. The Comment to Model Rule 3.7 rejects the narrow interpretation of "undue hardship" that courts had used under the predecessor provision of the old ABA Code. The Comment advocates a balancing test in which Curt's interest in having Annette as his trial lawyer must be balanced against Danforth's interest in not having to face Annette as both adversary counsel and adversary witness. On the facts stated in Problem 6, I think Curt's interest should be paramount, and Annette should not be disqualified.

A] If Annette's testimony would be favorable to Curt, would Annette's law partner, Elmwood, be allowed to serve as Curt's trial counsel?

B] Assuming that Curt consents under ABA Model Rule 1.7, then Elmwood could serve. ABA Model Rule 3.7(a) applies only to Annette, not to Elmwood. Thus, Danforth could not even make a tenable argument for having Elmwood disqualified. [*See* Comment 7 to ABA Model Rule 3.7.]

A] You mentioned that the analysis would be different under the CRPC. Please explain.

C] The California rule to be applied, CRPC 5-210, provides less direct guidance. Its intention seems to be to narrow the circumstances under which lawyer-witnesses must disqualify themselves.

A] Why do you say that?

C] First, the scope of the rule is limited to lawyer-witness testimony before a jury. It does not apply in trial to the court or even to testimony outside the jury's presence during a jury trial. It does not apply to non-adversarial proceedings. [*See* CRPC 5-210, *Discussion.*] Second, it substitutes the client's informed, written consent for the "substantial hardship" exception of ABA Model Rule 3.7(a)(3). This looks like a client-autonomy rule—it lets the client decide if the hardship outweighs potential prejudice to the client if his or her lawyer testifies—but I wonder if there isn't a danger that a lawyer's desire to remain in the case would color the client's decision, even if it is supposed to be "informed"?

A] You're right. In *Reynolds v. Superior Court*, 177 Cal.App.3d 1021, 223 Cal.Rptr. 258 (1986), the California court indicated it could and would disqualify client's counsel if counsel's testimony would be prejudicial to the client regardless of the client's consent to continuing the representation. [*See also Lyle v. Superior Court*, 122 Cal.App.3d 470, 175 Cal.Rptr. 918 (1981).] Maybe the California rule ends up more restrictive than the ABA rules. Regardless of client hardship and regardless of whether the testimony will be favorable or unfavorable to the client, unless the client gives her informed, written consent, the lawyer must withdraw if the lawyer is going to be called as a witness in a jury trial. But what does this mean for Annette, Curt and Elmwood?

C] If Annette is going to testify against Curt, it is difficult to see how Annette could seek Curt's consent to the representation either under the general conflict of interest rule, CRPC 3-310 (although 3-310(B) only requires written disclosure), or CRPC 5-210. Even if she got over her good conscience, and Curt gave his written, informed consent to the representation, the trial court could disqualify her according to the *Reynolds* and *Lyle* cases. Under the California rules, Elmwood would not automatically be barred, even in this circumstance. [*See* CRPC 5-210, *Discussion.*] Rather, the court would balance the harm to the client to be deprived of counsel of choice against the possible prejudice to Curt, Danforth, and the judicial process. If Elmwood's relationship to Annette can be kept from the jury, the court might well allow the representation. [*See Lyle, supra.*]

If Annette's testimony is going to be favorable to Curt, then Curt should be allowed to consent to the continued representation under both CRPC 3-310(B) and 5-210. If Curt gives his informed, written consent, the court will be reluctant to override the decision without proof that Danforth or the judicial process will be injured and that the injury outweighs Curt's interest in retaining his counsel of choice. [*See Reynolds, supra.*] If, on balance, Annette is nevertheless disqualified, Elmwood ought to be allowed to continue the representation.

## Discussion Problem 6

### Part (a)

A] Part (a) asks if attorney Alice may suggest herself as executrix in the will she is drafting for her aged client, Chadbourne. What do you think?

B] The ABA Model Rules offer no clear guidance on this one. [*But cf.* ABA Model Rule 1.8(c) relating to "substantial gifts" from client to lawyer.] Further, the general conflicts principle in ABA Model Rule 1.7(a) suggests that a lawyer should not pressure a client to bestow a favor on the lawyer, and that could include naming the lawyer as executor. [*See Wisconsin v. Gulbankian,* 196 N.W.2d 733 (1972); *see also* Anno., 57 A.L.R.3d 703 (1974).]

C] California, on the other hand, specifically prohibits a member from "induc[ing] a client to make a substantial gift, including a testamentary gift," to the member or the member's immediate family, except when the member and client are related. [CRPC 4-400.] The *Discussion* to 4-400 explains that a member may *accept* a client gift, "subject to general standards of fairness and undue influence." If the gift is fair and appropriate, the member may prepare an instrument to memorialize the gift. But, if the gift is the result of undue influence, discipline is appropriate. [*See Magee v. State Bar*, 58 Cal.2d 423, 374 P.2d 807, 24 Cal.Rptr. 839 (1962) (suggesting lawyers should avoid drawing wills containing substantial gifts to themselves under circumstances that could suggest overreaching or improper influence).]

A] Would that prohibit Alice from suggesting herself as Chadbourne's executrix?

B] No. Poor Chadbourne doesn't have any suitable relatives or friends, and he doesn't want to use a bank or other institution. He may not know that Alice would be available to serve, or he may be reluctant to ask. So long as she does not pressure him, but simply lets him know she'd be glad to serve if he wishes, I see no harm in it. [*Accord* N.Y. State Bar Op. 481 (1978).]

## Part (b)

A] Parts (b) and (c) deal directly with gifts from a client. What do you think about (b)—the gift of the picture frame?

B] ABA Model Rule 1.8(c) provides that a lawyer should not prepare an instrument giving the lawyer or a close relative of the lawyer "any substantial gift unless the lawyer or other recipient of the gift is related to the client." I assume no instrument is prepared for the simple gift of a picture frame. The problem says it is a "modest" picture frame, so I see no objection. My answer would be the same under CRPC 4-400 because the gift is not "substantial."

## Part (c)

A] What's your answer to part (c) where the gift is Chadbourne's valuable townhouse?

B] That's a different bag of cats. Alice cannot prepare the real estate documents or a will giving her such a gift. [ABA Model Rule 1.8(c).] Under CRPC 4-400, Alice has apparently not "induced" the gift, but the Discussion following that rule suggests that Alice better turn very square corners here. [*See* CAL. PROBATE CODE §§ 21350-51 (requiring independent legal review of donative transfers to lawyers and others).] If Chadbourne really wants Alice to have his townhouse, she'd better send him to an outside lawyer for independent advice. Discipline aside, Alice would be asking for trouble from the people who expect to inherit from Chad if she failed to take that step.

### Discussion Problem 7

## Part (a)

A] In Part (a) of Problem 7, we are told that lawyer Rhonda Howe finds herself personally attracted to client Curt Callen. Howe is representing Callen in dissolution of marriage proceedings. Howe's own marriage was recently dissolved, so she is especially sympathetic to Callen's situation. What advice you would offer Howe?

B] The ABA Model Rules offer no specific guidance about conflicts of interest that arise from matters of the heart. But they do offer a general principle that applies here: A lawyer must not try to represent a client if the lawyer's professional judgment may be affected by the lawyer's own personal interests. [ABA Model Rule 1.7(a).]

A] Might Howe's personal interest in Callen affect the attorney-client relationship between them?

B] Yes. If a lawyer and client have a personal relationship, the lawyer may find it more difficult to restrain the client's demands regarding the legal matter because the lawyer will not wish to harm the personal relationship. [*See* Callner & Portnoy, *Sharing Client Intimacies without Entanglements*, 9 FAMILY ADVOCATE 40 (Winter 1987).] Similarly, the client may feel constrained in asking the lawyer about certain matters, or questioning the lawyer's advice, or objecting to the lawyer's proposed course of conduct, or complaining about the lawyer's performance, all for fear of harming the personal relationship.

A] A number of other problems can arise when lawyer and client are simultaneously involved in a personal relationship. For instance, the lawyer's personal involvement with the client may give the lawyer a personal interest in the outcome of the legal matter. Or, the lawyer may find it difficult in the personal relationship not to take advantage of information that the client revealed to the lawyer in confidence. Or, the lawyer may unnecessarily prolong the professional relationship in order to prolong the personal relationship.

B] Lawyers who do domestic relations work are particularly at risk. Their clients need help at a time of personal tumult and crisis. Their clients routinely need advice on social and money matters, but sometimes also on matters of the utmost intimacy. Their clients are casting about for new guidance and direction in their lives. Further, their clients have generally just come to the end of a close emotional involvement with another person and are thus ripe for a new relationship. [*Id.*] Their clients are at a uniquely vulnerable time of life, and the lawyer must be careful not to take advantage of that vulnerability.

172

A]  So what advice should we offer lawyer Howe?

B]  The advice here is about the same as for other conflict of interest problems:

*  First, if the lawyer can see in advance that he or she is likely to become romantically entangled with the person who just walked in the door, then the lawyer ought to decline to act as that person's lawyer.

*  Second, once a lawyer has decided to begin a lawyer–client relationship with a potentially attractive person,  the lawyer ought to be mindful of the dangers that we have just discussed.  The lawyer should seek to avoid the flirtations and temptations that precede more serious involvement.

*  Third, a lawyer who has become romantically entangled with the client should withdraw as lawyer as soon as possible. [*Id.*] I suspect it would be very easy for the lawyer to convince him or herself that the romance would not really harm the professional relationship with the client.  But, ironically, a lawyer in that position is the world's least–qualified person to make that judgment call.  That's why prompt withdrawal ought to be the standard remedy.

*  Fourth, the ABA Model Rules expressly prohibit a lawyer from engaging in a sexual relationship with a client unless the sexual relationship predated the formation of the attorney–client relationship. [*See* ABA Model Rule 1.8(j); *see also* CRPC 3-120.]

C]  As a result of some highly-publicized allegations against a high-profile Los Angeles lawyer by his family-law clients, members of the California legislature first urged the bar to take action and then passed legislation to require the bar to adopt a rule governing lawyer-client sex. [*See* CAL. BUS. & PROF. CODE § 6106.8.] The rule adopted, CRPC 3-120, bans lawyer-client sex when the lawyer demands sex as a condition of employment; when the lawyer uses coercion, intimidation, or undue influence to enter into sexual relations; and when the sexual relationship causes the lawyer to render incompetent legal services.  Minnesota and Oregon also have rules with even broader bans on lawyer-client sex. [*See* Hazard & Hodes § 11.18; *see also* Note*, Keeping Sex Out of the Attorney-Client Relationship: A Proposed Rule*, 92 COLUM. L. REV.

887 (1992).] For the most part, the California rule duplicates existing rules against conflicts of interest, client coercion, and incompetent representation, but the continued reports of abuses suggest the need for greater vigilance by the bar. Discipline is not the only risk here. [*See McDaniel v. Gile*, 230 Cal.App.3d 363, 281 Cal.Rptr. 242 (1991) (lawyer who sexually harassed client and attempted to pressure her into sex with him may be liable for intentional infliction of emotional distress and legal malpractice). California has since adopted a statute that makes lawyers and other professionals civilly liable for sexual harassing clients. [*See* CAL. CIV. CODE § 51.9.]

## **Part (b)**

A] Part (b) of Problem 8 asks about lawyer Shubert who is asked to take on a litigated matter in which the adversary will be represented by Arnott, the person Shubert is soon to marry. What advice should we give Shubert?

B] Comment 11 to ABA Model Rule 1.7 would govern this question if Shubert and Arnott were already married. It says that they shouldn't represent adversary parties absent full disclosure and consent by the respective parties. [*See also* ABA Formal Op. 340.] An abundance of caution would suggest full disclosure and consent in Shubert's and Arnott's situation as well. The custody case may drag on past their wedding date. Further, the same sorts of problems could arise with engaged lawyers as with married lawyers.

A] For example?

B] For example, suppose Shubert is at Arnott's house one evening when Arnott has run down to the store for a pint of ice cream. Arnott's phone rings. Shubert answers it and innocently offers to take a message. The message would be meaningless to most people, but Shubert realizes that it is a scrap of confidential information that is exceedingly useful to her client in the child custody case. That is the kind of problem that can arise when lawyers for adversary parties have a close personal relationship with each other.

C] CRPC 3-320 would apply if Shubert and Arnott live together or have an "intimate personal relationship" even if they are not married. However, that rule requires only that each person informs his or her own client, in writing, of the relationship. That gives the client a chance to ask the lawyer to withdraw.

A] The problem says that Shubert believes that the senior associate in Shubert's firm could handle the child custody case. If Arnott handled the case for one side, and if the associate in Shubert's firm handled the case for the other side (and Shubert had nothing to do with the case), would that solve the conflict of interest?

B] Yes. This is not the kind of conflict of interest that is imputed to all the lawyers in a firm. [*See* ABA Model Rule 1.10 and Comment 11 to ABA Model Rule 1.7.] The same is true under CRPC 3-320.

## EMPLOYERS INSURANCE OF WAUSAU v. ALBERT D. SEENO CONSTRUCTION CO.
### U.S. District Court, N.D. California, 1988

Facts: Plaintiff, Employers Insurance of Wausau ("Wausau"), insured defendant, Albert D. Seeno Construction Company, in a construction contract for a large number of homes. Buyers of the homes brought a variety of claims against Seeno due to alleged construction defects. When Seeno submitted the claims, Wausau reserved its right to deny coverage, and Seeno engaged independent counsel paid by Wausau. Seeno asked that Wausau take responsibility for the unlitigated claims, but Seeno's independent counsel handled the claims that already reached litigation.

In August 1986, Wausau brought a declaratory judgment action against Seeno seeking a declaration that Wausau was not liable for the claims. Wausau also asserted that Seeno breached its contractual obligations and asked for the return of any advanced payments Wausau made to defend and settle the third party claims. Finally, Wausau moved to disqualify Seeno's counsel, the Archer firm, on the ground that Archer failed to adequately represent Wausau's interests. [Wausau also claimed that the court must disqualify Seeno's counsel because a member of the Archer firm once worked for a firm representing Wausau. Seeno responded by cross-moving to disqualify Wausau's primary counsel due to a conflict of interest in representing Wausau against Seeno and against claims brought by third parties against Seeno.]

Issues: 1) Should Seeno's *Cumis* counsel be disqualified on the ground that Seeno's *Cumis* counsel has failed to adequately represent Wausau's interests?

       2) Should Wausau's counsel be disqualified on the ground that primary counsel also represents Seeno and has inadequately protected Seeno's interests?

       3) Should Seeno's counsel be disqualified because an attorney from that firm (the Archer firm) once worked for a firm that represents Wausau?

Holdings:     1) No. Independent *Cumis* counsel chosen by the insured has a duty to the insured when a conflict arises between the insured and the insurer. The insured not only has a right to choose the independent counsel, but also the right to counsel who only represents the interest of the insured. Otherwise a conflict would arise in which counsel would represent the interest of opposing parties.

       2) No. Only in a case in which the insurer's counsel continues to represent the insured in liability issues after a conflict arises between the insurer and the insured does the insured have grounds to have the insurer's counsel disqualified. Wausau's primary counsel only acted on Wausau's behalf regarding the liability claims.

       3) No. Generally the concern for attorney-client confidentiality would justify disqualification of the Archer firm. However, Wausau had an opportunity to object to the Archer firm's representation of Seeno much earlier in the litigation and declined to do so. In addition, it would cause undue hardship on Seeno to disqualify the Archer firm.

Discussion:  California has clearly established the insured's right to select independent counsel when a conflict arises between the insured and the insurer in *San Diego Navy Federal Credit Union v. Cumis Ins. Society, Inc.*, 162 Cal. App. 3d 358, 208 Cal.Rptr. 494 (1984). When the insured chooses to exercise the right to *Cumis* counsel, the insurer must pay the counsel's fees. Wausau argues that since they must pay for the Archer firm, Seeno's *Cumis* counsel, the Archer firm in essence represents Wausau as well. Wausau argues that the representation of both parties constitutes a conflict of interest.

    *Cumis* counsel only owes a duty to the insured. Once the insurer decides to assert a coverage defense against the insured, the insurer's counsel cannot represent both parties. Therefore, the insured must receive *Cumis* counsel. The *Cumis* counsel may not serve as counsel for both insurer and insured due to the possibility of a conflict of interest. Since the Archer firm does not represent Wausau, no conflict of interest exists in its representation of Seeno.

[Seeno argued that the court should disqualify Wausau's counsel, the Robins firm. Seeno claimed that Robins represents Wausau in the coverage dispute and Seeno in opposing the liability of Seeno to third parties. Wausau argued that the dual representation causes a conflict of interest. In order to disqualify Robins, Seeno must prove that Robins actually represented Seeno at the same time it represented Wausau in the coverage dispute claim. Wausau does not represent Seeno simply because it represents Wausau with respect to third party claims against Seeno.

Robins has not represented Seeno. Seeno provided no evidence of a contract or letter that Robins has ever represented Seeno. Wausau retained Robins solely for representation of their own interests. Seeno has continually objected to the use of Robins in liability matters. Seeno has also had *Cumis* counsel during the entire period in dispute. The existence of *Cumis* counsel during this period suggests the Archer firm, not Robins, represented Seeno. Just as the insured may hire independent *Cumis* counsel to represent only the insured's interest, the insurer may also retain counsel who will have a duty only to the insurer.

Finally, Wausau argued that since a member of the Archer firm, Lageson, once worked for a firm that represented Wausau, the entire Archer firm cannot represent Seeno in the coverage dispute litigation. California Rule of Professional Responsibility 4-101 governs the area of prior representation of an adverse party. The relevant standard for disqualification is whether the former representation is substantially related to the present representation. Seeno concedes that Lageson worked on coverage and liability matters for Wausau until 1986 when he became a partner in the Archer firm. As the *Cumis* counsel at the Archer firm, Lageson has also handled numerous liability cases for Wausau's insured. Therefore, Lageson's past and present representations are substantially related. In addition, Lageson's move from the law firm of the insurer to the law firm of the insured creates the appearance of impropriety.

However, the Archer firm can continue to represent Seeno. Wausau waived its right to object to the Archer's firm representation of Seeno by the one year delay in making the motion to disqualify. Wausau had cause to make the motion earlier because Lageson became personally involved in a dispute with Wausau in state court immediately upon joining the Archer firm in 1986. In addition, neither Wausau nor their counsel made any objection on ethical grounds to Lageson's work for Seeno until they made the motion to disqualify. Finally, disqualification of the Archer firm would cause considerable prejudice and hardship to Wausau.

## PHILLIPS v. CARSON
### Supreme Court of Kansas, 1987

Facts: In 1978, client Phillips retained attorney Carson and his law firm to handle the estate of her deceased husband. Prior to that time Phillips and Carson had been personal friends. Phillips paid the firm $80,000 while the estate was pending to "take care of all her legal business." In 1980 Carson told Phillips he was having financial problems. She lent him $200,000. Carson gave her a note and a second mortgage on some Arizona property. These documents were executed, and the mortgage was recorded. 1981 Carson lent him $70,000 more. Later, Carson got Phillips to release the mortgage on the Arizona property and to accept instead a second mortgage on property in Wyandotte County. Carson failed to record the Wyandotte mortgage. Phillips never discussed the loans with any other partner of Carson's law firm. In 1982, she found out that the mortgage had not been recorded. She hired a new lawyer who got the mortgage and recorded it, and she demanded payment of the loans in full. Carson then filed for bankruptcy under Chapter 11. Phillips sued Carson and his law firm for malpractice. The trial court granted summary judgment against Carson but in favor of the law firm.

Issue: Was the trial judge correct in granting summary judgment against Carson but in favor of the law firm?

Holding: As to Carson, the trial judge was correct. As to the law firm, the trial judge was in error.

Discussion: There were no disputed facts concerning Carson's own liability. He breached his duties as an attorney by failing to record the Wyandotte mortgage, failing to properly advise Phillips, and failing to recommend that she seek outside counsel before lending him money. Thus the trial judge was correct in entering summary judgment against Carson.

As to the law firm's liability, there were unresolved issues of fact. Did Carson have apparent authority? Were the loans from Phillips to Carson apparently authorized by the law firm? Was Carson apparently carrying on the usual business of the firm? Were his acts and omissions within the usual course of the firm's business? Were they actually authorized by the firm? In light of these unresolved fact issues, it was error for the trial judge to grant summary judgment in favor of the law firm.

## AAA PLUMBING POTTERY CORP. v. ST. PAUL INS. CO. OF ILLINOIS
### United States District Court, N.D. Illinois, 1995

Facts: In two prior workers compensation actions brought by an AAA employee, Britton, AAA's insurance company, St. Paul, defended the actions on behalf of AAA. Around June 6, 1991, Britton's attorney proposed settling all of Britton's claims he might have against AAA for $200,000. St. Paul rejected the demand, but AAA claimed St. Paul never communicated the settlement offer to AAA. In November 1992, St. Paul and AAA settled the workers compensation cases for $75,000.

On June 7, 1991, Britton brought a civil action for fraud against AAA and others. Britton claimed that AAA had fraudulently induced him to return to work prematurely by misrepresenting that his doctor had approved his return to a specific job assignment, and that this conduct had led to his second back injury and permanent disability. While St. Paul was named a defendant in this action, AAA, according to St. Paul, never filed an employer's liability claim under their insurance policy. AAA asserts that St. Paul rejected its demand for defense and coverage regarding the lawsuit.

Near the end of the Britton trial, AAA contacted William Gifford, a partner at a Chicago law firm, Shefsky Froelich & Devine, Ltd. (SF&D), to ask for advice regarding settlement of the case. Gifford consulted with a senior partner, Gross, who recommended that Gifford inquire about insurance coverage for the suit and tell AAA to follow their Alabama counsel's advice since they were more knowledgeable about the case. AAA, against the advice of both SF&D and their Alabama counsel and recommendation of the presiding Alabama judge, refused to offer $100,000 to $125,000 to Britton. Instead, AAA offered only $50,000 which Britton rejected. The case went to the jury who awarded Britton $1,314,000 in compensatory damages and $2,000,000 in punitive damages.

Afterwards, SF&D prepared, either wholly or in part, a motion for judgment notwithstanding the verdict or alternatively, a new trial or remittitur on behalf of AAA. In support of its claim that the punitive damage award was excessive, AAA claimed that the judgment was uninsured and paying it would put AAA out of business.

SF&D then advised AAA to transfer security interests (or mortgages) in almost all of its fixed assets to affiliated corporations to protect them from attachment. AAA did so. Gifford's notes indicated that, after the conveyances, two SF&D partners who worked on the security interests informed him that the conveyances would be fraudulent but Gross instructed him to proceed with them anyway. Consequently, Britton was unable to collect his judgment.

Britton's attorney moved to have the mortgages set aside as fraudulent conveyances, pointing to the mortgages as additional evidence that the punitive damages award was proper. SF&D never received permission from the Alabama court to appear *pro hac vice*. At his deposition, Gifford explained that AAA did not want Britton or the court to see that it was being represented by a Chicago law firm at the same time they were claiming they did not have the money to pay the judgment. Gifford's contemporaneous notes also indicated that he was not to sit at the counsel table or be introduced.

Before the court ruled on the post-trial motions, AAA settled with Britton for $950,000, allegedly without St. Paul's knowledge. In return, Britton assigned his rights to the judgment and any claim he might have against St. Paul, to AAA's parent corporation, Kokomo.

A provision in the settlement agreement specifically releasing two additional claims, including one based upon AAA's failure to tend the Britton case to St. Paul, was eventually deleted. Based on Gifford's deposition, St. Paul suggests that Gross made the deletion, lumping all of Britton's claims together instead of dividing them. AAA seeks in this action to hold St. Paul responsible for the full amount of the settlement, even though two of the claims fall outside the provisions of the insurance policy.

In the present action, AAA asserted three causes of action: (1) bad faith on the part of St. Paul for failing to communicate the June 6, 1991 settlement offer; (2) negligence for the same reason; (3) breach of the policy terms because Britton's claim in the fraud case arose out of his work-related injury. Kokomo also asserted a claim on Britton's behalf for the portion of the judgment not paid under the settlement agreement ($2,364,000).

St. Paul filed a counterclaim, seeking a declaration that they did not act in bad faith and have no indemnification duty to AAA. Additionally, St. Paul asserted as one of its affirmative defenses that the Britton case settlement was made in bad faith, was collusive and fraudulent, unjustly enriched AAA and Kokomo, and violated public policy. SF&D represented both AAA and Kokomo, with Gross as the senior attorney. Gifford did not participate in this action.

St. Paul notified AAA and Kokomo that it intended to call Gross and Gifford as witnesses. St. Paul moved to have Gross disqualified and requested a protective order preventing Gross from participating in depositions for the case.

Issues:

A. Is an attorney who is called to testify in a trial in which he or she is participating as counsel disqualified?
B. Does the disqualification of an attorney prevent that attorney from participating in depositions in that proceeding?
C. Is the lawyer's disqualification imputed to the firm?

Holding:

A. No, unless the lawyer knows or reasonably should know that the lawyer's testimony will be prejudicial to the client.

B. Only if the depositions are videotaped so that it may be replayed at trial in place of the witness' trial testimony. In that case, the lawyer may not participate in the deposition or appear on the videotape.

C. No. Only when a party establishes that the other party's attorney has a conflict of interest can the disqualification of the attorney be imputed to the firm. Merely establishing that the attorney will be called as a witness does not suffice.

Discussion: Rule 3.7(b) of the Rules of Professional Conduct for the Northern District of Illinois [in substance ABA Code DR 5-102(B)] states that if a lawyer is to be called as a witness other than on behalf of the client, the lawyer may continue to act as an advocate in a trial or evidentiary proceeding unless the lawyer knows or reasonably should know that the lawyer's testimony is or may be prejudicial to the client.

However, the court has the discretion to decide whether an attorney appearing as a witness may continue as an advocate. The court also may forbid the lawyer being called as a witness if the information is available from other sources and no other "compelling reasons" exist for calling the attorney as a witness.

St. Paul contends that Gross is a necessary witness. Out of fifteen factual issues, the court found only two of merit, both centering on Gross' role in structuring the Britton settlement. St. Paul needed Gross to testify regarding the original intention to include the claims, the deletion of the specific mention of them, and the overall structure of the settlement. Gross was the only source of information regarding his precise role in drafting the settlement agreement; no other could testify regarding his reasoning and judgments.

In addition to finding that Gross was a necessary witness, the court also had to determine whether Gross' testimony would be prejudicial to AAA. Considering that Gross' testimony could be used to prove St. Paul's affirmative defense that the settlement agreement was made in bad faith, his testimony could easily be prejudicial to AAA. Consequently, the probability of the

182

prejudicial nature of his testimony was high enough to warrant disqualification.

St. Paul also argued that should Gross be disqualified, that disqualification should be imputed to SF & D. SF & D could only be disqualified under Rule 1.10 which required a conflict of interest under Rules 1.7, 1.8(c), or 1.9. St. Paul only established that Gross was a necessary witness, not that he had a conflict of interest. The court did note that that situation might change if the plaintiffs decided to use an advice of counsel defense to rebut St. Paul's affirmative defense. St. Paul also requested a protective order to prevent Gross from participating in depositions in the case. The court ruled that Gross would be barred from participating in depositions only when the deposition was videotaped so that it could be replayed at trial in place of the witness' trial testimony.

## CHAPTER TWELVE
## CONFLICTS OF INTEREST--
## CONFLICTS BETWEEN TWO CLIENTS

A] In Chapter 11 we discussed two of the three main kinds of conflicts of interest. In Chapter 12, we reach the third main kind: conflicts between two of the lawyer's clients. They might be two prospective clients, or they might be two present clients, or they might be one present client and one former client. At the outset, here are three general rules that may help you see the big picture:

*First:* For conflict of interest purposes, all the lawyers in a law firm are *usually* treated as a single unit. [By "law firm" or "law office," we mean lawyers who practice together in a private law firm, or in a corporate law department, or in an institutional or governmental law office, such as a public defender's office. *See* ABA Model Rule 1.0(c); Comment 1 to ABA Model Rule 1.10; California has no parallel disciplinary rule, but the case law uses the imputation principle in non-disciplinary matters.] Thus, if one lawyer in the office is barred from taking a case because of a conflict of interest, then no other lawyer can take the case either. [*See* ABA Model Rule 1.10.] This general rule has some exceptions. We have already discussed two of them in Chapter 11: ABA Model Rule 3.7 (trial counsel as witness), and ABA Model Rule 1.7, comment 11 (family relationships between lawyers).

*Second:* If a lawyer is asked to represent a client in a matter, and if that client's interests potentially conflict with the interests of another client, then the lawyer must decide whether her loyalty to one might adversely affect her representation of the other. [*See generally* Martha Neil, *Check, Please*, A.B.A.J., May 2006, at 50.] Unless the lawyer *reasonably* concludes that there will be no adverse effect, she must decline the employment. [*See* ABA Model Rule 1.7; *see also* CRPC 3-310, Discussion] Note that some conflicts are nonconsentable, "meaning that the lawyer involved cannot properly ask for such agreement or provide representation on the basis of the client's consent." [*See* ABA Model Rule 1.7, comment 14.]

*Third:* If the lawyer *reasonably* concludes that there will be no adverse effect on her representation of either client, then she must consult with each client and obtain the written consent of each. That means that the lawyer should fully explain the situation to each client; she should spell out the implications and the possible problems that could arise if she represents both clients, and she should give each client an opportunity to evaluate the need for independent representation, free of any potential conflict of interest. [*See* Comments to ABA Model Rule 1.7; CRPC 3-310(C)] Finally, if both clients consent after full disclosure, and if it later becomes apparent that the dual role will adversely affect the lawyer's representation of one client or the other, then the lawyer must *withdraw.* Failure to withdraw would constitute a disciplinary violation. [*See* ABA Model Rule 1.16(a) and 1.7(a); CRPC 3-700(B)(2) and 3-310(C)(2).]

## **Discussion Problem 1**

A] With those three general rules as background, let's consider Problem 1. Here an association of real estate dealers (CARED) hired Adler to draft a new standard form apartment lease to comply with the state's new plain English statute. Adler drafted the form, and it was sent out for use by CARED members. A CARED member used the form to lease an apartment to one Leon Beckner. Now Beckner comes to Adler asking Adler to represent him in a suit to have the form lease declared void for failure to comply with the plain English statute. Put yourself in Adler's position: Beckner has come into the office and has started explaining the background of his legal problem. What's the very first thing you'd do if you were Adler?

B] Stop him in mid–sentence, the second it becomes apparent that he's got a problem relating to the CARED lease form.

A] Why stop him in mid–sentence?

B] Because the moment Adler learns that Beckner has a problem with the lease form, Adler should be alert to the possibility of a conflict of interest. Fairness to Beckner, to CARED, and not least to himself, requires him to stop Beckner mid–sentence—before Beckner discloses any confidential information.

A] Is this something you've read in the CRPC or the ABA Model Rules?

B] No, it's a matter of courtesy and common sense. Suppose Adler sits back and quietly lets Beckner prattle on about the law suit he wants to bring. When

Beckner finally finishes his monologue, Alder tells Beckner that he can't represent him because he himself drafted the lease form. Wouldn't Beckner feel deceived by Adler's silence? Poor Beckner has walked right into the adversary's tent without realizing it. Thus, Adler's first duty is to stop Beckner, before Beckner can reveal anything remotely confidential.

A] What would be the consequence if Adler failed to do as you suggest?

B] Either CARED or Dearbourne Realty may want to hire Adler to defend the form lease against Beckner's challenge. If Adler had previously allowed Beckner to sit at his desk and spill out confidential information about the matter, then Beckner could move to disqualify Adler as defense counsel. [*See Bridge Products, Inc. v. Quantum Chemical Corp.*, 6 ABA/BNA LAWYERS' MANUAL ON PROFESSIONAL CONDUCT 158 (U.S.Dist.Ct., N.D. Ill., 4/27/90) (firm disqualified on the basis of information received in initial consultation).] Both the ABA in Formal Opinion 90-358 and the ALI in the Restatement (Third) of the Law Governing Lawyers, § 15, Comment *c* (2000) suggest ways to minimize the risk of disqualification due to information received in a prospective consultation. [*See also* RESTATEMENT § 132.] The information obtained must be no more than necessary to make conflicts checks, and the lawyers involved in the initial consultation should be screened from other lawyers in the firm. [*See also* Hazard & Hodes §§ 9.18, 13.9.] In other words, if Adler doesn't stop Beckner mid–sentence, Alder may deprive CARED or Dearbourne of their first choice in counsel, not to mention deprive himself of a chance to earn a nice fee.

A] Suppose <u>Beckner</u> wants to hire Adler to attack the lease that he himself drafted. After all, we lawyers learn in law school to argue either side of a case, and Adler has the advantage of being intimately familiar with this lease. Could Alder represent Beckner?

B] No. Technically, Alder's former client was CARED, but Adler doubtless knew that the real beneficiaries of his drafting work would be CARED members such as Dearbourne. [*See Glueck v. Jonathan Logan, Inc.*, 512 F. Supp. 223, 226-27 (S.D.N.Y. 1981), *aff'd*, 653 F.2d 746 (2d Cir. 1981). We must also assume that representatives of CARED, and perhaps some of CARED's members, discussed confidential information with Adler during the drafting process. If Adler now represents Beckner, those confidences may be compromised. [*See* ABA Model Rule 1.9(c); CRPC 3-310(E); *State Farm*

*Mutual Automobile Insurance Co. v. K.A.W.*, in the casebook; RESTATEMENT (THIRD) OF THE LAW GOVERNING LAWYERS, § 132, Comment *d(iii)* (2000).] Even if there were no confidential information, ABA Model Rule 1.9(a) is directly on point. The interests of CARED and Dearbourne are materially adverse to Beckner's interests, and the lawsuit and the lease drafting are substantially related. [*See also* the *Rosenfeld* case in the casebook, and CRPC 3-310(E).] Furthermore, it's downright tacky for a lawyer to attack a piece of legal work that he himself did! [*See* ABA Formal Op. 64 (1932) (lawyer must not represent his deceased client's heirs in attacking a will that the lawyer himself drafted); RESTATEMENT (THIRD) OF THE LAW GOVERNING LAWYERS § 132, Comment *d(ii)* (2000).] Even arguing opposing positions on the same legal question for unrelated clients in unrelated cases (so called "issue conflicts" or "positional conflicts") raises a possible conflict of interest under ABA Model Rule 1.7. [*See* RESTATEMENT (THIRD) OF THE LAW GOVERNING LAWYERS § 128, Comment *f* (2000); Ass'n of the Bar of the City of New York Comm. on Prof. and Judicial Ethics, Formal Opinion 1990-4, 5/22/90, 6 ABA/BNA LAWYERS' MANUAL ON PROF. CONDUCT 225; Philadelphia Bar Ass'n, Prof. Guidance Comm., Opinion 89-27, 3/90, 6 ABA/BNA LAWYERS' MANUAL ON PROF. CONDUCT 117. *But see* Cal. State Bar Standing Comm. on Prof. Resp. and Conduct, Formal Opinion 1989-108 (4/91). *See generally* Hazard & Hodes § 10.10.]

## **Discussion Problem 2**

A] In Problem 2, three car passengers (Aaron, Bropovski, and Carter) and the car driver (Duffy) have all asked you to represent them in a lawsuit against a truck driver (Emerson) and the truck driver's employer. May you represent all four occupants of the car in that civil suit?

B] It depends on whether Duffy was partly at fault in the crash. Suppose that when the four people come into my office and tell me their story, it's immediately apparent that Duffy was partly at fault. If I tried to represent all four of them, I'd be subject to discipline. [ABA Model Rule 1.7(a); CRPC 3-310(C).] The interests of Aaron, Bropovski, and Carter would require me to advise them to name Duffy as a party defendant in the suit, but Duffy's interest would require me *not* to give that advice to Aaron, Bropovski, and Carter. That's a hopeless conflict.

A] Very well, suppose you make a careful inquiry at the outset and conclude that there's no present evidence of any fault on the part of Duffy. What then?

B]  My first duty would be to make sure I could represent all four of them effectively. [ABA Model Rule 1.7(b).] My second duty would be to disclose to all of them the disadvantages of multiple representation and the possibility that some conflict may arise later in the case. If they understand all of that, and if they still want me as their lawyer, then I could represent all of them. [*Id.;* CRPC 3-310(C). *See generally* RESTATEMENT (THIRD) OF THE LAW GOVERNING LAWYERS § 128, Comment *d* (2000).]

A]  Suppose you are representing all of them, with their consent, after full disclosure of all the problems. Now the defense lawyer begins to take depositions. In these depositions, he develops some convincing evidence that Duffy was partly at fault in the accident. What now?

B]  I have to assess that evidence and decide whether I can continue to serve Aaron, Bropovski, and Carter along with Duffy. If the evidence is sufficient to give Aaron, Bropovski, and Carter a tenable claim against Duffy, then I've got to withdraw. [*See* ABA Model Rules 1.16(a) and 1.7(a); CRPC 3-700(B)(2) and 3-310(C).]

A]  Would you have to withdraw from the case entirely, or would it be sufficient simply to dump Duffy and go on representing Aaron, Bropovski, and Carter?

B]  Under ABA Model Rule 1.9(c) and CRPC 3-310(E), the clearest situation is where I've gotten confidential information from Duffy during the joint representation. If that confidential would be relevant to the claim against Duffy, then I could not represent Aaron, Bropovski, and Carter against Duffy. But even if I had never received a scrap of relevant confidential information from Duffy, ABA Model Rule 1.9(a) would require me to get Duffy's consent before I could represent Aaron, Bropovski, and Carter in a claim against Duffy. [*See also* CRPC 3-310(E) and the *Rosenfeld* case in the text; *Picker International, Inc. v. Varian Associates, Inc.*, 670 F. Supp. 1363, 1365 (N.D. Ohio 1987) (firm may not choose which of two clients with conflicting interests it will represent and which it will drop, even when "consent" has been obtained from one of the clients—the "hot potato" approach).] California law is essentially the same. [*Truck Ins. Exchange v. Fireman's Fund Ins. Co.*, 6 Cal.App. 4th 1050, 8 Cal.Rptr.2d 228 (1st Dist. 1992).]

## Discussion Problem 3

A] Problem 3 concerns Virgil McQuillan. First, Virgil owes your client, Sand Springs Hardware, some money on a past-due charge account. Second, he's accused of trying to burglarize a saloon.

## Part (a)

A] Part (a) asks whether the public defender is on sound ground in refusing to represent both McQuillan and his co–defendant in the burglary case.

B] Yes, she is on sound ground. Both men are indigent, and the Sixth Amendment guarantees each of them the effective assistance of counsel. There may be an inconsistency in the legal positions available to McQuillan and his co–defendant. One may want to blame it all on the other. One may seek lenient treatment in return for testifying against the other. One may have a strong defense and the other a weak defense. The trial tactics that would assist one might harm the other. If one lawyer (or even two lawyers from the same office) tries to defend both men, one or the other is likely to get short changed—and that will violate the Sixth Amendment. [*See Cuyler v. Sullivan*, 446 U.S. 335 (1980).]

## Part (b)

A] Part (b) asks how you should respond to the court's request that you serve as McQuillan's appointed defense counsel in the burglary case. What do you say?

B] In Chapter 3, we learned that a lawyer should not turn down a court appointment except for a compelling reason—but a conflict of interest is a compelling reason. I'd respectfully tell the court that I could not accept the case.

A] What is the conflict of interest?

B] I'm representing Sand Springs Hardware in a pending civil suit to collect money on his charge account. I'm willing to assume that the criminal and civil cases are totally unrelated, and further to assume that nothing I learn from McQuillan in confidence in the criminal case could be even remotely relevant to the civil case. Nevertheless, from McQuillan's point of view, I am "the enemy" in the civil case.  How can I expect him to treat me as "friend" in the criminal case at the same time?  In law school, we learn to compartmentalize our minds, to argue both sides of every proposition, and to be impersonal and dispassionate when thinking about legal problems.  But we can't expect the same Olympian dispassion from our clients.

A]  So you are proposing an ethics rule that generally a lawyer must not represent a client in one matter and oppose that same client in a different matter pending at the same time, even if the two matters are totally unrelated.  Can you cite any authority for such a rule as that?

B]  The best I can do is Comment 6 to ABA Model Rule 1.7:  "Ordinarily a lawyer may not act as advocate against a client the lawyer represents in some other matter, even if the other matter is wholly unrelated."  The Comment then points out that the rule may not apply if the client is sophisticated enough to have that Olympian dispassion I mentioned (for example, the government or a large, diverse business).  [*See also* Cal. State Bar Standing Comm. on Prof. Resp. and Conduct, Formal Opinion 1989-133 (7/6/90) (representation adverse to wholly-owned subsidiary of existing corporate client may be possible under some circumstances); New York County Lawyers' Ass'n Comm. on Prof. Ethics, Opinion 684, 7/8/91, 7 ABA/BNA Lawyers' Manual on Prof. Conduct 276 (same).  *But see Teradyne, Inc. v. Hewlett-Packard Co.*, 7 ABA/BNA Lawyers' Manual on Prof. Conduct 195 (N.D. Cal., 6/6/91) (firm representing wholly-owned subsidiary and retirement plans of parent may not represent plaintiff in patent infringement action against parent).]

## Discussion Problem 4

A]  In Problem 4, you have previously represented Mr. W in setting up a close corporation for his business and for some personal investments.  Now Mrs. W wants you to represent her in getting a divorce from Mr. W.  May you do so?

B]  No.  In setting up that close corporation for Mr. W, I am bound to have had access to confidential information about his business and personal assets.  I would undoubtedly have discussed those matters with him at some length, both for tax and corporate law reasons.  Problem 5 says there is a sharp disagreement between Mr. and Mrs. W about the division of property, child support payments, and alimony.  There's no way I could do a proper job of representing Mrs. W without making Mr. W feel that I'm abusing information he gave me in confidence. Unless I can get Mr. W's consent (and that seems quite unlikely), I cannot represent Mrs. W. [*See* ABA Model Rule 1.9(c); CRPC 3-310(E); Los Angeles Ethics Op. 448 (1987).]

## Discussion Problem 5

A] Problem 5 raises the thorny question of how far we should carry the taint of conflict of interest when lawyers move among firms, something that is more likely than not going to happen to all of you. For our facts, we return to the *Wausau* case from Chapter 11. A member of the law firm (the Archer firm) representing Seeno against Wausau—Lageson—was formerly associated with another firm (the B firm) that represented Wausau in actions of this sort.

## Part (a)

A] In order to reach the question of whether the entire Archer firm is disqualified from representing Seeno, we first must decide, in part (a)—is Lageson himself is disqualified from representing Seeno against Wausau?

B] The answer to that part is easy—yes. Because of Lageson's former association with the B firm, Lageson previously represented Wausau. At best, Lageson is now opposing a former client in similar kinds of cases. Both ABA Model Rule 1.9(a) and California through case law apply the "substantial relationship" test (*see Rosenfeld Construction Co., Inc. v. Superior Court* in the casebook) to representation adverse to a former client. Given Lageson's work on a number of Wausau cases raising similar legal and factual issues as recently as two years ago, it is highly likely that he gained familiarity with and special access to Wausau's policies, practices, and procedures for these cases. Even without a showing that he gained confidential information relevant to Seeno's action, Lageson has effectively "switched sides" and now represents a Wausau adversary against his former client. Thus, the matters should be considered "substantially related," and Lageson should be disqualified on this basis alone. At worst, as Wausau claims, Lageson has confidential Wausau information as a result of his former representation that he now could use against a former client in a related matter. Unless Wausau consents, this also bars Lageson from representing Seeno under ABA Model Rule 1.9(b) and (c) and CRPC 3-310(E).

## Part (b)

A]  Assuming you're right, and Lageson is personally disqualified from representing Seeno, Part (b) asks whether the entire Archer firm also disqualified. Is it?

B] It depends. Under ABA Model Rule 1.10(a), if Lageson is personally disqualified, then the entire Archer firm is disqualified regardless of whether or not there has been an actual sharing of confidences. California lacks a specific rule here. California has generally applied the same imputed disqualification standard. [*See Cho v. Superior Court* in the casebook; *Klein v. Superior Court*, 198 Cal.App.3d 894, 244 Cal.Rptr. 226 (1988); *William H. Raley Co. v. Superior Court*, 149 Cal.App.3d 1042, 197 Cal.Rptr. 232 (1983).]

## **Part (c)**

A]  Part (c) asks, if the Archer firm had seen the problem coming, is there anything it could have done to avoid finding it disqualified merely because the firm hired a tainted lawyer?

B] Now you're talking about "screening procedures." A bit of history may be in order.  Under the old ABA Code, imputed disqualification applied on a concurrent basis—whenever one lawyer was barred, all her current partners and associates were barred as well. [ABA Code DR 5-105(D).] The Model Rules' drafters realized that strictly applying the imputed disqualification rule to lawyers with extensive government experience would prevent most private firms from employing the former government lawyer. This, in turn, would deter lawyers from entering government service in the first place. As a result, after considerable debate, the Model Rules adopted a "screening procedure" to eliminate the automatic firm disqualification. [*See* ABA Model Rules 1.11, 1.12.] "Screening" involves prohibiting any communication with the former government lawyer and other firm members about a matter in which the former government lawyer "participated personally and substantially," and prohibiting the former government lawyer from sharing in any fees generated by the matter.  The government must also be notified, but need not consent to the representation. Despite recognizing the desirability of screening procedures in the context of government lawyers moving to private firms, for many years the Model Rules rejected the suggestion that screening procedures should also be permitted for lawyers moving between private firms.

In 2009, Model Rule 1.10 was amended to permit screening procedures as a method of avoiding potential disqualification.

A] Is screening all that is required under ABA Model Rule 1.10 to avoid potential disqualification?

B] The rule requires that the disqualified lawyer is "timely screened from any participation in the matter and is apportioned no part of the fee therefrom," and also that written notice and certifications of compliance are provided to the former client. The written notice must contain a description of the screening procedures used, that review may be available before a tribunal, and that the firm will respond promptly if the former client has any questions or objections about the screening procedures.

A] What about California. Is screening accepted here?

C] There is no disciplinary rule or statute. *Chambers v. Superior Court*, 121 Cal.App.3d 893, 175 Cal.Rptr. 575 (1981) refused to apply a rigid imputed disqualification rule in the case of a former *government* employee who had been screened to the satisfaction of the government agency concerned. Screening was also accepted as a possible solution to vicarious disqualification in *Higdon v. Superior Court*, 227 Cal.App.3d 1667, 278 Cal.Rptr. 588 (1991), a case involving a former court commissioner. In the purely private firm context, the California courts had rejected screening arrangements—*see William H. Raley Co. v. Superior Court* and *Klein v. Superior Court, supra* as well as *Cho v. Superior Court* in the casebook.

## Part (d)

A] Part (d) asks whether Wausau or any adversary might nevertheless feel uneasy when its opposing counsel says it has screened off the lawyer who formerly represented Wausau.

B] I know I wouldn't be reassured that the law firm opposing me tells me they have screened my former lawyer from participating in the case. It goes against all the notions of zealous advocacy and absolute client loyalty that my former lawyer kept reassuring me about when the lawyer was on my side. Now that she's on the other side, how can she continue to be loyal to me <u>and</u> her new associates. I agree with the Professor Wolfram's comment that, "In the end there is little but the self-serving assurances of the screening–lawyer foxes that they will carefully guard the screened-lawyer chickens." [WOLFRAM, MODERN LEGAL ETHICS § 7.6.4, at 402 (1986).]

## **Discussion Problem 6**

A] In Problem 6, we are asked whether attorney Barneo may argue an appeal for the Mandel Toy Company in a case in which she was involved during her tenure as a government hearing officer. May she argue the appeal?

B] No. To do so would violate ABA Model Rule 1.12(a). California has no direct counterpart.

A] The problem says that she was formerly an Administrative Law Judge for the State Consumer Protection Commission. Is that the kind of adjudicative position covered by the rules you cite?

B] Yes. Comment 1 to ABA Model Rule 1.12 specifically says so.

A] Suppose Barneo's only involvement with the case was to rule on a Commission motion for sanctions against Mandel for failing to make a timely response to the Commission's request for production of certain documents. Then would she be barred from representing Mandel in her later role as private attorney?

B] I believe that her earlier participation as hearing officer would <u>not</u> be regarded as "on the merits" (to use the old ABA Code phrase), but I believe it *would* be regarded as "personal, substantial participation" (to use the ABA Model Rules phrase). When Barneo ruled on the Commission's motion for a preliminary cease and desist order, she had to weigh whatever evidence was then available about the dangerousness of the toy rifles. She did that, and she apparently concluded that the evidence was too thin to support a preliminary cease and desist order. To me that is a ruling on the substance of the Commission's case as it then stood.

On the other hand, when Barneo ruled on the Commission's motion for discovery sanctions, she was not concerned with the dangerousness of the toy rifles. All she needed to consider was whether Mandel had or had not responded properly to the request for documents. To me that's administrative or procedural, not substantive. A judge's ruling could constitute "personal, substantial participation" even though it was not a ruling on the merits. The Comment and the Model Code Comparison following ABA Model Rule 1.12 indicate that 1.12 was intended to be broader than its counterpart in the ABA Code.

A] Is there any California authority to help us out here?

C] California has no counterpart to ABA Model Rule 1.12, but the *Cho* case in the text draws on ABA Model Rules 1.11 and 1.12, as well as CRPC 3-310(E) in disqualifying both the judge and the firm that hired him, because he had participated in settlement negotiations involving a client of his current firm and the adverse party.


## STATE FARM MUTUAL AUTOMOBILE INS. CO. v. K.A.W.
### Supreme Court of Florida, 1991

Facts: David Wilkerson was driving a rental car carrying his wife and daughter when another car struck them. Wilkerson hired the law firm of Sheldon J. Schlesinger to file suit against the driver and owner of the other vehicle for injuries suffered by Wilkerson and his family. Wilkerson also filed suit against State Farm Mutual Automobile Insurance Company (State Farm), the Wilkersons' insurer, for uninsured motorist coverage. The Wilkersons also hired the Schlesinger firm to bring a malpractice action against the health care providers who cared for their daughter after the accident. Two years later, the Schlesinger firm determined that David Wilkerson had driven negligently.

David Wilkerson subsequently found another attorney. Mrs. Wilkerson and her daughter added David Wilkerson as a defendant in an amended complaint and continued to employ the Schlesinger firm. The Schlesinger firm also continued to represent all three Wilkersons in the medical malpractice action. Petitioners objected to the Schlesinger firm representing the Wilkersons in the personal injury action due to the confidential information the firm could have obtained while representing Mr. Wilkerson. Wilkerson argued that he had disclosed everything in his deposition and he did not feel Mr. Schlesinger's representation of his wife and daughter disadvantaged him.

The trial court refused to disqualify the Schlesinger firm because the petitioners lacked standing to request disqualification based on Wilkerson's consent and because petitioner failed to show prejudice. The court of appeal denied the insurer's petitions for review.

<u>Issue</u>: Can the Schlesinger firm represent the Wilkersons in the personal injury action with Mr. Wilkerson's consent?

<u>Holding</u>: No. The insurers may "stand in the shoes" of the insured for purposes of seeking disqualification of the Schlesinger firm and can vitiate Mr. Wilkerson's consent.

<u>Discussion</u>: Petitioners have standing to request the law firm's disqualification because as the insured of Mr. Wilkerson they had an interest in the outcome of the case. Mr. Wilkerson has an adverse interest to his wife and daughter in theory only. The insurance company actually has a legitimate interest in preventing the opposing counsel from using confidential information.

Petitioners do not need to show actual proof of prejudice. Instead, the correct standard is the one set out in the Rules of Professional Conduct to determine whether a firm should be disqualified. One seeking to disqualify opposing counsel must show that: (1) an attorney–client relationship existed and (2) the matter in which the law firm subsequently represented the interest adverse to the former client was the same or substantially related to the matter in which it represented the former client.

An attorney-client relationship did exist between the Schlesinger firm and David Wilkerson before his wife added him as a defendant in her claim. In addition, the matter in which the firm represented David Wilkerson had a close relationship to the matter in which they represented his wife and daughter. Therefore, even with consent by David Wilkerson, the Schlesinger firm must be disqualified in order to avoid prejudice to the petitioners.

## ROSENFELD CONSTRUCTION CO., INC. v. SUPERIOR COURT
### California Court of Appeal, Fifth District, 1991

<u>Facts</u>: Petitioner construction company brought a motion to disqualify opposing counsel, the Wild Firm, because it had formerly represented petitioner in a related matter. The Wild Firm had represented petitioner in 1982 at the request of

petitioner's president, John Rosenfeld, in a dispute over payment for a home petitioner constructed. The Wild Firm acknowledged that it represented petitioner for four years, but claimed it worked on very few matters for the company.

Real parties in interest (Sivas') initiated a lawsuit against petitioner in 1988 and hired Steven Paganetti to represent them in a suit for breach of contract. In 1991, Paganetti joined the Wild Firm. Petitioner's attorney, at the request of his client, asked the Wild Firm to withdraw as counsel. The Wild Firm refused to withdraw.

Petitioner claimed that its president spent dozens of hours with counsel for the Wild Firm. The Wild Firm claimed Paganetti had never had any conversations with any of his fellow attorneys at the Wild Firm nor seen any documents concerning the petitioner's matters. The firm also claimed it had done very little work for petitioner. The trial court ruled that no actual or potential present conflict of interest existed.

Issue: Must the Wild Firm and Paganetti disqualify themselves from representing a client who brought a lawsuit against petitioner, a former client of the firm?

Holding: Yes. The Wild Firm must disqualify itself on the basis of the substantial relationship test. The work they did for petitioner on an earlier matter has too close a relationship to the case at bar to avoid a conflict of interest. Paganetti must disqualify himself on the theory of imputed disqualification. The knowledge the law firm obtained about petitioner is imputed to Paganetti, even if he does not have actual knowledge about the situation.

Discussion: According to Rule 3-310 of the State Bar Rules of Professional Conduct, counsel must avoid representation of adverse interests. When a question arises about a potential conflict of interest between a party and the opposing party's counsel, the court must use the "substantial relationship" test. Under the *T.C. Theatre Corp. v. Warner Bros. Pictures* standard "where any substantial relationship can be shown between the subject matter of a former representation and that of a subsequent adverse representation, the latter will be prohibited." If a substantial relationship is established, the court can presume a conflict will arise.

The next issue concerns what constitutes a substantial relationship. According to *H.F. Ahmason & Co. v. Salomon Brothers, Inc.*, a judge should consider the similarities between the facts of the two cases, the legal questions raised, and the nature and extent of the attorneys' involvement in each case. Because the trial court did not use the *Ahmason* standard in determining whether the Wild Firm and Paganetti had to withdraw, the case must be remanded to the trial court.

Petitioner argued that Paganetti must withdraw as counsel because of imputed disqualification. Real parties argued that the court can impose a screening procedure. A presumption exists that confidential information passed from the Wild Firm to Paganetti. Therefore, Paganetti cannot represent real parties. Screening off an entire law firm does not avoid the problems of conflicting representation. Although attorneys should not feel restricted in moving to a new firm with their clients, the interest of maintaining public respect for the legal system also must receive consideration. In determining whether a client should follow an attorney to a new firm, the firm and attorney must consider the conflicts of interest that may occur.

## CHO v. SUPERIOR COURT
### California Court of Appeal, Second District, 1995

Facts: Judge Younger presided in an action between petitioner Cho and real parties in interest, Cho Hung Bank. Judge Younger held three settlement conferences, during which he told the plaintiff's lawyer to speak candidly about the strengths and weaknesses of the plaintiff's case and what settlement the plaintiff would accept. Plaintiff's counsel did so under the assumption that the information divulged was in the strictest confidence. If it had not been in a confidential setting, plaintiff's counsel asserts the information would never have been given.

Judge Younger retired shortly and was hired by the law firm, Graham & James, as of-counsel. Graham & James was substituted into the action for Cho Hung Bank after Judge Younger's retirement. Before Judge Younger began his employment, the firm discovered that he had presided over the Cho action. To avoid any potential conflicts of interest, the firm decided to screen off Judge Younger by forming a "cone of silence" around Judge Younger. Graham & James circulated a memorandum directing all personnel that Judge Younger was not to be involved in the action, to have access to the files, and that no one could discuss the case, Judge Younger's role, or any information he had obtained while presiding over the case with Judge Younger.

In March, almost a month after Judge Younger began working for the firm, plaintiff's counsel learned of his employment. That same day, the court and involved counsel received a letter detailing Judge Younger's employment and the screening off process the firm had employed.

The petitioner moved to recuse or disqualify Graham & James in March. Judge Younger submitted a declaration which stated that he never received confidential information and if he did, he did not remember any of it.

In an evidentiary hearing on the motion to disqualify, the referee, Judge Dell (retired), decided that the screening-off process was sufficient and Judge Younger's position as of-counsel prevented any monetary interest in the outcome. The trial court adopted the referee's recommendations. The Court of Appeal issued an alternative writ, established a briefing schedule, and issued a stay of the trial in action.

Issue: Must a law firm be disqualified as counsel in a lawsuit after employing the retired judge who had presided over the action and had received ex parte confidences from the opposing party in the course of a settlement conference?

Holding: Yes. Screening procedures are not sufficient to preserve public trust in the justice system under these circumstances.

Discussion: No California Rule of Professional Conduct governed the situation. Nor did any prior case law, including *Higdon v. Superior Court*, 227 Cal.App.3d 1667(concerning a former court commissioner who did not receive confidences from either side) and *In re Marriage of Thornton*, 138 Ill.App.3d 906 (dealing with a judicial officer not privy to ex parte confidences). Instead, examples of screening off came from ABA Model Rules of Professional Conduct 1.11, governing public attorneys, and ABA Judicial Code of Conduct 1.12(a) concerning a judge representing a party. Both offered screening provisions although neither was directly applicable to the facts before the court.

The substantial relationship test from *Rosenfeld Construction Co. v. Superior Court, supra*, which looked to the connection between the former and current representation, did not apply in this factual situation. However, both situations recognize the importance of maintaining confidences disclosed in the course of litigation in order to keep the public trust in the judicial system.

## GOLDBERG v. WARNER/CHAPPELL MUSIC, INC.
### California Court of Appeal, Second District, 2005

Facts:    Ilene Goldberg filed a lawsuit against her former employer, Warner/Chappell Music, Inc., and her former supervisor for wrongful termination based on sex discrimination.    Goldberg subsequently moved to disqualify Warner's counsel, Mitchell Silberberg & Knupp, LLP (MS&K), on the ground that Goldberg previously had discussed her employment contract  with J. Eugene Salomon, a former partner of the MS&K firm, when Goldberg was employed by Warner.

Issue:   Do Goldberg's numerous contacts with the MS&K firm, including a former MS&K partner's review of her employment contract with Warner, serve to disqualify MS&K from representing Warner in the instant action?

Holding: No.   The attorney-client relationship between Goldberg and Salomon does not warrant the vicarious disqualification of MS&K in this lawsuit, in light of the fact that Salomon left MS&K three years before Goldberg filed this lawsuit and had no opportunity to inadvertently pass along confidential information to others at the MS&K firm.

Discussion: An attorney can and should be disqualified from representing a party adverse to a former client where the attorney possesses confidential information that could be helpful to the new client and harmful to the former client.  In determining whether the attorney possesses such confidential information, the California courts employ the substantial relationship test, which presumes the attorney's knowledge of confidential information when a substantial relationship exists between the former representation and the current representation, and when it appears that, by virtue of the nature of the former representation or the former attorney-client relationship, confidential information material to the current dispute would normally be imparted to the attorney or the attorney's subordinates.

Generally, when a lawyer is disqualified due to an ethical conflict, the lawyer's disqualification is imputed to the entire law firm.  However, a narrow exception exists in those circumstances where the lawyer can show that there was no opportunity for confidential information to be divulged.

If Salomon were still practicing at MS&K, the vicarious disqualification of the MS&K firm might well be necessary.  However, Salomon departed from the firm three years earlier, and none of the attorneys remaining at MS&K are privy to any confidential information that Goldberg may have shared with Salomon. Accordingly, vicarious disqualification of the MS&K firm is unwarranted. [*Accord* ABA Model Rule 1.10(b).]

## CHAPTER THIRTEEN
## LAWYERS IN LAW FIRMS
## AND SPECIALIZED PRACTICE AREAS

### Discussion Problem 1

A] Chapter 13 brings together materials that reflect issues in practice that are not as completely covered in the legal ethics rules as those topics in earlier chapters. In part, these are the issues of lawyers in group practice. We also deal with specialized practice areas. As the ABA's "MacCrate Report" noted:

> Since 1970 there has been a steady movement of law firms of all sizes from smaller unites into larger. Private practice has become a spectrum of different practice units, differentiated not only by size but by clients, by the kind of legal work performed, by the amount of specialization, by the extent of employment of salaried associates and other support staff, and by the degree of bureaucratization of the practice.

Report of The Task Force on Law Schools and the Profession: Narrowing the Gap, *Legal Education and Professional Development—An Educational Continuum* 31 (1992). The ABA's ethical rules have been relatively late in recognizing the special problems that group practice creates, and—with a few exceptions—the California rules are even farther behind the times. The ABA's Model Rules begin with the premise that an individual lawyer in sole practice represents a natural person as a client. And the rules clearly work most easily in this context. But today lawyers are as likely to practice in some type of group practice—from small firms to large, mega-firms, to the government or a prosecutor's office. New and specialized practice areas have arisen in the law. This chapter brings these practice areas to the forefront.

### Discussion Problem 1

A] Problem 1 takes up the issue of law firm supervision and division of responsibility.

## Part (a)

A] Allen, a new associate with Fimrite, Steele & Lasar, a 20-person firm, has chosen to do the best she could despite some practical and ethical doubts about a will and trust arrangement she worked on for one of the firm's clients. Did she do the right thing?

B] I don't know what you mean. She did what she was told, followed the firm's practice guidelines, and she's still working there. What more could you ask?

C] I'd ask for a little ethical responsibility. I thought we did away with the "I was just following orders" answer 50 years ago.

A] O.K. Did you find any help in the ABA's Model Rules?

C] Well, ABA Model Rule 5.1 and 5.2 sketch out the respective duties of supervisory and subordinate lawyers. Rule 5.2(a) tells Allen she is independently responsible for her actions under the rules and that there is no "Nuremberg" defense. It doesn't matter if she is ordered to do it or not. Under ABA Rule 5.2(b), however, if her ethical duties in a matter are debatable, she does not act unethically if she follows her supervisory lawyer's reasonable resolution of the issue. [California has no parallel to 5.1 and 5.2, but CRPC 1-100(B) and 1-120 could be stretched to reach the same results as above.]

A] So is Allen O.K. here under the ABA Model Rules?

C] No. Although she was acting under firm guidelines, she didn't ask for, or receive, Lasar's informed judgment about what she did. I don't think the rule can be stretched to reach "just doing what we always do here" as a "reasonable resolution of an arguable question of professional duty," to use the language of Rule 5.2(b). That leaves Allen just where she started, responsible for her actions, and teaches a valuable lesson. If you don't ask about ethical issues in practice when you see them, there is no shelter from full responsibility for what you do. Part of ethical practice in law is learning to recognize professional responsibility issues, and then seeking guidance in their analysis and resolution.

B] Aren't we forgetting about Lasar? Shouldn't he have some responsibility here too? How can you put the entire ethical burden on the most vulnerable members of the firm—the new associates?

A] Good question. This is the subject of part (b) of Problem 1.

## Part (b)

A] What are Lasar's ethical obligations in the matter?

B] Well, in the first place, he's just as responsible for the work product here; his name is probably on the documents Allen prepared; and possibly only his name. If something was done improperly under the rules, he's going to answer for it and won't simply be able to shift the blame to Allen.

C] Even more to the point, ABA Model Rule 5.1(c) makes Lasar, as Allen's supervisor, directly responsible for her acts if he either orders them or ratifies the conduct with knowledge of the conduct. Certainly, the Fimrite Steele practices fit within these provisions.

A] Anything else?

B] Yes. ABA Model Rules 5.1(a) and (b) impose affirmative duties on law firm partners, managers, and other supervising lawyers. Rule 5.1(a) requires law firm partners, managers, and supervising lawyers to see that the firm has measures in effect that will insure all lawyers will conform to the rules of professional conduct. Rule 5.1(b) requires all lawyers with supervisory responsibility for another lawyer to insure that lawyer will conform to the rules of professional conduct. CRPC 3-110, concerning failure to act competently, includes a duty to supervise the work of subordinate attorneys and non-attorney employees. [*Gadda v. State Bar*, 50 Cal.3d 344, 267 Cal. Rptr. 114 (1990); *In re Whitehead*, 1 Cal. State Bar Ct. Rptr. 354 (1991) (lawyer's failure to supervise associate is failure to perform services).]

A] What do these rules mean in practice?

B] If partners, managers, and other supervisory lawyers take them seriously, they mean firms (at least the larger ones) will have to create procedures for identifying and handling issues of professional responsibility, both for individual representations and for the firm as a whole. For example, virtually all firms now have conflicts checking procedures. Before a prospective client becomes a client of the firm, the firm gathers information about the client and checks against other clients the firm also represents to see that there are no disqualifying conflicts. This protection often came from the firm's malpractice carrier, but 5.1 makes the effort a part of the ethical duties of each partner, manager, and supervisory lawyer. As for Lasar and Fimrite Steele, it appears the partners as a group and Lasar as an individual supervisor have failed to take appropriate measures to ensure the associates at Fimrite Steele will be providing competent, ethical service to their clients through their associates.

## Part (c)

A] In part (c) of Problem 1, the question becomes more concrete—should the firm itself be held accountable in some way?

B] From what we just learned about ABA Model Rule 5.1(a), it appears that all the partners, managers, and supervisory lawyers have a responsibility for the professional conduct of all the lawyers in the firm, but I didn't find anything in the ABA Model Rules that suggests the firm could be disciplined *as a firm*.

A] You're right. Outside of the rules of professional responsibility, however, law firms can be held responsible for professional lapses. They have tort and contract liability, for example, as firms. And Federal Rule of Civil Procedure 11(c) allows the court to impose a sanction on a law *firm* that breaches the certifications of Rule 11(b) (that motions, pleadings, and other papers are not being presented to harass and are warranted by the law and the facts after reasonable inquiry). Several states, including New York and California, have studied possible discipline for law firms. But you can't disbar a firm, only its lawyer members; nor does suspending a firm from practice seem a likely sanction as a practical matter. As the casebook notes, no state has yet adopted a rule that provides for law firm discipline.

## Part (d)

A] Part (d) of Problem 1 asks whether Allen would have any recourse against Fimrite Steele if she ends up being fired for reporting her concerns about the firm's fiduciary practices to the appropriate regulatory agency. What limitations are there on firing lawyer employees?

B] If this makes out a wrongful termination claim in a non-law firm setting, surely the same claim should be available to her against Fimrite Steele.

C] What about the very limited acceptance of such a claim in the *General Dynamics* case? Don't you have to take into account the right of clients to fire their lawyers and threats to the attorney-client privilege, both recognized and accommodated in that case?

A] No and yes. The client firing problem is not present for associate employees of law firms. The firms are not the associate's clients. But there is some danger that litigation of claims like Allen's will potentially require the disclosure of client confidences. *General Dynamics* limited the wrongful discharge action for in-house lawyers to circumstances in which prevailing law permits any breach of attorney-client confidentiality rules required for the suit to go forward. The California court suggested that when the privilege must be breached in the lawyer's claim against the employer, but the law does not allow any disclosure of client confidences, the lawyer's action must be dismissed. Still, wrongful discharge claims by in-house lawyers and associate attorneys are rare, and more states have rejected such claims than recognized them. Cases brought by associate attorneys against their law firm employers are even rarer than cases by in-house attorneys against their corporate employers. Why is this?

B] One reason must be that suing your firm or employer alleging the employer violated an important public policy or the rules of professional responsibility or was forcing the lawyer-employee to violate the rules is not likely to make you more popular among future law firm or corporate employers, even if you were entirely in the right.

C] Also, isn't it possible these claims could be used by lawyer-employees who are otherwise out of favor or being fired for perfectly good reasons to hold up their employers? It's just one more burden of being on the low end of the firm or company ladder (but at the same time with significant professional responsibilities) that we are going to have to live with sharply limited rights to seek legal redress for being fired.

A] It is also part of being a lawyer, as we noted in Chapter 3 and as *General Dynamics* acknowledges, that you are subject to discharge rather freely as part of the structure of the lawyer-client relationship. The only issue is whether you *may* have some claim for some sort of monetary compensation when this happens. [For further insight into the *General Dynamics* case and the questions raised by wrongful discharge actions by lawyers, *see generally* Hazard & Hodes § 20.6, at 20-35 n.10.]

**Discussion Problem 2**

A] Problem 2 concerns Ayers & Alfred, the law firm that has been defending Clayton Industries in some massive products liability litigation. Clayton needs its line of credit renewed. The bank wants a candid evaluation of the products liability litigation, so that it can judge whether Clayton is a good credit risk. Clayton therefore asks Ayers & Alfred to prepare a candid evaluation of the litigation and to furnish it to the bank's loan department. The problem asks what are the ethical obligations of Ayers & Alfred in this situation? Once again, let's tackle it first under the ABA Model Rules; then we will go back and see how a California lawyer would handle it.

B] I think Ayers & Alfred ought to decline the task.

A] Is it improper for a client's lawyer to provide an evaluation of the client's affairs to a third party, upon the client's request?

B] No, it is not generally improper. ABA Model Rule 2.3 says that it is proper if it is compatible with other aspects of the lawyer's relationship with the client.

A] So what is the problem here?

B] I think the "candid evaluation" is incompatible with Ayers & Alfred's primary role as litigators for Clayton. It seems incompatible in three ways:

First, the lawyers of Ayers & Alfred have been steeped in this products liability litigation for four years. If they are vigorous litigators, they have become by now so thoroughly convinced of the correctness of their client's position that they couldn't possibly provide a "candid evaluation."

Second, doubtless a great deal of material in this products liability litigation needs to be protected, either by the attorney–client privilege, or by the work product rule, or by the attorneys' ethical duty to preserve confidential information. As litigators, Ayers & Alfred will be predisposed to withhold and protect information. Furthermore, litigators are used to operating under peculiar ground rules: never volunteer harmful information, and never say anything unless you are asked. I think it would be inordinately difficult for Ayers & Alfred to shift mental gears and become "candid evaluators." I suspect the bank would get a more accurate, complete picture if Clayton asked an outside law firm to take a fresh look at the litigation.

Third, suppose Ayers & Alfred did provide a candid opinion letter to the bank in which they stated that Clayton would probably win the products liability cases, but that there were several areas of real danger. And suppose the opinion letter then candidly explained those areas of danger. That letter could not be protected as confidential information because it was sent to the bank, an outsider. Can't you imagine the glee that would sweep the adversary camp when they got hold of that letter?

I think both the bank and Clayton would be better off here to have the evaluation performed by a different law firm—either a firm chosen and paid by Clayton or a firm chosen and paid by the bank itself.

A] Would your conclusion be different under California law?

D] Here again, California has no counterpart to ABA Model Rule 2.3, so a California lawyer would have to limp along with CRPC 3-310(B), which would seem to permit the firm to give the evaluation, provided that it discloses the problems to the client in writing. The rule does not require the client's consent, but as a practical matter, the client can always fire the lawyer after the client learns what the problems are. But, for all the reasons stated above, I think California litigators would be nuts to try to render this impartial evaluation.

**Discussion Problem 3**

Problem 3 concerns Powell, a former judge who has established a mediation practice.

## Part (a)

A] Part (a) asks if any ethical rules govern this situation. Did you find anything on point?

B] Yes. ABA Model Rule 2.4 addresses situations where a lawyer is serving as a third-party neutral, such as a mediator.

## Part (b)

A] Part (b) states that Snyder and Ramos have approached Powell with respect to a property dispute. If this is a traditional mediation, are Snyder and Ramos clients of Powell?

B] I don't think so. ABA Model Rule 2.4(a) states that, "A lawyer serves as a third-party neutral when the lawyer assists two or more persons who are not clients of the lawyer to reach a resolution of a dispute or other matter that has arisen between them." It sounds like one of the distinguishing characteristics of a third-party neutral is precisely the fact that he or she is "neutral." If the situation involves a lawyer who is representing both parties, we are then back in joint representation territory.

## Part (c)

A] Part (c) introduces the notion that Snyder and Ramos are each represented by separate legal counsel, which happens in many mediations. How might the presence of separate legal counsel complicate the mediation process?

B] In some cases, counsel might act in a manner that was obstructionist rather than facilitative. The presence of counsel may double the number of negotiating participants in the mediation process, causing additional posturing and delay.

A] If we have counsel representing the parties to a mediation, does the fact that we're in a mediation setting take us out of the ABA Model Rules?

B] No. Comment 5 to ABA Model Rule 2.4 expressly states that "[l]awyers who represent clients in alternative dispute-resolution processes are governed by the Rules of Professional Conduct."

A] Why might separate legal counsel be a benefit in a mediation?

B] Comment 3 to ABA Model Rule 2.4 talks in some detail about the "potential for confusion" when the parties to a mediation are not represented by counsel. I guess sometimes the parties to a mediation can be thinking that the mediator is representing them individually—and especially that the attorney-client privilege will apply to their discussions with the mediator.

A] Are there any other potential benefits?

B] I would imagine that it depends on the particular circumstances. In some cases, the presence of counsel might serve to keep clients focused on the matter at hand, or might serve as an effective buffer if a client is difficult, or might be helpful if a client is shy or unassertive. If a client has confidence in counsel, counsel's presence might also reassure the client that the process is operating fairly and inspire the client's confidence in the procedure and the outcome.

## Part (d)

A] In Part (d), a third party (Norris) seeks to retain Powell as counsel in a lawsuit in which Norris would be suing Brooks, who was one of the parties to a dispute mediated by Powell. May Powell represent Norris?

B] In this situation, comment 4 to ABA Model Rule 2.4 sends us back to ABA Model Rule 1.12, pertaining to former judges, arbitrators, mediators, and other third-party neutrals. The initial question appears to be whether the "matter" that was the subject of the mediation is the same as that over which Norris wishes to sue. If so, "all parties to the proceeding [must] give informed consent, confirmed in writing."

C] Since Norris is a newcomer who wasn't involved in the mediation, isn't it impossible for the same "matter" to be involved?

B] The facts state that the mediation concerned an "employment dispute," and now Norris seeks to sue the same employer for wrongful termination. Although we have different employees (now Norris instead of Caldwell), the same underlying issue may lie at the heart of the matter—an issue that perhaps was thoroughly disputed and discussed at length in the mediation. If so, surely Powell should not be permitted to undertake the representation of Norris without full disclosure and informed consent.

## Discussion Problem 4

A] In Problem 4, attorney Johnson held a judicial clerkship with the federal Court of Appeals. He then went to work for a law firm, and one of the partners wants Johnson to work on a brief that is to be submitted to that very Court of Appeals. May Johnson undertake this assignment?

B] Law clerks are mentioned in both ABA Model Rules 1.11 and 1.12. It seems pretty clear that if Johnson worked on this particular case while clerking for the judge, he cannot work on that case now that he is at the firm unless "all parties to the proceedings give informed consent, confirmed in writing." [*See* ABA Model Rule 1.12(a).]

C] The facts in this Problem don't say that the project concerns one of Johnson's prior case assignments for the judge. The partner asked Johnson to work on the brief due to Johnson's "expertise" in federal appellate work.

B] I think the answer comes from a supplemental source. The Federal Judicial Center issues a short publication entitled, "Maintaining the Public Trust: Ethics for Federal Judicial Law Clerks." [This publication is available online at http://www.fjc.gov/public/pdf.nsf/lookup/Ethics01.pdf/$file/Ethics01.pdf.] According to this publication, a former law clerk "should not handle any matter pending before her judge while she was clerking there. Also, many judges have policies about how much time must pass before a former law clerk can appear before the judge." [*Id.* at 16.] I understand that two years is a common waiting period before a former law clerk may appear before her judge.

A] Assuming that Johnson's judge has such a two-year policy, how would that affect Johnson's ability to accept the assignment?

B] If we are at the early stages of the appeal—if the brief that the partner wants Johnson to work on is the appellant's opening brief—then the three-judge panel hearing the case likely hasn't yet been assigned. If that's so, then there is a chance that Johnson's judge could be assigned to this case, and therefore Johnson should decline to work on the brief.

C] But the provision from the Federal Judicial Center publication talked about "appearing" before the judge. Even if Johnson's judge ends up hearing this case, can't Johnson work on the brief so long as he doesn't orally argue the case on appeal?

B] Essentially we're talking about a form of disqualification. If an attorney is disqualified from participating on a case, we don't say that she is barred from arguing motions, but may write the underlying points and authorities. Johnson can't work on the brief if his judge might be hearing this case.

**Discussion Problem 5**

Problem 5 concerns four real estate partners who are planning to split off and form their own firm.

**Part (a)**

A] Part (a) asks if the departing partners may take their clients with them.

B] I've heard references to this type of issue before, and I find it strange. It often sounds like lawyers think they "own" their clients. Aren't clients autonomous human beings who should make their own decisions?

C] I think the circumstances matter, in several respects. Sometimes a client seeks the legal expertise of a particular law firm because the client has heard good things about the firm. Sometimes a client seeks the legal expertise of a particular lawyer. In addition, I think *how* the departing lawyers are handling the departure would matter. Certainly it would not be appropriate for the departing partners to disparage the firm in an attempt to persuade the clients to come with them.

B] I think this gets back to my previous point. The ultimate decision rests with the client, who should not be subjected to pressure in either direction—

whether to stay with the firm or to follow the departing partners.

## Part (b)

A] Part (b) relates that the firm's partnership agreement prohibits departing lawyers from practicing within a 50-mile radius unless they change their field of practice. Does anything in the legal ethics rules address this?

B] Yes. ABA Model Rule 5.6(a) prohibits agreements "restricting the right of lawyers to practice after leaving a firm." Similarly, CRPC 1-500 prohibits agreements restricting the right to practice law. The comments to CRPC 1-500 state that although a partnership agreement can contain a clause that would prohibit "a separate practice during the existence of the [partnership] relationship," once the partnership relationship is over, the lawyer "is free to practice law without any contractual restriction except in the case of retirement from the active practice of law."

A] Why do the rules contain such a restriction?

B] Comment 1 to ABA Model Rule 5.6 says that permitting such agreements would harm both lawyers and clients by limiting lawyers' "professional autonomy" and limiting "the freedom of clients to choose a lawyer."

**Discussion Problem 6**

A] Problem 6 involves the settlement of a legal malpractice claim against attorney Atkins. Atkins agreed to take a case that was outside his area of expertise, and then messed up. Atkins has agreed to reimburse client Chamberlain for the $60,000 judgment and the legal fees incurred, but Chamberlain is also demanding that Atkins stay within his traditional area of expertise for two years so that the same problem won't happen to someone else. Is this type of demand covered by any of the ABA Model Rules?

B] Yes. ABA Model Rule 5.6(b) seems expressly to prohibit this type of agreement because it would contain "a restriction on the lawyer's right to practice" as "part of the settlement of a client controversy." [*Accord* CRPC 1-500.]

C] I've heard that this provision often comes up in situations where a client, in connection with a settlement, is demanding that a lawyer suspend his practice of law for a period of time, or agree not to represent particular individuals or entities. [*See also* ABA Model Rule 5.6, comment 2, and comments to CRPC 1-500.] So this prohibition would reach to a number of different situations.

## GENERAL DYNAMICS CORP. v. SUPERIOR COURT
### Supreme Court of California, 1994

Facts: General Dynamics employed Rose, an attorney, for fourteen years. Rose was in line for a promotion to division vice-president and general counsel when he was abruptly fired. General Dynamics claimed that Rose was fired due to a loss of confidence in Rose to adequately and zealously represent its interests. Rose claimed that the real reasons included his spearheading of an investigation into widespread drug use in the Pomona plant; his protest regarding the company's failure to investigate the "bugging" of the office of the chief of security, and his advisement to company officials that a particular salary policy might violate the federal Fair Labor Standards Act.

Rose sued General Dynamics for wrongful termination. Rose based his claim on two main theories. First, Ross contended that through its acts and assurances, General Dynamics impliedly represented to him that he would only be fired for "good cause" (implied-in-fact contract claim). Second, Ross contended that the real reasons he was fired violated fundamental public policy (public policy tort claim). General Dynamics filed a general demurrer, asserting that Rose failed to state a claim for relief. The company contended that since Rose had been employed as an attorney, he was subject to discharge at any time, "for any reason or no reason." The trial court overruled the demurrer and the Court of Appeal refused General Dynamics' petition for a writ of mandate, saying that the complaint, including both theories of relief, was sufficient to survive a general demurrer.

Issue: Does an attorney's position as in-house counsel bar the attorney from asserting implied-in-fact contract and discharge tort claims against the employer since those claims are more commonly the subject of suits asserted by non-attorney employees?

Holding: No. An attorney's position within a company does not preclude that attorney from bringing a retaliatory discharge claim, provided the claim can be established without breaching attorney-client privilege or "unduly endangering the values lying at the heart of the professional relationship."

Discussion: Rose did not challenge General Dynamics' right to terminate a legal department employee, but rather asserted that there was a cost to be paid for such action in these circumstances. Allowing the client's right of discharge to be used without consequences in all situations could produce "unconscionable results." California law has never specifically allowed a company to fire in-house counsel without liability of any sort.

In this situation, a reasonable expectation that the plaintiff-lawyer would not be terminated without good cause existed. Consequently General Dynamics had to honor its antecedent contractual obligations to fire only for good cause. However, the employer still has ways to limit liability because the employer is allowed wide latitude in determining what constitutes good cause for discharge. Plaintiff can pursue a wrongful discharge claim although a judgment ordering his reinstatement is not an available remedy.

The position of the in-house counsel differs greatly from that of the average outside attorney. First of all, the in-house counsel is economically dependent on his/her employer. Consequently, there are enormous pressures to conform to corporate goals even at the cost of ethical considerations.

Secondly, lawyers have dual allegiances, one to the interests and welfare of the client and the other to the code of professional ethics. In a corporate setting, those allegiances force a hard choice on the attorney. Even though attorneys are required to withdraw in certain situations, outside attorneys do not suffer the harm that in-house counsel do. So in-house counsel have, if anything, an even more powerful claim to judicial protection. Allowing the retaliatory discharge cause of action to exist in limited circumstances vindicates public policy and lessens the pressure on the attorney to silently conform.

In-house counsel should be allowed to pursue the same cause of action as non-attorney employees where non-attorney employees could do so and a statute or ethical rule provides an exception from the usual rule that client matters remain confidential. In the case of a mandatory ethical obligation, the plaintiff will most likely have a suitable cause of action. If the attorney's actions were merely ethically permissible, the court must answer two questions to see if an appropriate claim exists:

1. Would the employer's conduct give rise to a cause of action for retaliatory discharge for a non-attorney employee under *Gantt v. Sentry Insurance*, 1 Cal. 4th 1083, 4 Cal.Rptr.2d 874, 824 P.2d 680 (1992) (which states the plaintiff's actions must have a clearly established, fundamental public policy basis and the policy must be a public one)?

2. Does some statute or ethical rule specifically permit the attorney to depart from the usual requirement of confidentiality and engage in the "nonfiduciary" conduct for which he or she was terminated?

However, the plaintiff bears the burden of establishing the unequivocal requirements of the ethical norm at issue and that the employer's conduct was motivated by impermissible considerations under a "but for" standard of causation.

If the elements of retaliatory discharge cannot be established without breaching attorney-client privilege, the suit must be dismissed in the interest of preserving the privilege. The attorney-client privilege should not be diluted in context of in-house counsel and their corporate clients. But the extreme measure of dismissal will rarely if ever be appropriate at the demurrer stage of litigation.

## CHAPTER FOURTEEN
## JUDICIAL CONDUCT

### Judicial Ethics Bee

Obviously you can use the 62–question Judicial Ethics Bee questions for ordinary class discussion, or for individual study, but we hope you will consider using them to stir up some competitive enthusiasm among your students as they learn the 2007 CJC. Here are some suggestions for running a lively class discussion:

● Assign the 62 questions and the CJC reading at least a week in advance. Ask the students to work out their own answers and pencil them into their books.

● On the day of the competition, divide the students into two teams. A quick, visual way to divide them is to stretch and anchor a piece of string from the front to the back of your classroom. To kindle some team spirit, let each team pick a name for itself.

● All students compete with their books open, so they can use the answers they penciled in. The teams take turns answering questions. Within a team, the students take turns answering. Intra-team coaching is forbidden. Here's one way to keep score:

— If a student's yes–no answer is correct, and if she gives a satisfactory explanation for the answer, she wins two points for the team.

— If her yes–no answer is correct, but her explanation is not satisfactory, she wins one point for the team.

— If her yes–no answer is wrong, but her explanation is compelling, she wins one point for the team.

— If her yes–no answer is wrong, and her explanation is not compelling, she earns no points for the team.

● You have three jobs. The first is to read each question out loud, to refresh everybody's memory of what it asks. Take the questions in random order, not numerical order. That will focus the students' attention on the current question, not the one down the line that they will have to answer. Make a pencil mark beside each question you cover, so that you won't repeat a question.

● Your second job is to be the Decider. You must decide whether an explanation is satisfactory or compelling, and your decision must be absolutely final. (If you keep your sense of humor, you can get away with a surprising measure of arbitrary and capricious decision–making.)

● Your third job is to keep score accurately on the blackboard, or appoint a deputy to do it for you.

Here are our best efforts at devising correct answers for the 62 questions. We are re–printing the questions along with the answers, to avoid your having to juggle two books in the classroom.

1. The CJC's four Canons state "overarching principles of judicial ethics," and the various Rules prohibit or require specific kinds of conduct. If a judge's conduct offends a Canon but does not violate a Rule, is the judge *subject to discipline*? [*See* CJC, Scope ¶ 2.]

1. **No.** This point became important in the drafting of 2007 CJC, Canon 1, which requires a judge to avoid both impropriety and "the appearance of impropriety." Some people argued that the quoted words are satisfactory for an aspirational goal, but are too vague to be the basis of discipline. Others argued that the quoted words have a long history in earlier versions of the CJC and are therefore well enough established to be the basis of discipline. Ultimately the ABA House of Delegates approved CJC Rule 1.2, which authorizes discipline for a judge who fails to avoid "impropriety and the appearance of impropriety." Comment 4 states that the "test for appearance of impropriety" is whether "the conduct would create in reasonable minds a perception that the judge violated . . . [the CJC] or engaged in other conduct that reflects adversely on the judge's honesty, impartiality, temperament, or fitness to serve as a judge." In other words, don't be seen bending over in your neighbor's melon patch, even if only to tie your shoe.

2. The Comments in the CJC have two functions. First, they provide guidance on the purpose, meaning, and proper application of the various Rules. Second, they help explain the Rules and sometimes give examples

of conduct that is permitted or prohibited by a Rule. If a Comment says that judges "must" do X, can a judge be *subject to discipline* for failing to do X, even though the associated Rule doesn't specifically mention X? [*See* CJC, Scope ¶ 3.]

2. **Yes.** CJC, Scope ¶ 3 explains that the Comments "neither add to nor subtract from the binding obligations set forth in the Rules." If a Comment states that a judge "must" do X, that doesn't make the Comment itself mandatory. Rather, the Comment signifies that when the associated Rule is properly understood and applied, the Rule makes X mandatory. Thus, a judge who failed to do X would be *subject to discipline* for violating the Rule, not for violating the Comment.

3. While lawyer LB was litigating a case in Judge JT's court, LB committed a serious violation of the Rules of Professional Conduct. Judge JT learned of LB's violation from a trustworthy, non–confidential source. Judge JT considered reporting LB to the appropriate disciplinary authorities, but after careful deliberation, she decided not to. One of Judge JT's fellow judges found out about JT's failure to report LB, and that judge reported Judge JT to the Judicial Disciplinary Board. The Board investigated the matter and decided not to institute disciplinary proceedings against Judge JT. Was the Board's action *proper*? [*See* CJC, Scope ¶ 6 and Rule 2.15(B); ABA Model Rule 8.3, Comment 3.]

3. **Yes.** Judge JT had an ethical duty under CJC Rule 2.15(B) to report lawyer LB, but only if LB's misconduct raised a "substantial question" about LB's "honesty, trustworthiness, or fitness as a lawyer." Those qualifying phrases gave Judge JT a measure of judgment about whether to report LB. [*Cf.* ABA Model Rule 8.3, Comment 3.] Similarly, the Judicial Disciplinary Board had a measure of judgment about whether to pursue disciplinary proceedings against Judge JT. CJC, Scope ¶ 6 explains that not every violation of the CJC Rules will result in discipline:

> Whether discipline should be imposed should be determined through a reasonable and reasoned application of the Rules, and should depend upon factors such as the seriousness of the transgression, the facts and circumstances . . . , the extent of any pattern of improper activity, whether there have been previous violations, and the effect of the improper activity upon the judicial system or others.

4. Plaintiff PE sued his former employee DF for stealing PE's trade secrets. Judge JR failed to make timely rulings on PE's motions for a temporary restraining order and a preliminary injunction. Judge JR's delay caused PE to lose thousands of dollars. PE then sued Judge JR to recover his losses, alleging that JR's failure to make timely rulings was a tortious breach of judicial ethics. Does PE have a valid tort claim against Judge JR? [See CJC, Scope ¶ 7; Rule 2.5(A) and Comment 3.]

4. **No.** PE has no valid claim against Judge JR for two reasons. First, judges are generally immune from suit for tort claims based on their decisions and other conduct within the scope of their judicial duties. Second, even though a judge can be disciplined for failing to make timely decisions [CJC Rule 2.5(A) and Comment 3], the rules of judicial ethics are not intended to be a basis for criminal or civil liability. [CJC, Scope ¶ 3.]

5. CC is the Calendar Clerk of the Rosslyn County Trial Court, a position she has held for the past 28 years. Her employer is Rosslyn County, and her duties are to keep the court's calendar current and accurate. She does not perform any judicial functions, but every lawyer in the county knows that CC can make life difficult for lawyers who habitually forget court dates, fail to file papers on time, or the like. Can CC be *subject to discipline* under the CJC? [*See* CJC, Application I(B) and Rule 2.12(A).]

5. **No.** CC is not herself subject to professional discipline for violating the CJC, because she is not authorized to perform "judicial functions." [CJC, Application I(B).] Court officers who *do* perform judicial functions include justices of the peace, magistrates, court commissioners, special masters, referees, and (usually) administrative law judges. [*Id.*] But in one sense the CJC does constrain CC's conduct, because the judges who supervise her work must require her to "act in a manner consistent with" the judges' obligations under the CJC. [CJC Rule 2.12 (A).]

6. Retired Judge RJ is subject to recall, to serve as a trial judge when she is needed. When she is recalled, she is paid a generous *per diem* in addition to her ordinary retirement pay. As a judge subject to recall, she is not permitted to practice law. During a month in which she is certain not to be recalled as a trial judge, would it be *proper* for her to serve for pay as the mediator of a work–assignment dispute between two labor unions? [*See* CJC, Application II(A) and Rule 3.9.]

6. **Yes.** CJC Rule 3.9 prohibits full–time judges from serving as mediators or arbitrators (except as part of their judicial duties). But retired judges subject to recall are exempted from that rule [CJC, Application II(A)], and many retired judges work as mediators and arbitrators.

7. Judge JP is a continuing part–time judge who for many years has served roughly 10 weeks per year on the Lemon County Family Court. He has a continuing appointment, and he is called in whenever one of the regular judges becomes ill or goes on vacation. When he is not judging, he practices family law in neighboring Walnut County, where his office and home are located. *May* JP represent a woman who is seeking a divorce in the Lemon County Family Court? [*See* CJC, Application III(A)(2) and III(B).]

7. **No.** CJC, Application III(A)(2) permits a continuing part–time judge, such as JP, to practice law, but III(B) prohibits him from practicing in the court on which he serves.

8. Law professor LP serves sporadically as a pro tempore part–time judge on the Oregon Court of Medical Appeals, a court of limited jurisdiction that handles bioethics cases, medical malpractice cases, and other cases that turn on medical issues. When the court needs LP on a case, it appoints her separately to the panel that will hear that case. LP vehemently disagrees with the Florida Supreme Court's decision in a so–called "right to life" case, and she writes a hard–hitting op–ed piece for the New York Times, hoping to influence public opinion and to encourage the U.S. Supreme Court to grant certiorari and reverse the Florida decision. Is LP *subject to discipline*? [*See* CJC, Application V(A) and Rule 2.10(A).]

8. **No.** A pro tempore part–time judge is exempt from the ordinary rule that prohibits judges from making a "public statement that might reasonably be expected to affect the outcome . . . of a matter pending or impending in any court." [*See* CJC, Application V(A) and Rule 2.10(A).] What if LP were a *full–time* judge and wanted to publicly express her views on the Florida decision? Comment 1 to Rule 2.10 asserts that the limitation on judicial speech is "essential to the maintenance of the independence, integrity, and impartiality of the judiciary." Do you think that the rule can withstand a free-speech challenge under the First Amendment?

9. PL is a practicing lawyer who also serves on the board of directors of InterCorp, a large, publicly held telecommunications company. Last

month, PL was sworn in as an appointed member of the State Intermediate Court of Appeals. Will PL be *subject to discipline* if he does not immediately resign his InterCorp directorship? [*See* CJC, Application VI and Rule 3.11(B).]

9. **No.** PL need not resign *immediately.* CJC 3.11 prohibits a full–time judge from being a director of a publicly held corporation like InterCorp. Application VI and Comment 1 allow a new judge a *reasonable period* within which to comply with the rule, but not longer than one year.

10. Justice JZ sits on the State Supreme Court. To reduce their state and federal income tax burden, JZ and his wife knowingly and grossly overstated the fair market value of some property they donated to a charity. The Internal Revenue Service charged them with willful failure to pay income tax, a serious criminal offense. Eventually the IRS dismissed the case in return for full payment of all the taxes due, plus interest and a stiff penalty. Is JZ *subject to discipline*? [*See* CJC Rule 1.1, 1.2, and Comments 1–3.]

10. **Yes.** CJC Rule 1.1 requires judges to obey the law, and Rule 1.2 requires them to act at all times in a manner that promotes public confidence in the integrity of the judiciary. Willful failure to pay income tax is a fairly common ground for disciplining lawyers, and judges should not be held to any lesser standard of conduct.

11. The North Virginia Legal Assistance Corporation (NVLAC) is a tax–exempt, publicly chartered corporation that seeks charitable donations and in turn grants funds to locally operated Legal Aid offices. Those offices provide legal services to needy people in non–criminal matters. Justice JL sits on the North Virginia Circuit Court of Appeal. She allows her name and judicial title to be used on the letterhead that the NVLAC uses to solicit contributions from the public and memberships from lawyers. The Justice also makes speeches at bar association meetings, urging lawyers to become dues–paying members of NVLAC and to provide pro bono services. Finally, the Justice serves as an unpaid instructor in quarterly workshops that train lawyers how to do Legal Aid work. Are Justice JL's activities *proper*? [*See* CJC Rule 1.2, Comments 4 and 6; Rule 3.7(A), Comments 3 and 4; Rule 3.7(B), Comment 5.]

11. **Yes.** CJC Rule 1.2, Comment 4 encourages judges to participate in activities that promote "access to justice for all." Comment 6

says judges should participate in community outreach activities to promote public understanding of and confidence in the administration of justice. Rule 3.7(A)(3) allows judges to solicit dues-paying memberships for law–related organizations, and Rule 3.7(A)(4) allows judges to speak at a fund–raising event for such an organization. Rule 3.7(B) allows judges to encourage lawyers to do pro bono legal work, and Comment 5 allows judges to train lawyers for such work.

12. On her way to work one morning, Superior Court Judge JE was stopped by a State Highway Patrol Officer for driving her little red sports car 83 miles per hour through a 45 mph construction zone. The officer gave JE a $400 speeding ticket. In response, JE ordered the officer to appear at 10 a.m. the following day in her courtroom. The officer appeared as ordered, in uniform and wearing his service pistol on his belt. JE ordered him to place his pistol on her bench. She picked it up and pointed it at the officer's mid–section, saying that: "Officer, the next time you see my car on your little piece of highway, think carefully about this moment." With that, she handed the pistol back and dismissed him. She later paid the speeding ticket on time and without complaint. Is JE *subject to discipline*? [*See* CJC Rules 1.2 and 1.3, Comment 1.]

12. **Yes.** CJC Rule 1.2 requires judges to act in a manner that promotes public confidence in the independence, integrity, and impartiality of the judiciary. They must also avoid impropriety and the appearance of impropriety. Rule 1.3 prohibits judges from abusing the prestige of the judicial office to advance their personal or economic interests. Rule 1.3, Comment 1 offers as an example a judge who alludes to his judicial status to gain "favorable treatment in encounters with traffic officials."

13. After graduating from law school, LG served for a year as law clerk to State Supreme Court Justice JJ. When LG started looking for a law firm job, Justice JJ volunteered to write recommendation letters for her. Using Supreme Court stationery, stamps, and secretarial services, JJ wrote letters to a dozen top law firms, enthusiastically recommending LG as "among the best two or three law clerks I have ever had." Is Justice JJ *subject to discipline*? [*See* CJC Rule 1.3, Comment 2.]

13. **No.** CJC 1.3 prohibits judges from using the prestige of the judicial office to advance the personal or economic interests of themselves or others, but Comment 2 allows a judge to use official stationery to write recommendations letters based on personal knowledge if there is no

likelihood that the recipients will misinterpret them as an attempt to exert undue pressure of the judicial office. Justice JJ's use of the court's stamps and secretarial service was also proper; everyone in the legal profession understands that recommendation letters for clerks and former clerks are a routine part of a justice's job.

14. Judge JW wrote a thinly disguised "novel" based on an infamous murder committed by a Hollywood film star. Earlier JW had presided at the film star's jury trial, which resulted in a publicly unpopular acquittal. In JW's novel, the wise trial judge permitted the prosecutor to use some evidence that JW had excluded from the real trial, and the fictional jury came back with a conviction. The book publisher heavily advertised the novel as having been written by "Trial Judge JW, The Man Who Knows the Truth." Is JW *subject to discipline*? [*See* CJC Rule 1.3, Comment 4; *see also* Rule 1.2.]

14. **Yes.** Judge JW is subject to discipline for allowing the book publisher to tout JW's position as trial judge to sell books, which produces royalties for JW and profits for the publisher. [*See* CJC Rule 1.3, Comment 4.] Moreover, JW probably shouldn't have written the book in the first place, because it could lead to public distrust of the legal system in general and jury verdicts in particular. [*See* CJC Rule 1.2.]

15. Justice JU is serving her third term as an elected State Appellate Court Justice. She lives with her aged parents, who are both in the mid–stages of Alzheimer's disease. They require full–time, watchful care, and thus far they have vigorously resisted JU's efforts to obtain outside help or to place them in an appropriate care facility. Justice JU attempts to do her reading, legal research, and opinion writing at home, but she finds it hard to concentrate, and she is frequently unavailable to come to the court for conferences and oral arguments. Will Justice JU be *subject to discipline* if she does not either resign or make other arrangements for the care of her parents? [*See* CJC Rule 2.1.]

15. **Yes.** CJC Rule 2.1 says that a judge's judicial duties must take precedence over all personal and extra judicial activities. If Justice JU wants to avoid discipline, she must either get other care for her parents or resign her judicial position.

16. Administrative Law Judge JA came to the United States from his native country as a penniless immigrant 38 years ago. He learned to speak fluent

English, earned a law degree, and now sits on the Social Welfare Appeals Court. Judge JA has an unshakeable faith in the ability of immigrants from his native country to make their own way in the U.S. through hard work and frugal living. Without exception, whenever JA hears a welfare appeal involving an immigrant from his native country, he rules against the immigrant and delivers a little lecture on his own life story. Is Judge JA's conduct *proper*? [*See* CJC Rule 2.2, Comments 1 and 2; Rule 2.3(B); Rule 2.11(A)(1); *see also* CJC, Application I(B) and n.1.]

16. **No.** At the outset, you should assume that administrative law judges *are* governed by the CJC, unless the state in question has excluded them from coverage. [*See* CJC, Application I(B) and n. 1.] CJC Rule 2.2 requires judges to uphold the law and to judge fairly and impartially. Comment 1 requires judges to be fair and impartial to all parties and to be objective and open-minded. Comment 2 recognizes that each judge comes to the bench with a unique background and philosophy, but it requires all judges to interpret and apply the law whether or not they personally approve of it. Here JA has apparently prejudged the welfare appeals of immigrants from his native country. [*See* CJC Rule 2.3(B).] He should disqualify himself from hearing such cases [CJC Rule 2.11(A) and (A)(1)], and if he does not, he is subject to discipline under Rule 2.2 and 2.11.

17. Despite his advanced age, crumbling countenance, and perpetual halitosis, Appeals Court Justice JK regards himself as uncommonly attractive to women, especially young ones. In hiring law clerks, JK invariably selects young women, and in dealing with them he is always oleaginously attentive. He buys them little presents, compliments their hair, brings them flowers from his garden, pats them on the knee, and never requires them to work to capacity. In return, he expects them to fetch him coffee, run personal errands, accompany him to the occasional movie, and listen to his ancient jokes about traveling salesmen and farmers' daughters. Surely JK is an oily old creep, but is he *subject to discipline*? [*See* CJC Rule 2.3(A), (B), and Comments 2–4.]

17. **Yes.** Justice JK is subject to discipline for sexual harassment. [*See* CJC Rule 2.3(B) and Comments 3 and 4.] The most obvious indicators are the pats on the knee, the movies, and the jokes.

18. Judge JH is assigned to handle the bail hearing in a street–gang murder case against gang leader GL. JH received an anonymous telephone call, telling him to free GL on bail or else "prepare to find your precious

sixth–grader dead and floating in the river." The police could not find the source of the call, and they could not guarantee the safety of JH or his sixth–grader. JH was so unnerved that he felt he could not rule fairly on GL's motion to set bail, and the Chief Judge urged JH to recuse himself and let a different judge handle the bail hearing. JH reluctantly recused himself. Was JH's recusal *proper*? [*See* CJC Rule 2.4(B); Rule 2.7; and Rule 2.11(A)(1).]

18. **Yes.** The telephone call put JH in an untenable position. He didn't want to capitulate to the illegal threat, nor shirk his duty to rule on difficult matters, but he felt that he could not rule fairly on GL's motion for bail. In those circumstances, his least odious choice was to follow the Chief Judge's advice and recuse himself. [*Compare* CJC Rule 2.7 and Comment 1 *with* Rule 2.11(A)(1).]

19. This morning Judge JD's courtroom is overflowing with angry citizens who have come to hear JD rule on the habeas corpus petition of ST, an alleged terrorist who has been confined without a hearing for four years in a Navy brig in JD's judicial district. The bailiffs cannot stop the angry citizens from shouting and stamping their feet, so JD asks the local police to eject them from the courtroom, which the police do with dispatch. Is JD's action *proper*? [*See* CJC Rules 2.4 and 2.11(A)(1).]

19. **Yes.** A judge must not be swayed by public clamor or fear of criticism [CJC Rule 2.4(A)], and a judge must require order and decorum in proceedings before the court. [CJC Rule 2.8(A).] A criminal defendant's Sixth Amendment right to a public trial is not implicated in this habeas corpus proceeding; even if it were, the judge could properly eject people who were disrupting the proceedings.

20. Court Commissioner CC performs judicial functions in the Labor Relations Court of First Instance. CC's late father was a respected union leader, and CC's siblings are all members of various labor unions. CC's younger brother, Benny, often tells other union members things like this: "Hey, don't worry about it—if you end up in court, my brother CC will take care of it." CC had admonished Benny not to say such things, but CC knows that Benny does it anyway. Is CC *subject to discipline*? [*See* CJC, Application I(B); CJC Rule 2.4().]

20. **Yes.** As a Court Commissioner who performs judicial functions, CC is subject to the CJC. [CJC, Application I (B).] CJC Rule

2.4(C) says that a judge must not "convey or permit others to convey the impression that any person or organization is in a position to influence the judge." The CJC doesn't explain what a judge is supposed to do to muzzle a brother like Benny, but a good starting point might be for CC to seriously and patiently explain to Benny how CC could get in trouble if Benny continues to make inappropriate statements.

21. Justice JQ sits on the State Court of Criminal Appeals (CCA), which in this state is the highest appellate court for criminal matters. The CCA's own Rule of Court 400–4 requires each Justice to *personally* read and prepare bench briefs for a pro rata share of the Petitions for Discretionary Review that the court receives every month. Justice JQ thinks that rule is foolish and that the Justices should have their law clerks read the petitions and prepare the bench briefs, to free up the Justices for more demanding work. JQ's efforts to get the rule changed have been in vain, so he simply refuses to follow it—his share of the petition work is done by his law clerks, and they do it quite well. Is JQ's conduct *proper*? [*See* CJC Rule 2.5(A) and (B).]

21. **No.** Justice JQ is *subject to discipline* for his refusal to follow the local court rule. CJC Rule 2.5(A) requires a judge to perform both his judicial and his *administrative* duties competently and diligently, and 2.5(B) requires a judge to "cooperate with other judges and court officials in the administration of court business." Apparently JQ has not convinced the other Justices to change the disputed rule of court. Until he does convince them, he must obey the rule.

22. State Supreme Court Justice JN used to be one of the two or three best judges on the high court, and she is still excellent during the morning hours. After lunch, however, she has become alternately belligerent and somnambulant, which some court observers attribute to the amount of alcohol she drinks with lunch. She is frequently late in returning from the noon hour, which prevents the court from resuming on time. Some afternoons she flies into a rage when one of the arguing lawyers cannot satisfactorily answer her questions. Other afternoons she goes quietly to sleep during the oral arguments. Is JN *subject to discipline*? [*See* CJC Rule 2.5.]

22. **Yes.** CJC Rule 2.5 requires a judge to be competent and diligent. At a minimum, that includes staying awake during oral argument, not belittling the arguing lawyers, getting back from lunch on time, and

exhibiting basic courtesy to her fellow judges, to counsel, and to the parties.

23. For many years Judge JG has been the only judge assigned to the Law and Motion calendar in Centertown, the commercial and population hub of the state. JG wrote the state's leading treatise on pre–trial civil procedure, the topic that controls most law and motion issues. The book publisher advertises the treatise with cartoons that depict angry clients berating their dull–eyed lawyers with statements like this: "My *next* lawyer will look in Judge JG's book!" When the State Commission on Judicial Performance inquired about the advertising, JG responded that he just writes the treatise, and the advertising is up to the publisher. Is JG's *position* proper? [*See* CJC Rule 1.3, Comment 4.]

23. **No.** The cartoons play on lawyers' fear that they will lose on law and motion day if they don't align their arguments with the judge's treatise. When Judge JG contracts with his publisher, he should retain enough control over the treatise advertising to make sure that it doesn't exploit JG's judicial position. [CJC Rule 1.3, Comment 4.]

24. Judge JY prides herself in keeping her trial calendar current by insisting that the parties do everything possible to settle their differences before resorting to trial. At the final pre–trial conference, she almost always tells the parties and their lawyers something like this: "All of you are being unreasonable babies. I want you to settle this case this afternoon, and none of us will go home tonight until you get it done." She puts the plaintiffs in one room and the defendants in another room, and then she moves from one room to the other, carrying settlement offers, debunking legal arguments, threatening stubborn clients, humiliating self–important counsel, and finally bringing the sides together with a settlement agreement. Is Judge JY's conduct *proper*? [*See* CJC Rule 2.6(B) and Comment 2.]

24. **No.** Judge JY's approach may be perfect for some cases, but the question suggests that she almost always uses that approach, and it is likely to be too heavy–handed for many cases and litigants. CJC Rule 2.6(B) advises judges that in seeking to settle cases, they must not coerce any party into settlement, and Comment 2 includes a useful list of factors judges should consider when picking an approach to settlement.

25. Judge JJ is taking her two–year turn in Small Claims Court, where litigants represent themselves in civil matters valued at $5,000 or less.

Behind JJ's back, her fellow judges call her Saint Jean, because she is endlessly patient with every litigant who appears in her court, no matter how ineptly they present their case, and no matter how foolish their contentions. JJ listens serenely to shameless liars, hallucinating addicts, and selfish quibblers, giving each of them equal and undivided attention. According to the court's statistical records, JJ is not handling as many small claims cases as other judges have in the past. On the other hand, in litigant surveys, the litigants who appear in her court rate her "outstanding" in both "fairness" and "ability." Is JJ *subject to discipline*? [*See* CJC Rule 2.5 and Rule 2.8(B).]

    25. **No.** Judges are human, and humans are not uniform in their strengths and weaknesses. Apparently Judge JJ is strong in the virtues described in CJC Rule 2.8(B) (patience, dignity, and courtesy), but not strong in processing cases, as described in CJC Rule 2.5 (promptness and efficiency in handling the court's caseload). Many citizens' only experience with the judicial system comes from appearing in small claims court. Would we prefer to have our judges known for their efficiency, rather than their fairness?

26. Next November, Judge JT will be running in a contested election to retain his seat on the Superior Court bench. Five other judges sit on JT's court. The court clerk assigns cases randomly, by drawing judges' names from an old tin can. The clerk draws JT's name and assigns him *Dinsmore v. Unified School District*, in which an outspoken atheist is suing the local school board to stop the teaching of Intelligent Design as an "alternative theory" to Darwinian evolution. JT has no personal convictions about how the world began, but he does know that 68% of the voters in his district are fundamentalist Christians who believe in the literal truth of the Bible. *May* JT disqualify himself from hearing the case for the honest reason that he does not want to become embroiled in this kind of case so close to the election? [*See* CJC Rule 2.7 and Comment 1.]

    26. **No.** None of the proper grounds for disqualification listed in CJC Rule 2.11 appear to apply in this situation. Therefore JT must hear the case for the reason explained in Comment 1 to CJC Rule 2.7—a judge can't use disqualification to duck difficult cases.

27. District Attorney DA is the elected criminal prosecutor in Judge JE's court. The citizens keep electing DA, term after term, because of the tough–guy cowboy image he conveys. DA always wears a big cowboy hat,

expensive boots, and Levi jeans with a rodeo belt buckle as big as a coffee saucer. In the courtroom, DA struts and swaggers, berating witnesses, pandering to jurors, and browbeating hapless defendants. Judge JE occasionally tries to moderate DA's antics, but mostly she just lets him perform. Is Judge JE *subject to discipline*? [*See* CJC Rule 2.8(B).]

27. **Yes.** CJC 2.8(B) requires a judge to be "patient, dignified, and courteous" to everyone who works in or appears in her court. Likewise, judges must require the same kind of behavior from the lawyers, staff, and court officials who are subject to their direction and control. [*Id.*] DA's cowboy costume is probably beyond JE's control, but she should make him sit at counsel table rather than strut and swagger around the courtroom, and she is subject to discipline if she continues to tolerate DA's misbehavior toward witnesses, jurors, and defendants.

28. Judge JS sat as the trier–of–fact in a breach of contract case involving the sale of a race horse named Sassy Sue. One evening during the trial, JS attended a cocktail party where he overheard some well–dressed strangers chatting and laughing about the Sassy Sue case. JS pricked up his ears and heard one of them say: "I don't blame the buyer for backing out of that sale—any decent vet could see that Sassy Sue is prone to shin splints." The next morning when the seller was on the witness stand, Judge JS posed his own line of questions about Sassy Sue and shin splints. Those questions turned out to be the most critical ones in the whole case. JS did not tell the litigants what he had overheard at the cocktail party. Was JS's conduct *proper*? [*See* CJC Rule 2.9(A) and (B).]

28. **No.** Judge JS should not have pricked up his ears at the cocktail party; he should have walked away, so as not to overhear stray information about the case. [*See* CJC Rule 2.9(A).] Moreover, even if JS *inadvertently* overheard the shin splint conversation, he should have told the litigants what he heard and should have given them a chance to respond. [*Id.* Rule 2.9(B).]

29. The Chief Judge assigned trial judge JT to hear a complex pension law case involving the Employee Retirement Income Security Act (ERISA). Because JT didn't know the first thing about pension law, he bought and carefully studied the best legal treatise in the field. Then JT contacted one of the treatise authors, Professor BW, and arranged to get BW's help on difficult ERISA questions. Finally, whenever such a question arose during the case, JT telephoned BW, who helped JT work out the right answer. JT

did not tell the litigants about the help he got from BW, but when they did find out later, they were pleased about the extra effort JT put into their case. Is JT *subject to discipline*? [*See* CJC Rule 2.9(A)(2).]

29. **Yes.** CJC Rule 2.9(A)(2) is specific about what a judge must do if he wants to get an outside expert's help on the law that applies to a case. First, the judge must give the parties *advance notice* of the subject and the person consulted. Second, the judge must give the parties a chance to object. Third, the judge must give the parties a further chance to respond to advice the judge gets from the outside expert. Judge JT didn't do any of those things, so he is *subject to discipline.*

30. Judge JZ is newly appointed to the bench and does not yet fully trust his judicial instincts. Whenever he is bothered by an issue of fairness or equitable application of the law, he talks it through with JV, the most senior member of JZ's court. These conversations frequently result in JZ changing his mind about the issue at hand. Is JZ's conduct *proper*? [*See* CJC Rule 2.9(A)(3).]

30. **Yes.** CJC Rule 2.9(A)(3) permits a judge to consult other judges about a pending matter. In doing so, the judge must make reasonable efforts to avoid hearing facts that are not in the record, and of course the judge must still take personal responsibility to decide the matter.

31. The court on which Judge JW and Judge JQ sit is located near many communication technology and biological technology companies. As a result, much of their court's business involves those fields of science. Whenever JW sits as trier–of–fact in such a case, he researches the scientific issues thoroughly, using both his computer and the nearby university's science library. Whenever JQ presides in a case that involves difficult questions of law, she doesn't limit herself to the lawyers' briefs to find out what the law is. Rather, she does her own legal research, using both her computer and the nearby university's law library. Are both JW's and JQ's actions *proper*? [*See* CJC 2.9(C).]

31. **No.** Judge JQ's personal research is proper, but Judge JW's is not. *See* CJC Rule 2.9(C), which prohibits judges from doing their own research on issues of fact. Judges are allowed to consider only evidence in the record plus facts that can be judicially noticed (such as facts of common knowledge, and facts that can be indisputably established from unquestionably accurate sources). In contrast, judges have traditionally

been allowed to do their own legal research, based perhaps on the fiction that all judges and lawyers are well trained as experts in finding out what the law is. Another explanation may be that the appellate courts can more easily discover and correct a judge's mistake of law than a judge's mistake of fact.

32. Lawyer LL filed a complaint on behalf of Friends of the Birds to enjoin developer Knoxous Korp. from buying and building on a certain 500 acre parcel of virgin wetlands. One day later, before Knoxous was even served with the complaint, LL showed up at the chambers of Judge JR with a petition for an immediate temporary restraining order that would stop Knoxous for 21 days from closing the land purchase transaction. Nobody was present on behalf of Knoxous, but Judge JR invited LL into his chambers, glanced over the petition, and—without hearing anything from LL—denied the petition without prejudice to later renewal, on the ground that he could not grant the petition ex parte without giving Friends of the Birds a tactical advantage over Knoxous. Was Judge JR's action *proper*? [*See* CJC Rule 2.9(A)(1).]

32. **Yes.** Local court rules typically allow ex parte communications in emergency situations, including a request for a TRO that will preserve the status quo until all parties can be present. However, CJC Rule 2.9(A)(1) forbids ex parte communications that will give a tactical advantage to one side or the other. If Judge JR were to grant LL's petition for a 21 day TRO, the developer's land purchase might fall through, which would give Friends of the Birds a huge tactical advantage, and maybe even give them the ultimate relief their suit seeks. Judges are understandably loath to use their equity powers in that manner.

33. Judge JE was presiding at criminal defendant CD's jury trial for drug dealing. CD was defended by a court–appointed defense lawyer who seemed more intent on augmenting his hourly fee (paid from the public purse) than on effectively defending CD. The prosecution relied heavily on testimony from three shifty–eyed witnesses, and CD's lawyer offered no character evidence to attack their credibility. When JE got home, he did a bit of Internet research and discovered that each of the three shifty–eyed witnesses had multiple convictions for crimes involving dishonesty or false statement—convictions that the defense could have used for impeachment. After careful thought, JE decided not to interfere with CD's lawyer's handling of the case. The jury found the defendant guilty as charged, but the following day JE granted the defendant's motion for a new trial based

on incompetence of defense counsel. JE based his decision, in part, on the defense counsel's failure to impeach the three shifty–eyed witnesses. Were JE's actions *proper*? [*See* CJC Rule 2.9(C).]

33. **No.** CJC Rule 2.9(C) and Comment 6 forbid judges to do their own fact investigating, including fact investigating on the Internet. A witness's credibility is a question of fact, a question to be decided by the jury. Trial judges generally try not to interfere with a trial lawyer's tactical decisions, and that is probably why JE decided not to second–guess the defense lawyer during the trial. JE's granting of the new trial motion produced a just result in this case, but JE should not have done his own fact investigation, no matter the just result.

34. Crescent Corp., the world's richest oil company, made a hostile tender offer for shares of USA Petro, the largest U.S. producer of crude oil. The Antitrust Division of the U.S. Department of Justice sued Crescent, alleging that the tender offer was part of a plan to monopolize the global oil business. While the government's motion for a preliminary injunction was pending before a federal district judge, United States Supreme Court Justice JM appeared on television for an interview about the architecture of the beautiful white–marble building that houses the Court. The interviewer surprised him with a pointed question about the preliminary injunction motion in the Crescent antitrust case, and Justice JM blurted out the following response: "No federal judge could be dumb enough to deny a preliminary injunction in that case." *May* a judge make such a comment in a public forum? [*See* CJC Rule 2.10(A); *see also Republican Party of Minnesota v. White*, 536 U.S. 765, 122 S.Ct. 2528, 153 L.Ed.2d 694 (2002), noted in the text.]

34. **No.** The CJC does not officially bind the U.S. Supreme Court Justices, but it is nevertheless persuasive authority when they seek ethical guidance. CJC Rule 2.10(A) forbids a judge to make any public statement "that might reasonably be expected to affect the outcome or impair the fairness of a matter pending or impending in any court . . . ." The government's preliminary injunction motion will essentially determine the outcome of the whole case, because if the federal district court enjoins the tender offer, Crescent's proposed deal will almost certainly fall apart. Further, the federal district judge will be exercising the equity powers of a chancellor, and he will be acting all by himself, under time pressure, with billions of dollars at stake. In those circumstances, Justice JM's blunt

response to the interviewer's question seems likely to affect the district judge's decision.

35. Lawyer LC was a candidate for an appellate court judgeship in a contested election. During the campaign season, a radio reporter asked LC whether, if elected, she would vote to uphold the constitutionality of a physician–assisted suicide statute that the state legislature recently enacted. LC replied: "I don't know how I would vote, because that would depend on the procedural posture of the case and the precise legal issue before the court, but I can tell you what general legal principles would guide me. First, I think the individual states are the appropriate units of government to deal with issues of health care, including end–of–life decisions. Second, I think people have an inherent right of privacy, which is protected by our state constitution, and perhaps also by the federal constitution. Third, I think that, absent constitutional constraints, the will of the people, expressed through their legislators, should govern." Was LC's response *proper*? [*See* CJC Rule 2.10(B) and Rule 4.1(A)(13) and Comment 13.]

35. **Yes.** CJC Rule 2.10(B) and Rule 4.1(A)(13) forbid judges and judicial candidates from making promises that are inconsistent with an open mind on issues that are likely to come before their court. Thus it would be improper for a judge or candidate to say: "I believe that physician–assisted suicide, under the safeguards provided by our legislature, is part of every person's constitutional right to be let alone, free from interference by the government, and that belief will guide me in whatever physician–assisted suicide cases come before me." Lawyer LC's response to the radio reporter was proper, because he expressed the basic legal principles that would guide his thinking, without saying how he would resolve a particular case. That's roughly the same approach Chief Justice Roberts and Justices Alito, Bryer, and Ginsburg took on various issues in their Senate confirmation hearings.

36. A jury of his peers convicted arson defendant AD on seven separate counts of arson, each of which involved the burning of a family residence while the family was asleep inside. At the end of the trial, after the sentencing, the post–trial motions, and the housekeeping details had been disposed of, trial judge JS turned to the jury and said: "Before I excuse you, ladies and gentlemen of the jury, I want to commend you for your hard work, for your patience in grappling with some difficult expert testimony, for your sympathetic concern for the victim witnesses, and for the wisdom demonstrated in your guilty verdicts. I am proud of you, and your

community is proud of you, for a job well done. Now, ladies and gentlemen, you are excused." Is JS *subject to discipline* for that little speech? [*See* CJC Rule 2.8(C) and Comment 2.]

36. **Yes**. CJC Rule 2.8(C) forbids a judge from commending or criticizing jurors for their verdict, other than in a court order or judicial opinion. Comment 2 to the rule explains that the judge's approval or disapproval may "imply a judicial expectation in future cases," and "may impair a juror's ability to be fair and impartial in a subsequent case."

37. Trial judge JI disqualified himself from presiding at the trade libel trial of P Inc. v. D Corp., because JI was one of P Inc.'s lawyers in the early stages of the case. The case then passed to trial judge JG. Because JG had never handled a trade libel case before, he cornered JI in the judges' lunch room one day and asked her for a little lecture on the applicable law and on the facts and personalities involved in the case. JI politely declined to talk about the case with JG. Was JI's action *proper*? [*See* CJC 2.9(A)(3) and Comment 5.]

37. **Yes.** One judge may consult another judge about a pending matter if both are careful not to transmit fact information that is not in the record, and if conversation doesn't lead the consulting judge to shirk responsibility for personally deciding the case. [CJC Rule 2.9(A)(3)] But Comment 5 to the rule says that a judge must not have ex parte discussions with a judge who is disqualified from hearing the matter. Comment 5 should be read as an *exception* to Rule 2.9(A)(3) [*see* CJC, Scope ¶ 3], thus making JG subject to discipline if he had discussed the case with JI. Therefore, JI did JG a favor by refusing to discuss the case with him.

38. For many years before her appointment to the bench, lawyer LM was a business litigator. She usually defended large corporations in securities, antitrust, intellectual property, and contract cases, and she usually won. Over the years, she developed a deep loathing for attorney AS, who often represented her opponents. LM regards AS as dishonest, lazy, unethical, and ignorant. The very sight of him gags her with disgust. Whenever AS shows up as counsel in a case assigned to her, LM gets the urge to disqualify herself. *May* she do so? [*See* CJC Rule 2.11(A)(1).]

38. **Yes**. CJC Rule 2.11(A)(1) not only permits but *requires* LM to disqualify herself when she has a personal bias or prejudice against a party's lawyer.

39. Trial judge JO lives with and has an intimate relationship with his domestic partner DP, who is a news anchor for a local television station. DP has a married sister whose husband is the sole owner and operator of a dry–cleaning shop. The State Environmental Protection Agency has sued the husband to enjoin him from pouring toxic dry–cleaning chemicals down the storm sewer behind his shop. If the case is assigned to JO, would it be *proper* for him not to disqualify himself? [*See* CJC 2.11(A)(2)(a) and (c).]

39. **No.** CJC Rule 2.11(A)(2)(a) requires JO to disqualify himself. The disqualifying relationship traces out like this: JO's domestic partner DP is a disqualifying person, the same as a spouse would be. DP's sister is related to DP within the "third degree of relationship." [*See* the definition of that term in the CJC Terminology section.] DP's sister's husband is the spouse of a disqualifying person, and therefore JO must disqualify himself.

40. Appellate Justice JC is married to HC, the wealthy owner of a wide variety of businesses. One of HC's businesses is AmeriNet, a re–insurance company that insures other insurance companies against extraordinary losses due to natural disasters. Justice JC takes care not to learn the nature of extent of HC's business holdings, so as to insulate herself from possible bias in her role on the appellate court. *May* JC sit on the appellate panel that hears AmeriNet's appeal from a multi–billion dollar judgment in a case arising out of recent tornadoes in the Midwest? [*See* CJC Rule 2.11(A)(2)(c) and (A)(3); Rule 2.11(B).]

40. **No.** CJC Rule 2.11(B) requires a judge to make reasonable efforts to keep informed about her spouse's economic interests, so that she will know when she needs to disqualify herself. HC's ownership interest in AmeriNet will disqualify JC under either CJC Rule 2.11(A)(2)(a) or (c) or (A)(3). Therefore, JC ought to disqualify herself from sitting on the appellate panel.

41. Before State Supreme Court Justice JB took his present position, he was the elected Attorney General of the state. As Attorney General, he participated personally and substantially in writing Attorney General's Opinion 179, which takes the position that the state's current procedure for administering lethal injections in capital cases does not violate the state or federal constitutions. *May* Justice JB participate when his court decides a condemned man's challenge to the lethal injection procedure under the cruel and unusual punishment clauses of the state and federal constitutions? [*See* CJC Rule 2.11(A)(6)(b).]

41. **No.** Justice JB's personal and substantial role in the Attorney General's Opinion will disqualify him from sitting as judge in the condemned man's challenge to the constitutionality of the lethal injection procedures. [*See* CJC Rule 2.11(A)(6)(b).]

42. Trial judge JX owns 15 shares of common stock in Consolidated Gold Holdings, Inc. JX inherited the stock when his grandfather died, some 30 years ago. The stock trades in the $3 to $5 range. Consolidated is either wealthy or worthless, depending on whether gold is found someday in Consolidated's California mines. Consolidated employee Clem Whittle sued Consolidated for back injuries he claims to have suffered when he fell off a stool in Consolidated's employee lunch room. JX is assigned to be the trial judge in *Whittle v. Consolidated.* Would it be *proper* for JX not to tell counsel about his 15 shares of Consolidated, provided that JX truly believes that the stock ownership is clearly not disqualifying? [*See* CJC Rule 2.11(A)(2)(c) and (A)(3) and Comment 5.]

42. **No.** Justice JX should disclose his ownership of the Consolidated stock, even though he believes that it is not grounds for disqualification. [CJC Rule 2.11, Comment 5.] However, JX is probably right about the lack of grounds for disqualification. The stock is worth somewhere between $45 to $60, which seems de minimis. [*See* CJC Rule 2.11(A)(2)(c) and (A)(3); *see also* CJC, Terminology.] Moreover, JX's financial interest in the company is not likely to be significantly affected by whether the company has to pay Clem Whittle for his lunch room tumble.

43. Judge JA presided and served as trier–of–fact in *PL v. DF*. The critical issue was whether a particular stop sign was obscured from DF's line of sight by the trunk of an ancient oak tree. Unfortunately neither counsel offered satisfactory evidence on that issue. Before the trial ended, JA asked her law clerk to drive out to the intersection in question, stop half–a–block southeast, and determine whether he could see the stop sign despite the oak tree. The clerk reported that the sign was clearly visible, and JA decided the case accordingly. Were JA's actions *proper*? [*See* CJC Rule 2.9(C) and Rule 2.12(A).]

43. **No.** CJC Rule 2.9(C) would make judge JA *subject to discipline* if she had gone out to the intersection herself, because judges must not do their own fact investigating. Here JA is *subject to discipline* for sending her law clerk out to do something that she herself could not ethically do. [*See* CJC Rule 2.12(A).]

44. During Judge JJ's public election campaign, lawyer LY's husband contributed $1,000 to JJ's election campaign committee. [In this state, the judicial ethics code says that a contribution above $1,500 will result in the judge's disqualification from matters involving the donor.] JJ took pains not to learn the names of his campaign contributors. Six months later, JJ selected LY from among several qualified candidates to be the Special Master in some complicated patent cases. Special Masters in patent cases are very well compensated in this state. JJ selected LY because of her fine reputation among patent lawyers. Is JJ *subject to discipline*? [*See* CJC Rule 2.13.]

44. **No**. JJ picked LY based on merit, not based on favoritism. [*See* CJC Rule 2.13.] The $1,000 campaign contribution from LY's husband is below the disqualification point, and the question offers no grounds to suspect that the contribution influenced the choice of LY for the job.

45. Family Court Judge JG supervised the placement of 10–year–old orphan O in a loving foster home, and JG appointed lawyer LE to serve as guardian of O's financial interests until O reached age 21. Shortly after O's 15th birthday, O inherited a large sum of money from his aunt. LE took over the management of the money, subject to review by Judge JG every 60 days. At 10 a.m. in one of these review sessions JG smelled whiskey on LE's breath, and JG found that LE's computer records of O's money were garbled and incomplete. Further investigation revealed that LE had become a serious drunk and that he was diverting some of O's money for his own use. JG gave LE a vigorous talking–to. At the next reporting session, 60 days later, JG concluded that LE was still drinking, that the financial records were still a mess, and that more of O's money was missing. Is JG *subject to discipline* for failing to take stronger action 60 days earlier? [*See* CJC Rules 2.14 and 2.15.]

45. **Yes.** CJC Rule 2.14 required JG to take "appropriate action" when he discovered that LE had become a "serious drunk." In some cases the appropriate action might be to refer LE to a substance abuse program, but in other situations, the appropriate action might be reporting the lawyer to the disciplinary authority. [*See id.*, Comment 2.] Apparently JG's "vigorous talking–to" was not sufficient. Worse yet, JG had a special responsibility to O, because it was JG's job to review LE's performance every 60 days. When JG first discovered that LE was embezzling O's money, he probably should have found a new guardian for O and disclosed

LE's misdeeds to the disciplinary authorities and the prosecutor. [*See* CJC Rule 2.15.] JG's failure to do that makes him subject to discipline.

46. For more than 25 years, attorney AH divided his time about 50–50 between practicing law and helping his wife operate their charming small hotel on the edge of town. Last year AH was appointed to be a County Court Judge, and at that point his wife took on most of the hotel work, to give AH ample time for judging. Now the County Board of Supervisors is proposing a 17% tax on all hotel guests in the county—a tax that would drive small hotel owners out of business. AH plans to speak in opposition to the tax at the next Board of Supervisors meeting. Is it *proper* for AH to be involved in the hotel business with his wife, to spend a few hours per week on hotel work, and to speak against the tax at the Board of Supervisors' meeting? [*See* CJC Rule 3.1(A), 3.2(C), and 3.11(B)(1).]

46. **Yes.** A judge may be involved with the operation of a closely held family business. [CJC Rule 3.11(B)(1).] A judge may also participate in outside activities, so long as they don't interfere with his judicial duties. [*See* CJC Rule 3.1(A).] Finally, a judge may appear at a public hearing before a legislative or executive body and speak against a proposal that will harm his legal or economic interests. [*See* CJC Rule 3.2(C) and Comment 3.]

47. Appellate Justice JA got to know law student EJ well when she served for two semesters as his unpaid judicial extern, and he developed a high opinion of her moral character and legal abilities. At the time, EJ was an exchange student from Thailand, who was in the U.S. on a student visa. Now, a few years later, EJ wants to return as a permanent resident and eventually become a naturalized citizen, and she needs a good–character witness to testify on her behalf at an administrative hearing held by the U.S. Immigration and Naturalization Service. When she asked Justice JA to do that for her, he declined to do so voluntarily, but he said that if she did not have anyone else, and if she subpoenaed him, he would testify for her. Was JA's response *proper*? [*See* CJC Rule 3.3]

47. **Yes.** CJC Rule 3.3 prohibits a judge from testifying voluntarily as a character witness, but it permits such testimony when the judge is "duly summoned." Comment 1 to the rule says that, "except in unusual circumstances when the demands of justice require," a judge should "discourage" a party from requiring the judge to testify as a character

witness. We think Rule 3.3 is a tedious elevation of form over substance, so we regard JA's response as sufficient "discouragement" in EJ's case.

48.  After serving for seven years as the U.S. Treasury Secretary, SS became an Associate Justice of the U.S. Supreme Court, where she served for a decade with great distinction. While SS was still on the Court, U.S. President PR needed a person of undoubted wisdom and rectitude to chair a newly–created Presidential Commission on Foreign Relations, and he selected SS for that task. President PR's unexpressed hope was that the Commission would take the heat off of him for a series of foreign policy blunders. SS respectfully refused to serve, explaining that to do so would be inconsistent with her responsibilities on the Court. Was SS's refusal *proper*? [*See* CJC Rule 3.4.]

48.  **Yes.** The CJC is not binding on U.S. Supreme Court Justices, but when they seek ethical guidance, it is persuasive authority. CJC Rule 3.4 prohibits judges from serving on governmental committees, commissions, and the like, other than those related to the law, the legal system, or the administration of justice. President PR's new Commission is not that sort. Chief Justice Earl Warren let President Johnson talk him in to chairing the commission that investigated President Kennedy's assassination, but Warren was criticized for doing so. Associate Justice Sandra Day O'Connor served on the non-partisan Iraq Study Group, but she accepted that appointment after she had retired from the Court.

49.  To rule on a summary judgment motion, Judge JY had to read some confidential discovery material that was filed in her court under seal. From it she learned that MagnaTherm Energy Corp. was about to publicly announce its development of a new non–carbon–based fuel for generating electricity. JY knew that her scientist brother–in–law would be fascinated to learn of the new development, so she told him about it in strict confidence. Without revealing the secret to anyone, the brother–in–law bought 1,000 shares of MagnaTherm common stock on the open market at $54 per share. When MagnaTherm made its public announcement, the share price increased to $76 per share. Is JY *subject to discipline*? [*See* CJC Rule 3.5.]

49.  **Yes.** CJC Rule 3.5 prohibits a judge from disclosing or misusing nonpublic information that she gains in her judicial capacity. JY and her brother–in–law may also have violated the federal securities laws.

50. JW retired from the U.S. Army after 30 years in the Judge Advocate General's Corps. He was then appointed to the State Intermediate Court of Appeal, and a few months later he was offered membership in the Armed Forces Memorial Club, which operates excellent but inexpensive guest facilities in major cities of the U.S. The club offers membership to active duty or honorably discharged men and women from the Army, Navy, Marine Corps, or Coast Guard, except for homosexuals and lesbians. *May Judge JW join the club?*

50. **No.** CJC Rule 3.6 prohibits judges from joining or using an organization that invidiously discriminates based on race, sex, gender, religion, national origin, ethnicity, or sexual orientation. Comment 5 says the rule doesn't apply to national or state military service, but that exception is beside the point. The military services persist in discriminating against gays and lesbians, but the issue here is not whether JW may join one of the military services. Rather the issue is whether he may join a discriminatory *club,* and the answer is no.

51. Trial court Judge JT is known as the driving force behind his state's Legal Aid Institute. The institute helps fund legal aid offices, which provide pro bono legal services to poor people in civil matters. For years, Judge JT has helped the institute plan fund–raising events and manage its money. JT's name and judicial title are listed on the institute's fund–raising letterhead. JT also helps recruit lawyers to be "sustaining members" of the institute. To be a sustaining member, a lawyer must donate at least $5,000 per year to the institute and must personally perform at least 100 hours per year of pro bono work for poor people. JT's recruiting tools are good humor and appeal to virtue; he avoids anything remotely coercive. Is it *proper* for Judge JT to help plan fund–raising events, to help the institute with money management, to appear on the letterhead, and to recruit sustaining members? [*See* CJC Rules 3.1 and 3.7.]

51. **Yes.** CJC Rule 3.7(A)(1) authorizes the planning of fund raisers and the help with money management. Rule 3.7(A)(4) and Comment 4 authorize the fund–raising letterhead. Rule 3.7(A)(3) and Rule 3.7(B) authorize the recruitment of sustaining members.

52. Empire County trial judge JO's father FA has long been a gambling addict, and JO has always had to look out for him. A year ago FA won $15 million dollars playing poker in Las Vegas. JO convinced FA to put two–thirds of the money in trust, with JO as trustee and FA as beneficiary.

JO carefully researched the leading publicly held companies in Empire County, and she invested part of the trust money in the best eight. Those companies frequently show up as litigants in JO's court, but since she holds the investments as trustee, rather than as beneficial owner, she does not disqualify herself. Is it *proper* for JO to serve as trustee and for her not to disqualify herself, as described above? [*See* CJC Rule 2.11(A), Rule 3.8 and Comment 1, and Rule 3.11(C)(2).]

52. **No.** CJC Rule 3.8(A) does not prohibit JO from being trustee for her father, because he is a family member. But CJC Rule 2.11(A)(3) treats a trustee the same as a beneficial owner for the purposes of disqualification. Therefore JO has to disqualify herself whenever one of the eight companies shows up as a litigant in her court, assuming that the trust's investment is more than de minimis. [*See id.* and CJC Rule 3.8, Comment 1.] Better, JO should not have invested the trust money in companies that were likely to be litigants in her court. [CJC Rule 3.11(C)(2).] Now JO will have to be nimble to thread her way between the frequent disqualification rule and her fiduciary duty not to churn her father's trust account.

53. In the big city of Gotham, the court calendars are so crowded that civil litigants must often wait two or three years after their final pre–trial conference to get a trial date, a judge, and an open courtroom. As a consequence, many litigants now stipulate to use a "Rent–a–Judge," meaning an experienced judge who will decide their case under ordinary court rules and ordinary law, but who is paid a per diem fee by the litigants rather than a monthly salary by the government. In contrast, in the nearby sleepy village of Blossom Grove, the trial court calendar is never clogged, so the local judge, JZ, seldom has enough work to occupy his time. When nothing is going on in Blossom Grove, JZ moonlights as a Rent–a–Judge in Gotham. *May* he do so? [*See* CJC Rule 3.9.]

53. **No.** CJC Rule 3.9 prohibits a judge from acting as arbitrator or mediator, or performing "other judicial functions" apart from her official duties as judge. Of course it is proper and quite common for judges to arbitrate, mediate, or use other settlement techniques as part of their official judicial duties. [*See* CJC Rule 3.9, Comment 1.]

54. Judge JR no longer sits full–time on the State Seventeenth Circuit Appeals Court, but as a continuing part–time judge, she regularly substitutes for other judges when needed. JR's grandson GS came home

from high school a few months ago with two broken teeth, a broken nose, and two black eyes, all due to a beating by the Filthy Four, a notorious quartet of high–school bullies. JR promised GS she would represent him for free in bringing the bullies to justice. On GS's behalf, she sued the bullies in the Lake View trial court, which is under the appellate jurisdiction of the Seventeenth Circuit. JR won GS a judgment for $18,000. Were JR's actions *proper*? [*See* CJC, Terminology, definition of "member of the judge's family"; CJC, Application III(B); and CJC Rule 3.10.]

54. **No.** CJC Rule 3.10 prohibits full–time judges from practicing law, subject to some exceptions where the client is a "member of the judge's family." A grandson is a "member of the judge's family," but the exceptions don't allow a judge to appear on behalf of a family member in any kind of forum. CJC, Application III (A) might at first seem to rescue JR—it says that continuing part–time judges are not subject to Rule 3.10. But that hope is dashed by CJC, Application III (B), which says that a continuing part–time judge must not practice law in a court that is subject to the appellate jurisdiction of the court on which the judge sits. Therefore JR is subject to discipline for representing her grandson in the Lake View trial court.

55. LV was a successful appellate lawyer. He and five other successful appellate lawyers were joint venturers in a real estate deal; their objective was to restore the old buildings in the historic center of their city and to turn the area into an attractive and profitable shopping venue. When LV died, his share of the real estate venture passed to his daughter, Justice JE, who sits on the State Supreme Court. JE got along well with the five other venturers, and she enjoyed their regular Tuesday breakfast meetings, where they discussed their strategies and progress. Her five co–venturers frequently argue cases before the State Supreme Court, but she disqualifies herself from participating in those cases. Are her actions *proper*? [*See* CJC Rule 3.11.]

55. **No.** CJC Rule 3.11(A) and (B) generally allow a judge to hold and manage her and her family's financial and business affairs, but Rule 3.11(C) prohibits a judge from doing that if it will lead to frequent disqualification, or if it will involve the judge in frequent or continuing business relations with lawyers or other persons who are likely come before her court. Rule 3.11, Comment 2, advises a judge in JE's situation to divest herself of the real estate venture as soon as she can do so without serious financial harm.

56. The State of East Dakota five–judge Condemnation Court handles cases in which the government exercises the power of eminent domain to take private property for a public use. East Dakota condemnation lawyers formed the Eminent Domain Association. About half the members work for the government as condemnation lawyers, and the other half routinely represent private citizens whose property is being taken. The association holds annual meetings, always in some remote and scenic location around the state. At these meetings, the members attend continuing legal education sessions, debate condemnation policy, hear presentations on pending legislation, play an annual touch football game, and socialize at luncheons and dinners. This year the Association invited Condemnation Court Judge JC to attend the annual meeting and to be the keynote speaker at one of the dinners. The Association waived its usual $200 annual meeting registration fee for JC, and it reimbursed her travel, lodging, food, and incidental expenses. It also paid her its usual $400 honorarium for giving the keynote speech. JC publicly reported these sums in accordance with East Dakota's version of the CJC. Was it *proper* for JC to attend the meeting, give the speech, and accept the fee waiver, expense reimbursement, and honorarium? [*See* CJC Rules 3.12, 3.14, and 3.15.]

56. **Yes.** CJC Rule 3.12 allows JC to accept the honorarium. Rule 3.14(A) approves the waiver of the registration fee, and Rule 3.14(B) approves the reimbursement of expenses. Rule 3.15 states the public reporting requirement.

57. Juvenile Court Judge JQ's wife sells life insurance policies. Last week she won first prize in a sales contest put on by her employer. Her employer has never appeared in the Juvenile Court and is not likely to do so in the future. The prize is a two–week, all–expense–paid vacation in Tahiti for the winner and one guest. If JQ goes as his wife's guest, will he be *subject to discipline*? [*See* CJC Rule 3.13.]

57. **No.** CJC Rule 3.13(B)(8) allows JQ to accompany his wife because she won the prize in her own job, and the benefit to JQ is just incidental.

58. Land developer LD recently lost a zoning case that he plans to appeal to the 15 judge State Intermediate Court of Appeals. JY is a judge on that court. The clerk of that court randomly assigns judges to three–person panels, so litigants never know what judges they will get. JY and LD were college roommates, but they haven't corresponded or seen each other in

years. LD recalled that LY is an avid wildlife photographer; LD owns a rustic cabin high in a mountain range that teems with wildlife. Without mentioning the zoning case, LD telephoned JY and invited him to spend a few days together at the cabin, hiking in the mountains, and photographing the animals. The trip was a great success; JY got plenty of photos and fresh air, and the total cost for the two of them was under $100. Of course LD never mentioned the zoning case, and JY wasn't even aware of the case or of LD's plan to appeal. As luck would have it, JY was not selected for the three–person panel that ultimately heard LD's case. Is JY *subject to discipline*? [*See* CJC Rule 3.13.]

58. **No.** We think this is a borderline case, and that JY shouldn't be disciplined: JY did not realize at the time that LD might have an improper motive in inviting him to the cabin. The trip does not fit easily within any of the categories listed in CJC Rule 3.13(B) or (C). The closest category may be Rule 3.13(B)(3), "ordinary social hospitality," but we'd characterize this social hospitality as "unusual," not "ordinary." If JY had known of LD's plan to appeal, then JY should have declined the invitation under CJC Rule 3.13(A), because a reasonable person could believe that the trip would undermine JY's impartiality. JY did not know about LD's case, so we think he shouldn't be disciplined for making the trip. If, after making the trip, JY had been selected for the three–judge panel in LD's case, then we think he should disqualify himself under CJC Rule 2.11(A), because his impartiality might reasonably be questioned. [*But cf. Cheney v. U.S. Dist. Ct. for the Dist. of Columbia*, 541 U.S. 913, 124 S.Ct. 1391, 158 L.Ed.2d 225 (2004) (Justice Scalia, sitting as single Justice), noted in the text.]

59. Judge JZ is an appellate court judge in East Virginia, where appellate judges enjoy lifetime tenure. JZ's son is an up–and–coming young politician, a member of the Independence Party. He hopes to become the first Independence U.S. President, but for now he is working his way up by running in a contested public election for Lieutenant Governor of East Virginia—the state's second–highest elective office. JZ wants to support her son's candidacy in any way she can. *May* she publicly endorse him, make speeches on his behalf, contribute money to his campaign fund, and vote for him in the primary and general elections? [*See* CJC Rule 4.1(A) and Comments 3 through 6.]

59. **No.** She can vote for him [CJC Rule 4.1, Comment 6], but she must not publicly endorse him [*Id.*, Comment 5], nor make speeches for

him, [*Id.*, Comments 4 and 5], nor contribute to his political campaign [*Id.*, Rule 4.1(A)(4).]

60. Attorney AZ became so fed up with the local trial court's inefficiency that she vowed to get herself appointed to the next vacant judgeship. The Governor appoints new judges, based on recommendations from a State Bar committee. AZ's application letter to the committee promised that, if appointed, she would work to clean up the court's backlog of civil cases, streamline its probate calendar, and fire and replace the fossilized chief of records and the tyrannical jury commissioner. Was her application letter *proper*? [*See* CJC Rule 4.1, Comment 14, and Rule 4.3.]

60. **Yes.** CJC Rule 4.3 permits AZ to communicate her interest in a judgeship to the State Bar Committee. CJC Rule 4.1, Comment 14 allows her to promise to work for reform of the local court—that kind of promise is not inconsistent with impartial performance of her adjudicative duties.

61. Lawyer LY is one of seven candidates running in a partisan election for three vacant positions on the Superior Court bench. Within the time period specified by law, LY identified himself as a member of the Democratic Party, and he obtained and publicized the Democratic Party's endorsement of his candidacy. LY's main adversary is Republican Party candidate RP; the other five candidates are not well known or well financed. At a Democratic campaign rally, LY spoke vigorously on his own behalf, and he overtly and candidly criticized RP's suitability to be a judge. Is LY *subject to discipline*? [*See* CJC Rule 4.2(B)(2) and (3); Rule 4.2(C) and Comment 6.]

61. **No.** CJC Rule 4.2(C) permits LY to identify himself as a Democratic candidate and to seek and use the Democratic Party's endorsement within a time period specified by local law. Rule 4.2(B)(2) and (3) permit a candidate for elective judicial office to speak on his own behalf and to publicly oppose other candidates who are running for the same office. Comment 6 to the Rule 4.2 explains that candidates are considered to be running for the same office if several positions on the same court will be filled by the election.

62. State law requires all trial and intermediate appellate judges to run in a public "retention" election every seventh year. To retain his or her seat, a judge must get a majority vote. This year all of these retention candidates received a long questionnaire from the ATPW Coalition. (ATPW stands for

All Things Pure and Wholesome.) ATPW calls itself an "issues advocacy" group. The object of the questionnaire is to find out and publicize what each candidate believes about an assortment of controversial legal, social, and political issues, such as animal rights, prison reform, global warming, the death penalty, whales, gay clergy, welfare fraud, preemptive war, globalization, child abuse, coyotes, campaign finance reform, immigration, organic food, and urban sprawl. When Judge JI received her ATPW questionnaire, she sent it back without answering any questions. She included a handwritten note explaining that she opposes all such questionnaires on the ground that reasonable people might view them as undermining a judicial candidate's independence and impartiality. Was JI's response *proper*? [*See* CJC Rule 4.1, Comment 15.]

62. **Yes.** CJC Rule 4.1, Comment 15 states that this is one proper way to respond to such a questionnaire. Questionnaires of this kind have become common in some jurisdictions, and we, the authors, applaud judges who don't respond to them, because we believe that issue politics is inconsistent with the judicial role in our system of government. But reasonable people can differ on this question.